Solving Education's Problems Effectively

A Guide to Using the Case Method

Gerard Giordano

ROWMAN & LITTLEFIELD EDUCATION
Lanham • New York • Toronto • Plymouth, UK

Published in the United States of America
by Rowman & Littlefield Education
A Division of Rowman & Littlefield Publishers, Inc.
A wholly owned subsidiary of The Rowman & Littlefield Publishing Group, Inc.
4501 Forbes Boulevard, Suite 200, Lanham, Maryland 20706
www.rowmaneducation.com

Estover Road
Plymouth PL6 7PY
United Kingdom

British Library Cataloguing in Publication Information Available

Library of Congress Cataloging-in-Publication Data

Giordano, Gerard.
Solving education's problems effectively : a guide to using the case method / Gerard Giordano.
p. cm.
Includes bibliographical references and index.
ISBN 978-1-57886-998-5 (cloth : alk. paper) — ISBN 978-1-57886-999-2 (pbk. : alk. paper) — ISBN 978-1-60709-000-7 (electronic)
1. Case method. 2. Education—United States—History. 3. Problem solving. I. Title.
LB1029.C37G56 2009
370.7'22—dc22 2008046568

∞™ The paper used in this publication meets the minimum requirements of American National Standard for Information Sciences—Permanence of Paper for Printed Library Materials, ANSI/NISO Z39.48-1992.
Manufactured in the United States of America.

This book, which was inspired by my students, is dedicated to them.

Contents

List of Tables

Preface

THE CASE METHOD

This book is intended for persons who wish to study the roots of current educational problems. It is intended for educators, university students, parents, and community leaders. It is intended for persons who have been searching for information that is timely, practical, and engrossing.

This book is based on the case method. Although the case method may be relatively new in education, it has a storied reputation in other disciplines. Some experimentally minded law professors began to employ it during the late 1800s at Harvard University. Several decades later, business professors introduced it into their courses at Harvard. Eventually, professors on numerous campuses and in multiple disciplines experimented with it.

Students were aware that their professors were attracted to the case method; most of them were attracted as well. They were attracted because it was a style of learning that was stimulating and challenging. Moreover, they realized that it developed skills that they could transfer directly to their professions.

DISTINCTIVE FEATURES OF THIS BOOK

This book contains information about several topics. It contains information about students, teachers, methods of instruction, learning materials, curricula, and politics. It is organized to help readers identify and use this information.

Several of the chapters present information on the same topic. Nonetheless, they present it distinctively. For example, four chapters present information about learners. One of these chapters focuses on immigrant learners. Another chapter focuses on learners with disabilities. The two remaining chapters focus on the ways in which race, ethnicity, gender, and religion have affected learners.

Passages discuss current educational practices; they highlight the relevance of the historical cases. They are situated near the beginning of each chapter. They are followed by contextual information about the political, social, and cultural milieu that surrounded the cases.

The cases themselves review historical incidents. They explore ways in which those incidents were influenced by students, teachers, school administrators, and the other persons who worked in the schools. They also explore the ways in which they were influenced by persons outside of the schools. The outsiders include parents, businesspersons, professors, politicians, military leaders, and members of the public.

This book encourages readers to place themselves in the positions of historical characters. To help them make these transpositions, special activities are included. These activities follow the cases.

The special activities can guide persons who are involved in seminars; they can facilitate their dialogues and deliberations. They also can guide readers who are not participating in case-based seminars but who wish to make deliberations that are similar to those that these participants make.

Those readers who complete the special activities can rely on the information in the case studies. However, they also can rely on other types of information, such as those that are listed at the end of each chapter.

ADDITIONAL READINGS

Ashley, K. D. (1990). *Modeling legal argument: Reasoning with cases and hypotheticals.* Cambridge, MA: MIT Press.

Barnes, L. B., Christensen, C. R., & Hansen, A. J. (1994). *Teaching and the case method: Texts, cases, and readings* (3rd ed.). Boston: Harvard Business School Press.

Barrett, J. T. (1995). *Microbiology and immunology casebook.* Boston: Little, Brown.

Barrows, H. S. (1980). *Problem-based learning: An approach to medical education.* New York: Springer.

Barton, B. (2008). A tale of two case methods. *Tennessee Law Review, 75* (3). (Retrieved on 6 November 2008 from: http://ssrn.com/abstract=1021306.)

Berne, R. M., & Levy, M. N. (Ed). (1994). *Case studies in physiology* (3rd ed.). St. Louis, MO: Mosby.

Burlette, C. W. (1997). Reconstructing Langdell. *Georgia Law Review, 32* (4), 1–139.

Cabot, R. C. (1906). *Case teaching in medicine.* Boston: Heath.

Colbert, J., Desberg, O., & Trimble, K. (Eds.). (1996). *The case for education: Contemporary approaches for using case methods.* Boston: Allyn & Bacon.

Easton, G. (1983). *Learning from case studies.* London: Prentice Hall.

Erskine, J., Leenders, M., & Mauffette-Leenders, L. (1998). *Teaching with cases.* London, Ontario: Ivey.

Gray, D. L., & Smith, A. E. (2007). *Case studies in 21st-century school administration: Addressing challenges for educational leadership.* Thousand Oaks, CA: Sage.

Hutchings, P. (1993). *Using cases to improve college teaching: A guide to a more reflective practice.* Washington, DC: American Association for Higher Education.

Kimball, B. A. (2004). The Langdell problem: Historicizing the century of historiography, 1906–2000s. *Law and History Review, 22,* 277–338. (Retrieved on 6 November 2008 from: http://www.historycooperative.org/journals/lhr/22.2/kimball.html.)

Masoner, M. (1988). *An audit of the case study method.* New York: Praeger.

Mauffette-Leenders, L., Erskine, J., & Leenders, M. (1997). *Learning with cases.* London, Ontario: Ivey.

McAninch, A. R. (1993). *Teacher thinking and the case method.* New York: Teachers College Press.

McNair, M. P., & Hersum, A. C. (Eds.). (1954). *The case method at the Harvard Business School.* New York: McGraw-Hill.

Randrup, N. (2007). *The case method: Road map for how best to study, analyze and present cases* (2nd ed.). Rodovre, Denmark: International Management Press.

Silverman, R., Welty, W. M., & Lyon, S. (1991). *Case studies for teacher problem solving.* New York: McGraw-Hill.

Stenzel, A. & Feeney, H. (1970). *Learning by the case method: Practical approaches for community leaders.* New York: Seabury.

Thaller, E. A. (1994). *Bibliography for the case method: Using case studies in teacher education.* (ERIC Document Reproduction Service No. ED C367610). (Retrieved on 6 November 2008 from: http://www.eric.ed.gov/ERICWebPortal/custom/portlets/recordDetails/detailmini.jsp?_nfpb=true&_&ERICExtSearch_SearchValue_0=ED367610&ERICExtSearch_SearchType0=no&accno=ED367610.)

Wasserman, S. (1994). *Introduction to case method teaching: A guide to the galaxy.* New York: Teachers College Press.

Wilkerson, L., & Gijselaers, W. H. (Eds.). (1996). *Bringing problem-based learning to higher education: Theory and practice.* San Francisco, CA: Jossey-Bass.

Chapter One

Teachers: Using the Past to Understand the Present

Early teachers were expected to instruct children, develop their character, and design curricula for them. Many of them failed to meet these ambitious goals. Some failed because they lacked facilities, equipment, and supplies; others failed because they lacked training. This chapter explores the ways in which early teachers responded to their problems. This chapter also explores the ways in which theories of history have influenced our understanding of education.

TEACHERS IN TODAY'S CLASSROOMS

Parents worry about the schools. They worry about the equipment, the curricula, and the textbooks. They especially worry about the teachers. They are concerned because of teachers' inordinate influence on their children.

Scholars and researchers have agreed with the parents about teachers' influence (e.g., Solmon and Schiff, 2004; Solmon and Agam, 2007). They have alleged that even students who are assigned to schools with rundown facilities, inadequate equipment, outdated textbooks, and confusing curricula had a good chance of succeeding when they are paired with talented teachers.

In view of parents' and scholars' attitudes about the importance of teachers, school administrators have attempted to hire extraordinary professionals. Nonetheless, they had difficulty convincing talented persons to teach. Those who recruited talented teachers still faced another challenging problem: they had to retain them.

Some analysts attributed the recent problems with hiring and retaining teachers to changing patterns of employment (e.g., Bowsher, 2001; Cockburn and Haydn, 2003; Ginsburg and Lindsay, 1995; Greene, 2006; Heller, 2004;

McCluskey, 2007; Paige, 2007; Podsen, 2002). Labor union representatives, school administrators, journalists, politicians, scholars, and journalists offered distinct explanations for these shifting patterns.

Historians and social analysts have agreed that brilliant females originally pursued teaching careers because they had few other employment opportunities. Once alternatives became available to them, they took advantage of them. They pursued alternative careers for diverse reasons, including greater prestige, salary, personal freedom, and job satisfaction.

Residents in some communities, regions, and states have had to deal with shortages of teachers. To solve this problem, they have expanded their educator training programs. However, they have been distressed when the teachers that they trained have chosen to work in other career fields or other communities.

When current teachers make decisions about the careers that they will pursue and the regions in which they will reside, they consider a range of factors. Many of them consider personal, social, political, and economic factors. Earlier generations attended to remarkably similar factors when they made decisions about careers and locations.

EARLY TEACHERS

Colonial ministers, priests, and rabbis took charge of education. Some of them appointed educated congregation members to serve as teachers; others personally assumed the responsibility. They led the initiatives to build schoolhouses and attract professional teachers to their communities.

Because budgets were limited, the residents in many communities hired a single teacher. After providing a salary and a one-room schoolhouse, they assigned this person a broad set of responsibilities. They expected the teacher to instruct and design curricula for children who might range from seven to eighteen years in age. Furthermore, they expected the teacher to foster patriotism, craft character, dispense discipline, nurture religion, and monitor morality.

The early teachers had a hard time meeting the expectations that had been set for them. Their challenges were compounded by a shortage of professional resources. For example, most of them lacked books. To deal with this shortage, they required their students to bring printed materials from home. Although some students brought textbooks, others brought a Bible, Tanakh, dictionary, or the single volume that their family possessed.

Early teachers had explicit tasks for which they were accountable. Aware that they were expected to be firm disciplinarians, they punished students

Easton, G. (1983). *Learning from case studies.* London: Prentice Hall.

Erskine, J., Leenders, M., & Mauffette-Leenders, L. (1998). *Teaching with cases.* London, Ontario: Ivey.

Gray, D. L., & Smith, A. E. (2007). *Case studies in 21st-century school administration: Addressing challenges for educational leadership.* Thousand Oaks, CA: Sage.

Hutchings, P. (1993). *Using cases to improve college teaching: A guide to a more reflective practice.* Washington, DC: American Association for Higher Education.

Kimball, B. A. (2004). The Langdell problem: Historicizing the century of historiography, 1906–2000s. *Law and History Review, 22,* 277–338. (Retrieved on 6 November 2008 from: http://www.historycooperative.org/journals/lhr/22.2/kimball.html.)

Masoner, M. (1988). *An audit of the case study method.* New York: Praeger.

Mauffette-Leenders, L., Erskine, J., & Leenders, M. (1997). *Learning with cases.* London, Ontario: Ivey.

McAninch, A. R. (1993). *Teacher thinking and the case method.* New York: Teachers College Press.

McNair, M. P., & Hersum, A. C. (Eds.). (1954). *The case method at the Harvard Business School.* New York: McGraw-Hill.

Randrup, N. (2007). *The case method: Road map for how best to study, analyze and present cases* (2nd ed.). Rodovre, Denmark: International Management Press.

Silverman, R., Welty, W. M., & Lyon, S. (1991). *Case studies for teacher problem solving.* New York: McGraw-Hill.

Stenzel, A. & Feeney, H. (1970). *Learning by the case method: Practical approaches for community leaders.* New York: Seabury.

Thaller, E. A. (1994). *Bibliography for the case method: Using case studies in teacher education.* (ERIC Document Reproduction Service No. ED C367610). (Retrieved on 6 November 2008 from: http://www.eric.ed.gov/ERICWebPortal/custom/portlets/recordDetails/detailmini.jsp?_nfpb=true&_&ERICExtSearch_SearchValue_0=ED367610&ERICExtSearch_SearchType0=no&accno=ED367610.)

Wasserman, S. (1994). *Introduction to case method teaching: A guide to the galaxy.* New York: Teachers College Press.

Wilkerson, L., & Gijselaers, W. H. (Eds.). (1996). *Bringing problem-based learning to higher education: Theory and practice.* San Francisco, CA: Jossey-Bass.

who were disrespectful. They punished those who behaved inappropriately. They even punished students who had not mastered their lessons. Confident that corporal punishment would improve classroom behaviors, raise academic achievement, and nurture character, they required students to sit in corners on three-legged stools and wear dunce hats. They did not hesitate to strike them with paddles or rods.

EARLY SCHOOLS

At the beginning of the 1800s, many communities lacked schoolhouses and full-time teachers. Nonetheless, they had high aspirations. For example, the citizens of Boston set extremely high educational goals. During the 1600s, the Bostonians established high schools at which young males could study in Latin. Worried that some students could not attend and succeed when classes were offered in Latin, they later began to offer high school classes in English. They also established a high school for females. Although they relied on state taxes to cover some of their educational expenses, they supplemented these with local taxes.

Like the Bostonians, citizens in other parts of Massachusetts assigned a high value to education. During the mid- and late 1800s, they established educational programs for persons with disabilities, college programs for women, and training programs for teachers. They also established a state board to monitor and promote education.

The community leaders, school administrators, teachers, and parents in neighboring states were inspired by the citizens of Massachusetts. They replicated many of Massachusetts's policies and practices, but set relaxed timetables.

EARLY TEACHING MATERIALS

Teachers encountered problems because they lacked space, furniture, equipment, and textbooks. They encountered problems because they knew little about pedagogy. They encountered problems because they had to instruct very young children, intermediately aged youths, and adolescents, all grouped together in one-room schoolhouses. They encountered problems because they had to develop their own curricula.

To create curricula and refine instruction, some teachers relied on their own knowledge and personal experiences. Others relied on books. Because many of those who wished to rely on books did not have them, they requested that their students bring books from home. They were pleased when the children brought textbooks; they were frustrated when the children brought prayer books or collections of sermons.

Most teachers prized textbooks. They appreciated the ways in which textbooks identified and sequenced skills. They admired the first reading textbooks, which required students to recognize the letters of the alphabet, interpret illustrations, and comprehend textual passages. They used these tasks, which were arranged hierarchically, as rudimentary curricula.

EARLY TEACHING METHODS

Some parents may have questioned the value of curricula, learning materials, and textbooks. However, they did not question the value of teachers. They viewed teachers as the experts who could identify and inculcate the knowledge that children needed.

As for the teachers, they accepted the status that was bestowed upon them. Realizing that they were seen as experts, they searched for a method of instruction that complemented this status; they searched for a method that emphasized their own knowledge.

When teachers discovered the recitation method, they concluded that this was an ideal type of instruction for educational experts. They would read aloud information from books, restate it in lectures, and write it on chalkboards. They then would require that their students repeat the information. Sometimes they required them to repeat it in unison; at other times they required them to take turns repeating it.

Both experienced and novice teachers relied on recitation. However, school administrators and parents eventually began to discern weaknesses in it. As a result, they discouraged its use. Like school administrators and parents, professors of education began to detect weaknesses in recitation. After judging that the weaknesses outweighed the strengths, they encouraged teachers to employ new instructional methods. They introduced the teachers to instructional methods that placed an emphasis on students rather than teachers.

TEACHERS OF BILINGUAL STUDENTS

Serious educational problems were apparent in the nineteenth-century schools. Although these problems were addressed, they were not eliminated. Instructing learners with limited English was an example of an issue that had been and remained problematic.

The instruction of learners with limited English was complicated by problems in the community, among them prejudice, racial bias, and ethnic discrimination. Socially and economically established American citizens worried about immigrants who were poor, unable to speak English, and unfamiliar with American culture. Some of them feared that the immigrants would alter their neighborhoods, communities, states, and regions; some of them feared that they would irreparably damage the nation.

In diverse parts of the country, citizens feared different racial or ethnic minorities. In the Northeast, they feared Italian Americans. On the West Coast, they feared Chinese and Japanese Americans. In the West, they feared American Indians, who were not immigrants but who spoke distinctive languages, were poor, and represented a different culture. In the South, white residents feared African Americans, who were poor and represented a distinct culture.

In the West and the Southwest, residents feared Mexican Americans. Aware that the Mexican government had ceded vast portions of the Southwest to the United States under controversial circumstances, some of them worried about reprisals from displaced families. Some others feared Mexican Americans for subconscious reasons.

Those U.S. citizens who feared and resented Mexican Americans still depended on them. They depended on them to plant, cultivate, harvest crops, maintain herds of cattle, clean their homes, cook their meals, and care for their children; they also depended on those who were highly skilled professionals.

Just as residents showed ambivalent attitudes toward Hispanic Americans in the West and the Southwest, citizens in other regions exhibited ambivalent attitudes toward the Hispanic Americans in their own communities. Although they aggressively recruited Puerto Ricans, Cubans, and Latino Americans to fill jobs, they simultaneously scorned them.

Inevitably, tension developed between Hispanic Americans and their employers, coworkers, and neighbors. This tension influenced Hispanic American youths in the schools; it also influenced the teachers who instructed them.

THEORIES OF HISTORY

Some scholars have focused their attention on the academic factors that have influenced education; they have emphasized teachers, curricula, learning materials, and facilities. Some scholars have focused on nonacademic factors; they have concentrated on social, cultural, economic, and political forces. Some have focused on emotional forces.

Sigmund Freud was a scholar who focused his attention on emotional forces. He was sure that these forces influenced human behavior. In fact, he alleged that they had influenced communities, regions, nations, and civilizations. Freud was convinced that these forces would continue to influence future events.

Although relatively few persons adopted Freud's psychoanalytically oriented views of history, all persons who have contemplated the past have made some assumptions about historical incidents. They have relied on theories of history to explain the ways in which historical incidents were linked to each other and to current events. They have made historiography an indispensable component of history.

Case Study 1.1: Nineteenth-Century Teachers

American teachers were a heterogeneous group during the 1800s. Although some of them had attended college, many had attended only high school. Few of them had formal training in pedagogy. Needless to say, they worried about whether they would be able to instruct children.

To make the best of their stressful situations, early teachers relied on repetition. They referred to this type of instruction as recitation. They detected several advantages to it: They could use it to organize learning and instruction. They could use it to compensate for the lack of textbooks. They could use it to impose discipline, assess learning, and foster rhetorical skills.

Although the recitation method had advantages, it was not always the ideal approach. It was employed in some communities because it was the most suitable method of instruction; it was employed in others because no other method was practicable.

Opponents of recitation believed that it was expendable. In fact, they depicted its benefits as deficits. While admitting that it enabled teachers to work with heterogeneous groups of learners, they claimed that it reduced their sensitivity to individual students. While admitting that poorly trained teachers prized recitation, they claimed that they prized it only because they were unable to use the other types of instruction.

Opponents depicted recitation as a competitive process that eroded students' confidence. They cited examples of students who had become ashamed during oral recitations and then transformed their shame into resentment and anger. They cited examples of incidents in which the damage from recitations had been increased through publicly administered punishments.

The preparation of teachers influenced the types of instruction that they employed. Preparation was informal during the early 1800s. Some teachers succeeded not because of their training but because they were sensitive, ingenious, or resourceful; others succeeded because they had extraordinary mentors. As for those teachers who failed, some of them may have lacked talent or independence; others may have lacked chances to collaborate with mentors.

American school administrators searched for better ways to train teachers. They asked their European colleagues for advice. The Europeans had established model schools to which they sent future teachers. They expected the staffs at these schools to assess whether candidates had mastered the academic knowledge they would teach.

Staff at the European model schools also were expected to act as mentors to the teacher candidates. They insisted that candidates attend lectures, act as aides in their classrooms, and eventually teach under their supervision. Teachers in France referred to a teacher-preparation institution as an *école normale*. Translating this phrase as *normal school*, the Americans used this nomenclature to describe their own training institutions.

In the late 1830s, the citizens of Massachusetts established an American normal school. Although only three women were attracted to the initial class, larger numbers were drawn to subsequent classes. In addition to using the normal school to train teachers, it was used as a site for pedagogical experiments.

Prior to the Civil War, only a few states had established normal schools: California, Illinois, Massachusetts, Michigan, Minnesota, Pennsylvania, Missouri, and Washington. During the second half of the nineteenth century, many more states started them.

In the early 1860s, members of churches and philanthropic organizations provided the funding to establish a postsecondary institution for African Americans in Hampton, Virginia. After the Civil War, this institution was converted into a normal school for African American teachers. African American normal schools eventually were established throughout the South. Most of the graduates from these institutions worked in the segregated schools of the South.

Activity: Understanding Nineteenth-Century Teachers

Many early teachers relied on recitation, a procedure in which their students orally recapitulated key pieces of information. How did different groups react to this pedagogical procedure? To help answer this question, create a chart.

Along the vertical axis of the chart, place the following groups: students, parents, teachers who were not graduates of normal schools, teachers who were graduates of normal schools, school administrators, religious leaders, and professors of education.

Along the horizontal axis of the chart, arrange several columns. In one column, indicate whether each group primarily supported (+), opposed (-), or showed a mixed commitment (+/-) to recitation.

Your indications about the responses of the groups should be based on assumptions about the vested interests, values, and goals of their members. Although you can use the information in the case study to make some of these assumptions, you may wish to rely on a broader foundation of information.

Table 1.1. Nineteenth-Century Teachers

Group	*Support**	*Explanation*
Students		
Parents		
Teachers—Not Graduates of Normal Schools		
Teachers—Graduates of Normal Schools		
School Administrators		
Religious Leaders		
Professors of Education		

* (+) Supported
(-) Opposed
(+/-) Mixed Commitment

You may gather additional information from the materials that are listed at the end of this chapter. You may gather it from lectures or classroom discussions.

On a separate page, summarize your assumptions about each group.

Case Study 1.2: Twentieth-Century Teachers of Bilingual Students

American citizens were wary of persons who were entering their country during the 1800s. They distrusted poor immigrants because of their distinctive languages, customs, and religions. In the Southwest they distrusted the poor immigrants from Mexico.

Frontier settlers in that region clashed with Mexicans over military, political, social, and economic matters. They declared that Texas was independent, made it into a state, waged a war, defeated the Mexican army, negotiated a treaty, and annexed Mexican land. In fact, they annexed a vast amount of Mexican land. They annexed what are now California, Nevada, and Utah, and parts of Arizona, Colorado, New Mexico, and Wyoming.

After the military hostilities ended, the citizens of the United States and Mexico continued to quarrel. They argued about wages, livestock, and land;

they argued about politics, laws, and culture. Unable to resolve their disputes, they stormed back and forth across the border.

Because of these feuds, some Americans had begun to view Mexican citizens pejoratively. They extended these biased impressions to the citizens of other Hispanic countries. Just as they had extolled the martial superiority of American troops over Mexican soldiers during the Mexican-American War, they boasted about the ease with which Americans had dominated Hispanic soldiers in other conflicts.

Americans took particular delight in eulogizing the bravery that Theodore Roosevelt and his regiment of Rough Riders had exhibited during the Spanish-American War. They crowed about the territory that Spain had ceded to the United Sates in the treaty that ended this 1898 conflict. Spain had surrendered Guam, the Philippines, and Puerto Rico; it had relinquished its dominion of Cuba.

Some American citizens looked down on Hispanic Americans because their ancestral countries had not waged formidable wars; others had distinct pretexts for their prejudice. Some of them were influenced by economic factors. They noted that most of the Mexican laborers who crossed into the United States were poor. In spite of the fact that they encouraged these immigrants to take menial jobs, they looked down on them afterwards.

Hispanic Americans were resented for reasons other than their poverty and the menial jobs that they assumed; in fact, they frequently were feared. They were feared because they the American media depicted them as dangerous banditos, gang members, or drug dealers.

Hispanic Americans eventually were associated with dangerous politics. During the nineteenth and the twentieth centuries, citizens of the United States had derisively dismissed Latin American countries as "banana republics." However, they changed their minds after Fidel Castro established a communist government in Cuba.

Government leaders, political analysts, and journalists feared that Castro was a menace to the residents of Cuba and Latin America. Some of them worried that he was a menace to the United States. They feared that he would invite the Soviet Union to use Cuba as the staging ground for an attack on the United States.

The American public was unusually attentive to Cuba during the early 1960s. This was the era when the United States had begun to construct missile sites near the Soviet Union. However, the Soviet Union also had begun to prepare missile sites in proximity to the United States. The United States had built sites in Turkey; the Soviet Union had built sites in Cuba.

Each nation was dismayed by the other's audacity. In October of 1962, the government leaders of the United States and the Soviet Union came close to a military confrontation. These terrifying events convinced many Americans that the warnings about the danger of Cubans had been justified.

During the twentieth century, Hispanic Americans were oppressed by cultural, social, and political stereotypes. Nonetheless, they battled the stereotypes.

They battled them by assuming greater visibility in American popular culture. They battled them by becoming high-profile contributors to sports, film, television, music, and literature. They battled them by amassing greater cultural, social, political, and economic power.

Although Hispanic Americans combated stereotypes indirectly through their achievements, they also combated them directly. During the 1960s, they were impressed with the ways in which African Americans secured educational opportunities. They noticed that African Americans used legislation, litigation, and the support of a broad coalition to make changes. Hispanic Americans decided to borrow political strategies from African Americans.

Aware that African Americans had demanded an end to racially segregated schooling, Hispanic Americans pointed out that many Hispanic children had been subjected to either de jure or de facto segregation. Just as African Americans had demanded a system of education in which their children would be taught with sensitivity and respect, Hispanic Americans made similar demands.

Even though they were advocating for educational equity, Hispanic Americans questioned the need for fully integrated schools. They insisted that the optimal type of education did not have to be completely inclusive; they recommended a system in which Hispanic American children would be taught by Spanish-speaking teachers. They argued that this type of education would boost the children's confidence, ethnic pride, and academic achievement.

During the 1960s and the 1970s, schools implemented programs in which the teachers taught in Spanish. Sure that this instruction would have a profound and discernible impact, advocates urged the government to sustain it. Although some constituencies agreed with them, others opposed them. Controversy ensued.

In response to the controversy, supporters conducted research to demonstrate the effectiveness of the bilingual teachers. However, unconvinced opponents challenged the validity of the research.

In the early 1980s, President Reagan designated new national priorities for education; he withdrew the federal funds that had supported the training and hiring of bilingual educators. Although some state leaders, such as those in California, insisted that they would support bilingual teachers, they faced political challenges.

Activity: Bilingual Education

During the 1960s and the 1970s, the federal government sponsored and funded bilingual education programs in the schools. How do you think different social, political, and professional groups responded to these programs? To help answer this question, create a chart.

Along the vertical axis of the chart, place the following groups: Hispanic American parents, non-Hispanic American parents, teachers of students who

Table 1.2. Twentieth-Century Teachers of Bilingual Students

Group	*Support**	*Explanation*
Hispanic American Parents		
Non-Hispanic American Parents		
Teachers of Students with Limited English		
Teachers of Students Fluent in English		
School Administrators		
Professors of Education		
Politically Liberal Legislators		
Politically Conservative Legislators		

* (+) Supported
(-) Opposed
(+/-) Mixed Commitment

spoke limited English, teachers of students who were fluent in English, school administrators, professors of education, politically liberal legislators, and politically conservative legislators.

Along the horizontal axis of the chart, arrange several columns. In one column, use symbols to indicate whether each group primarily supported (+), opposed (-), or showed a mixed commitment (+/-) to the bilingual education initiatives.

Your indications about the responses of the groups should be based on assumptions about the vested interests, values, and goals of their members. Although you can use the information in the case study to make some of these assumptions, you may wish to rely on a broader foundation of information.

You can gather additional information from the materials that are listed at the end of this chapter. You may gather it from lectures or discussions.

On a separate page, summarize your assumptions about each group.

Case Study 1.3: Theories of History

When scholars investigated historical issues, they confronted vast amounts of information. They had to make decisions about the data that they would retain and those that they would discard. They depended on theories to help them make these decisions.

In a book about the collapse of civilizations, Diamond (2005) explained the theory on which he had relied in order to sort mountains of information. He noted that he had sorted information with the aid of categories such as environmental fragility, relations with neighboring countries, and political institutions. Using these categories as intellectual sieves, he incorporated the information that passed through them into his study.

Not all historians have been as straightforward and articulate as Diamond about the theoretical assumptions on which they have relied. Nonetheless, all of them have relied on theoretical assumptions.

Chroniclers

Some scholars were chroniclers; they assumed that events and the details associated with them could be parsed into encyclopedia-like records. Arnold Toynbee, an eminent nineteenth-century British scholar, was not a chronicler; on the contrary, he decried the chroniclers. Toynbee wrote gruffly that they treated history as "just one damned thing after another."

During different eras of the twentieth century, textbook publishers were criticized for creating biased school materials; they were accused of creating materials that fostered racial, gender, ethnic, and nationalistic biases. As a result of these accusations, some publishers suppressed the political voices of their authors. Although the publishers placated some of their critics, they angered others. The angered critics accused the publishers of transforming once-vibrant accounts into lackluster chronicles.

Continuity Theorists

Some scholars were continuity theorists. Unlike the chroniclers, they searched for patterns between past and present events. Once they found patterns, many of them used them to make moral generalizations; others simply identified recurring patterns and assumed that their readers would draw the appropriate implications. George Santayana, an American scholar, may have encapsulated the credo of the continuity theorists when he remarked that "those who cannot remember the past are condemned to repeat it."

Great Man/Great Woman Theorists

Some scholars were great man/great woman theorists. Like the investigators who subscribed to other theories, they had to select the information that they would use to depict complex historical events; they selected information that related to highly visible leaders.

Great man/great woman theorists not only called attention to important individuals but crafted heroically sized images of them. They were convinced that their character-centered depictions of events were justified because those characters had altered the course of historical events.

Dialectical Theorists

Some scholars were dialectical theorists; they emphasized the ways in which social, political, and economic clashes were essential components of historical events. Georg Hegel was a nineteenth-century German philosopher who wrote about the dialectical nature of historical events. He argued that significant events invariably elicited significant reactions.

Hegel detected a continuing dialectical tension between events and the counterevents that they spawned; he alleged that this tension ensured that additional forces would continue to emerge. Hegel predicted that the new forces would incorporate salient elements of the earlier forces. As such the new forces would have greater momentum than the forces from which they had arisen.

Eventually, the new forces would be confronted by counterforces. The tension between the new forces and the counterforces would create the conditions from which novel forces would emerge. Hegel predicted that this dynamic cycle would go on indefinitely.

Hegel might have attracted little attention through his abstruse philosophical books had it not been for one of his most avid readers, Karl Marx. Marx used Hegel's ideas to explain economic and political events. Marx argued that history illustrated the dialectical routes through which an increasing numbers of persons had accumulated wealth and political power.

Although he agreed with Hegel on most points, Marx challenged one of his mentor's predictions. He challenged the prediction that the turbulent dialectical cycle would continue indefinitely. Marx forecast that this cycle would halt once a utopian communist state had been achieved.

Marx was able to bring Hegel's theoretical insights to the attention of a massive international audience. Vladimir Lenin expanded that audience even more. Lenin calculated that Marx's economic predictions would not transpire unless poor and oppressed workers revolted against the social and economic establishment. Demonstrating this process, Lenin personally led the revolution in Russia.

Psychological Theorists

Some scholars were psychological theorists; they emphasized the ways that subconscious forces affected the course of historical events. Sigmund Freud may be the most famous psychological theorist.

Although earlier scholars had recognized that the actions of historical characters were influenced by their subconscious attitudes, Freud extended this theory to new conceptual realms. He argued that culture, society, religion, and even civilization itself was influenced by subconscious attitudes. He believed that these attitudes were primordial and animalistic; in fact, he was convinced that they were largely sexual.

Political analysts and journalists relied on psychological theories when they tried to rationalize the actions of contemporary world figures. One analyst (Coll, 2008) used Freud's views about fathers and sons to explain Osama Bin Laden's terrorist actions; another analyst (Weisberg, 2008) used these views to explain President George W. Bush's invasion of Iraq.

Social Theorists

Some scholars were social theorists; they alleged that the unique spirit of each era influenced the courses of events. In his historical novel *Memories of the Ford Administration*, John Updike articulated the assumption on which the social theorists relied. He wrote that "there is a difference between an event viewed statistically, as it transpired among people who are absorbed into a historical continuum, and the same even taken personally, as a unique and irreversible transformation in one's singular life, with reverberations traveling through one's whole identity, to the limits of personal time" (Updike, 1992, p. 52).

Edward Hallett Carr was a British scholar who used social theory to explain shifting attitudes toward controversial historical issues. He made a profound impression on American scholars, who relied on this theory to explain the attitudes that journalists, scholars, politicians, and members of the public exhibited during different eras.

Scholars relied on social theory to explain changing attitudes of the lawyers, government leaders, and judges who engaged in debates about the United States Constitution. They used this approach to explain the arguments of the nineteenth-century United States Supreme Court justices who curtailed the social, civic, and political rights of African Americans; they used this approach again to explain the arguments of the justices who eventually reversed the earlier decisions.

Hybrid Theorists

Some scholars were hybrid theorists; they realized that several theories were compatible with each other. Instead of selecting a single explanation for historical change, they combined several explanations.

Some hybrid theorists combined psychological theory with the great man/great woman theory. This group of scholars searched for individuals who had altered the course of history; they also searched for evidence that those individuals had been influenced by subconscious attitudes.

David McCullough relies on a hybrid approach in his popular accounts of American presidents. He employs psychological and social theories as well as the great man/great woman theory.

Nihilistic Theorists

Some scholars were nihilistic theorists; they claimed that historical scholarship was impossible because of the idiosyncratic factors to which events were inextricably bound. George Meade, a Civil War general, seemed to be advancing a nihilistic theory when he stated, "I don't believe the truth will ever be known, and I have a great contempt for history."

Some nihilistic theorists have warned that scholars are unable to disentangle the many idiosyncratic features of historical events. Paul Valéry, a French scholar, warned that history "teaches precisely nothing, for it contains everything and furnishes examples of everything."

Although some nihilistic theorists have argued that historians are unable to extract historical events from the extraneous details with which they are entangled, others have argued that they are unable to extract them from their own personal biases. Samuel Butler, the witty British author, may have characterized the latter viewpoint when he observed that "God cannot alter the past; historians can."

Referring to themselves as postmodern and deconstructionist scholars, some theorists identified gender, race, ethnicity, religion, and wealth as factors that influenced persons' comprehension of earlier events. They claimed that these factors also influenced their comprehension of current events. They concluded that the ways in which historians and contemporaries viewed events were equally flawed but equally valid.

Activity: Categorizing Historians

From ancient to present eras, scholars have made assumptions about the ways in which historical events are comprehended. Some of these scholars are listed in table 1.3. Next to each scholar's name is a quotation about historical knowledge. Two theories are identified in the cell next to each quotation. Select the theory that provides the most plausible explanation for the quotation. Briefly explain the reason for your selection.

Needless to say, a scholar's thoughts cannot be categorized on the basis of isolated remarks. Be aware of this limitation, and do not think of this activity as an attempt to definitively categorize the theory to which scholars subscribed.

Table 1.3. Theories of History

Scholar	*Quotation*	*Theories (Choose One)*	*Rationale*
Polybius, Greek Historian, 203 BC–120 BC	If we [historians] knowingly write what is false, whether for the sake of our country or our friends or just to be pleasant, what difference is there between us and hack writers?	Chronicler *or* Continuity Theorist	
Cicero, Roman Statesman, 106 BC–43BC	History . . . illuminates reality, vitalizes memory, [and] provides guidance in daily life.	Chronicler *or* Continuity Theorist	
Titus Livius, Roman Historian, 59 BC–17 AD	[In] the study of history . . . you can find yourself and your country both examples and warnings.	Chronicler *or* Continuity Theorist	
Anna Comnena, Byzantine Scholar, 1083–1153	Time in its irresistible and ceaseless flow carries along on its flood all created things and drowns them in the depths of obscurity. . . . But the tale of history forms a very strong bulwark against the stream of time, and checks in some measure its irresistible flow.	Chronicler *or* Nihilistic Theorist	
Machiavelli, Italian Scholar, 1496–1597	Whoever wishes to foresee the future must consult the past; for human events ever	Dialectical Theorist *or* Continuity Theorist	

Scholar	*Quotation*	*Theories (Choose One)*	*Rationale*
	resemble those of preceding times.		
Edward Gibbon, British Historian, 1737–1794	History . . . is indeed little more than the register of the crimes, follies, and misfortunes of mankind.	Nihilistic Theorist *or* Continuity Theorist	
Georg W. F. Hegel, German Philosopher, 1770–1831	What experience and history teach is this—that people and governments never have learned anything from history.	Chronicler *or* Continuity Theorist	
Emma Willard, American Scholar, 1787–1870	An epoch is an important event in any history, which, having happened on some certain day, or in some one year, is regarded but as a point in time.	Chronicler *or* Social Theorist	
Leopold von Ranke, German Historian, 1795–1886	History ought to judge the past and to instruct the contemporary world as to the future.	Psychological Theorist *or* Continuity Theorist	
Ralph Waldo Emerson, American Scholar, 1803–1882	There is properly no history; only biography.	Great Man/Great Woman Theorist *or* Continuity Theorist	
Francis Parkman, American Historian, 1823–1893	Faithfulness to the truth of history involves far more than a research, however patient and scrupulous, into special facts.	Continuity Theorist *or* Social Theorist	

(*continued*)

Table 1.3. ***(continued)***

Scholar	*Quotation*	*Theories (Choose One)*	*Rationale*
	. . .The narrator must seek to imbue himself with the life and spirit of the time. . . . He must himself be, as it were, a sharer or a spectator of the action he describes.		
Karl Marx, German Philosopher, 1830–1883	History itself is nothing but the activity of men pursuing their purposes.	Dialectical Theorist *or* Continuity Theorist	
Henry Adams, American Scholar, 1838–1918	History is simply social development along the lines of weakest resistance.	Dialectical Theorist *or* Continuity Theorist	
Sigmund Freud, Austrian Psychologist, 1856–1939	Historical residues have helped us to view religious teachings, as it were, as neurotic relics, and we may now argue that the time has probably come, as it does in an analytic treatment, for replacing the effects of repression by the results of the rational operation of the intellect.	Psychological Theorist *or* Continuity Theorist	
Frederick Jackson Turner, American Historian, 1861–1932	Each age writes the history of the past anew with reference to the conditions uppermost in its own time.	Nihilistic Theorist *or* Continuity Theorist	

Scholar	*Quotation*	*Theories (Choose One)*	*Rationale*
James Harvey Robinson, American Historian, 1863–1936	History includes every trace and vestige of everything that man has done or thought since first he appeared on the earth.	Continuity Theorist *or* Chronicler	
George Santayana, American Scholar, 1863–1952	Those who cannot remember the past are condemned to repeat it.	Great Man/Great Woman Theorist *or* Continuity Theorist	
Virginia Woolf, British Novelist, 1882–1941	History is too much about wars; biography too much about great men.	Great Man/Great Woman Theorist *or* Hybrid Theorist	
Samuel Eliot Morison, American Historian, 1887–1976	An historian should . . . become immersed in the place and period of his choice.	Chronicler *or* Social Theorist	
E. H. Carr, British Historian, 1892–1982	The function of the historian is . . . to master and understand [the past] as the key to the understanding of the present.	Chronicler *or* Continuity Theorist	
Joseph Freeman, American Scholar, 1897–1965	The best we can say of any account is not that it is the real truth at last, but that this is how the story appears now.	Chronicler *or* Nihilist Theorist	
Karl Popper, Austrian/British Philosopher, 1902–1994	There is no history, only histories.	Chronicler *or* Continuity Theorist	

(*continued*)

Table 1.3. (*continued*)

Scholar	*Quotation*	*Theories (Choose One)*	*Rationale*
Hannah Arendt, German Philosopher, 1906–1975	If history teaches anything about the causes of revolution . . . it is that a disintegration of political systems precedes revolutions.	Chronicler *or* Dialectical Theorist	
Yosef Hayim Yerushalmi, American Historian, 1932–	[The historian] constantly challenges even those memories that have survived intact.	Chronicler *or* Continuity Theorist	
Kevin Starr, American Historian, 1940–	Historians have properly emphasized the continuities between one era and the next.	Chronicler *or* Continuity Theorist	

Some of the quotations were retrieved on 10 June 2007 from: http://www historyguide org/history html, http://psychology about com/od/psychologyquotes/a/freudquotes htm and http://hnn us/articles/1328 html.

Instead, think of it as a way to develop your own acquaintance with historical theories.

USING THE PAST TO UNDERSTAND THE PRESENT

Because well-trained teachers were scarce, instructors with minimal qualifications were hired. Once they were appointed, unprepared teachers encountered problems. They encountered problems because they lacked pedagogical skills. They encountered problems because they lacked textbooks. They encountered problems because they lacked curricula.

The teachers attempted to deal with their problems. Attempting to compensate for inadequate pedagogical skills, they required their students to memorize key pieces of information.

Attempting to compensate for the textbooks that they lacked, the teachers asked parents to purchase them. They then used the books that their students brought to school to solve still another problem, the absence of curricula. They extracted a table of contents from a textbook and made this into a curriculum.

Teachers eventually did have opportunities for training, textbooks, and curricula. However, they still faced substantive challenges. For example, they had to figure out a way to instruct students who spoke limited English.

Do the issues that were problematic during earlier eras remain problematic today? To answer this question, consider the historical difficulties that school administrators encountered when they attempted to recruit and retain teachers. Compare these problems with those that school administrators have recently faced when they attempted to recruit and retain teachers.

Alternatively, consider the historical problems that teachers encountered when they attempted to instruct students who spoke limited English. Compare these problems with those that teachers recently have faced when they have attempted to instruct students with limited English. Attempt to locate incidents that took place in your own state or community.

CHAPTER SUMMARY

Parents set high goals for nineteenth-century teachers. They expected them to instruct and discipline their children. They expected them to create curricula. They expected them to nurture character, instill patriotism, and reinforce religion.

Teachers were influenced by the expectations of parents. They were influenced by the facilities in which they taught and the resources to which they had access. They were influenced by their academic and professional educations.

To deal with stressful situations, teachers turned to expedients. They asked their students to bring books from home. They transformed books into curricula. They relied on a repetition-based style of instruction. As their situations improved, teachers were able to address these challenges methodically.

ADDITIONAL READING

Introductory Passages

Giordano, G. (2000). *Twentieth-century reading education: Understanding practices of today in terms of patterns of the past.* New York: Elsevier.

Case Study 1.1: Nineteenth-Century Teachers

Edwards, J. (2002). *Women in American education, 1820–1955: The female force and educational reform.* Westport, CT: Greenwood.

Harper, C. A. (1970). *A century of public teacher education.* Westport, CT: Greenwood.

Kliebard, H. (1994). *The Struggle for the American curriculum: 1803–1958* (2nd ed.). London: Routledge.

Nash, M. A. (2005). *Women's education in the United States, 1780–1840.* New York: Palgrave Macmillan.

Ogren, C. A. (1995). *The American state normal school: "An instrument of great good."* New York: Palgrave.

Tyack, D., & Cuban, L. (1995). *Tinkering toward utopia: A century of public school reform.* Cambridge, MA: Harvard University Press.

Case Study 1.2: Twentieth-Century Teachers of Bilingual Students

Allison, G., & Zelikow, P. (1999). *Essence of decision: Explaining the Cuban Missile Crisis.* New York: Longman.

Eisenhower, J. (1989). *So far from God: The U.S. war with Mexico.* New York: Random House.

Foos, P. W. (2002). *A short, offhand, killing affair: Soldiers and social conflict during the Mexican-American war.* Chapel Hill, NC: University of North Carolina Press, 2002.

Frazier, D. S. (1998). *The U.S. and Mexico at war.* New York: Macmillan.

Fursenko, A., & Naftali, T. (1998). *One hell of a gamble—Khrushchev, Castro and Kennedy, 1958–1964.* New York: Norton.

Graff, H. J. (1995). *Conflicting paths: Growing up in America.* Cambridge, MA: Harvard University Press.

Hendrickson, K. E. (2003). *The Spanish-American War.* Westport, CT: Greenwood.

Krashen, S. D. (1997). *Under attack: The case against bilingual education.* London: Butterworth-Heinemann.

Meed, D. (2003). *The Mexican War, 1846–1848.* New York: Osprey.

Porter, R. P. (1998). The case against bilingual education. *Atlantic Monthly, 281 (5),* 28–39.

Ruiz, R. E. (1992). *Triumph and tragedy: A history of the Mexican people.* New York: Norton.

Stern, S. M. (2005). *The week the world stood still: Inside the secret Cuban Missile Crisis.* Palo Alto, CA: Stanford University Press.

Tebbel, J. (1996). *America's great patriotic war with Spain: Mixed motives, lies, and racism in Cuba and the Philippines, 1898–1915.* Tucson, AZ: Marshall Jones.

Tone, J. L. (2006). *War and genocide in Cuba, 1895–1898.* Chapel Hill: University of North Carolina Press.

Valencia, R. R. (Ed.). (1991). *Chicano school failure and success: Research and policy agendas for the 1990s.* Philadelphia: Falmer.

Case Study 1.3: Theories of History

Beardsworth, R. (1996). *Derrida and the political.* London: Routledge.

Bennington, G. (2000). *Interrupting Derrida.* London: Routledge.

Caputo, J. D. (1997). *Deconstruction in a nutshell.* New York: Fordham University Press.

Carr, E. H. (1961). *What is history?* Harmondsworth, UK: Penguin.

Elam, D. (1994). *Feminism and deconstruction.* London: Routledge.

Gilderhus, M. T. (1987). *History and historians.* Englewood Cliffs, NJ: Prentice Hall.

Holland, N. J. (Ed.). (1997). *Feminist interpretations of Jacques Derrida.* University Park: Pennsylvania State University Press.

Loewen, J. W. (1996). *Lies my teacher told me: Everything your American history textbook got wrong.* Carmichael, CA: Touchstone.

McCullough, D. (1993). *Truman: The life and times of the thirty-third president of the United States.* New York: Simon & Schuster.

McCullough, D. (2004). *John Adams: The adventurous life-journey of John Adams.* New York: Simon & Schuster.

Smith, B. G. (2000). *The gender of history: Men, women, and historical practice.* Cambridge, MA: Harvard University Press.

Updike, J. (1992). *Memories of the Ford administration: A novel.* New York: Knopf.

Chapter Two

Instruction: Selecting Reading as the Base for Education

Colonial parents ascribed religious, academic, social, and vocational benefits to literacy; they insisted that teachers provide effective instruction. Although teachers initially attempted to nurture literacy through spelling activities, they were disappointed with the results. They later developed a full range of instructional methods, including remedial and computer-aided instruction.

READING IN CONTEMPORARY AMERICA

Reading has been the foundation for American education. It has occupied this position because of its consequences. It has enabled students to progress academically. It also has enabled them to progress economically, culturally, and politically.

Like literacy, illiteracy has consequences. Some consequences are obvious: problems in school, society, and employment are obvious. Some of the consequences are subtle: shame, loss of confidence, and emotional suffering are subtle.

Wishing to thoroughly investigate the consequences of literacy and illiteracy, researchers differentiated academic literacy from functional literacy. Although they recognized that these two types of literacy were interdependent, they ascribed distinctive characteristics to each.

Researchers viewed academic literacy as the ability to comprehend the printed information that was connected to scholastic routines. They viewed functional literacy as the ability to comprehend the printed information that persons encountered in their daily lives.

Few educators quarreled about the distinction between academic and functional literacy. However, they did quarrel about the details associated with the distinction. For example, they quarreled about phonics, the ability to verbalize groups of letters. They argued about whether phonics characterized academic literacy, functional literacy, or both types of literacy (Giordano, 1996).

Just as educators disagreed about definitions of literacy, they disagreed about the ways to measure it. Some of them even challenged whether functional literacy could be measured (Giordano, 1996). These critics questioned whether each person's unique circumstances precluded the assessment of functional literacy. They objected to assessments that did not reflect those unique circumstances.

The critics might have conceded that comprehending the information on a bus schedule was a functional literacy task for adults who relied on public transportation. However, they would have questioned whether it was a functional literacy task for residents who were not served by mass transportation.

Although some educators questioned whether functional literacy could be measured, even those who insisted that it could be measured disagreed among themselves about appropriate assessment procedures. Because of this feuding, educational researchers found it difficult to estimate rates of functional literacy and illiteracy.

In spite of the academic turmoil about functional literacy, some researchers have attempted to make estimates about the levels of functional literacy and illiteracy. Their estimates have been shockingly high. For example, some of them estimated that at least 30 percent of American adults were functionally illiterate (United States Department of Education, 1993; 2007a; 2007b). Others estimated that nearly 800 million adults in the world were functionally illiterate (United Nations Educational Scientific Cultural Organization, 2007).

Scholars agree that the failure to read may devastate individual lives. Some of them contend that this failure also may devastate nations. Canadian government leaders, industrialists, and businesspersons have noted a positive correlation between their nation's rate of literacy and its rate of economic development; they have argued that this correlation reflects a causative relationship (Statistics Canada, 1994; 1996; 1998).

Businesspersons who are convinced that the literacy of their workers affects productivity have recommended distinctive interventions. Some of them began to train laborers in the workplace (Belfiore, Defoe, Folinsbee, Hunter, and Jackson, 2004; Melendez, 2004).

EARLY LITERACY

The colonists in America faced pressing problems; they had to build homes, gather food, and secure their safety. In spite of these challenges, they preserved a remarkable commitment to religion. They regularly read the Bible, the Tanakh, collections of sermons, and other religious books.

Church leaders insisted that children learn to read. Some of them personally taught literacy. Some of them relied on their spouses or other educated members of their congregations to provide this instruction.

Although the colonial-era settlers may have seen worship as the primary purpose of their churches and synagogues, they did assign civic functions to these facilities. They frequently made them the central sites for community activities.

As their communities prospered, settlers were able to replace small buildings with larger ones. Many of them resolved to vacate their religious buildings and replace them with churches and synagogues that had the grandeur of those that they had left in Europe. They then converted the vacated buildings into other types of facilities. They frequently converted them into schoolhouses.

The settlers believed that buildings dedicated exclusively to education had advantages. For example, schoolhouses were the minimal resources that they required to lure professional, full-time teachers.

The New England settlers excelled at establishing schools and hiring teachers. Although the precise number of elementary schools and high schools that they established is difficult to ascertain, the number of colleges that they established is documented clearly. During the period from 1636 to 1770, fourteen colleges were founded; eleven of them were located in New England.

NINETEENTH-CENTURY LITERACY

The colonists judged that reading enabled persons to lead full spiritual lives. For this reason alone, they would have made it a key competency in their communities. However, they also judged that reading was important for other reasons. For example, it indicated social and economic status; it characterized members of the military, government, clergy, and the business community.

Parents realized that reading was necessary for their children. Wealthy parents wanted their children to read so that they could maintain their social and economic status. Working-class parents wanted their children to read so that they could become apprentices in key trades and professions. If their children secured choice apprenticeships, they might have opportunities to acquire respect and wealth.

In addition to attributing social prestige and utilitarian value to reading, citizens believed that reading had a central role in a democratic republic. Because of the immense size of the United States and the poor conditions of its roads, citizens could not expect politicians to visit their communities. Under these circumstances, they had to be able to read newspapers and periodicals to stay informed about political developments.

The American colonists valued reading because of its symbiotic relationship with religion, social status, vocational training, wealth, and politics. Additionally, many of them valued it because of its aesthetic rewards. They believed that the value of great books, like the value of great music, sculpture, painting, and architecture, enriched their lives. For all of these reasons, they insisted that their children learn to read.

Case Study 2.1: Nineteenth-Century Reading Education

The early colonists placed a high priority on learning to read. Nonetheless, they had to address other educational issues. They had to build schoolhouses, recruit teachers, and pay for education.

When settlers built new churches and synagogues, they transformed their former places of worship into schoolhouses. They then used the schoolhouses to attract full-time teachers. After they designated schoolhouses, hired teachers, and amassed educational budgets, they expected their children to learn. They expected them to learn to read.

However, the settlers and the teachers they hired needed to resolve a critical problem. They needed to identify the type of instruction that would enable children to become successful readers.

Alphabet Method

Teachers employed the alphabet method during the 1700s, and many of them continued to use it throughout the 1800s. They valued this method because it complemented recitation, a classroom procedure in which students restated key pieces of information. Most teachers depended heavily on recitation, using it for all of the subjects in the curriculum.

When they taught with the alphabet method, teachers asked students to read orally. If they detected problems, they would ask students to recite the names of the letters in words. In effect, they would ask students to spell the troublesome words. The teachers believed that this approach provided the students with the mnemonic associations that they needed to master reading.

Whole-word Method

Although many teachers used the alphabet method, some of them began to experiment with other approaches. During the early 1800s, they experimented with the whole-word method. This new method focused students' attention on entire words. From the first day of instruction, teachers encouraged students to memorize the pronunciation of short and familiar words.

Teachers claimed that the whole-word approach was easy to master; they explained that it was simple because it did not require students to spell and read simultaneously. They noted that it also provided an alternative for students who had tried learning with the alphabet approach but failed.

Phonic Method

Teachers were aware that many students were frustrated by the alphabet approach, so some teachers turned to the phonic method. They used the phonic method to teach students to recognize the sounds of letters. When their students were baffled by words, they encouraged them to say the sound of the letters in those words.

If students did not recognize the word *cat,* they would say the sound of the letter *c,* the sound of the letter *a,* and the sound of the letter *t.* They then would blend those sounds together. Hopefully, they would recognize their utterance as the word *cat.*

Advocates pointed out that students could use the phonic method to recall words that they had forgotten. They claimed that they could even use it to decipher words that they had never encountered in print but which they had heard in conversations. They claimed that this method could work even when teachers or adults were not present to assist learners.

Phonetic Method

Proponents of phonics considered it an improvement over the alphabet approach. Nonetheless, they conceded that students would be unable to pronounce some words by sounding out the individual letters in them. They were aware that students who lived in *Connecticut* could not use phonics to pronounce that state's name.

Critics were able to identify thousands of frequently occurring words that could not be pronounced with phonics. Upset by these irregularities, some teachers began to spell words differently. They claimed that they had been inspired by Noah Webster.

Webster had written a popular set of dictionaries in which he had changed the spellings of words. He wanted words to be spelled more like the ways in which they were pronounced. He urged Americans to abandon traditional British spellings such as *colour* and replace them with such spellings as *color.* He made comparable suggestions for many other words with traditional British spellings.

In his bestselling dictionaries, Webster introduced new ways of spelling. He also introduced another strategy to help readers. He used phonetic symbols to indicate pronunciations. By relying on the sounds associated with phonetic symbols, adult readers were able to decipher words with which they were unfamiliar.

Like Webster, proponents of the phonetic approach began to create materials with phonetically transcribed words. Unlike Webster, they aimed their materials at children.

The proponents of the phonetic approach chose to depict the pronunciation of words in a new way. For instance, for the word *cake,* to reveal the pronunciation of the first vowel, they substituted the symbol *ā* for *a.* Because the second vowel is a silent letter, they eliminated it. Because the consonant sounds at the beginning and end of *cake* are identical, they used the same letter in both positions. When they had finished, the word *cake* was depicted as *kāk.* Using comparable logic, they depicted the word *bomb* as *bōm.*

Kinesthetic Method

Some approaches to literacy instruction emerged out of academic turmoil. They emerged after critics belittled the alphabet method. They emerged after critics claimed that teachers who relied on the alphabet method failed to recognize the individual needs of students.

The advocates of the alphabet method responded to their critics. They adapted their approach to make it more effective. They transformed it into phonics-based instruction. They eventually transformed it into phonetic instruction.

Teachers had opportunities to join multiple pedagogical factions. Some of them chose the alphabet faction, some chose the phonics faction, and some chose the phonetic faction. Some of them joined the kinesthetic faction.

Teachers who used the kinesthetic method encouraged learners to remember letters and words through movements. Some of them required students to make refined movements. For example, they required them to trace letters that had been printed on worksheets. They predicted that refined movements would create the mnemonic associations that students needed to read.

Some of the teachers who used the kinesthetic method required students to make large movements. For example, they required them to twist their bodies into the shapes of letters. They predicted that large movements would help students recognize letters, recognize words, and read.

Pictorial Method

Proponents of the phonic, phonetic, and kinesthetic methods realized that these methods were variations of the alphabet method. They had adapted the alphabet method in response to criticism.

Like other teachers, the proponents of the whole-word method made changes in response to criticism. Because they had been criticized for teaching children to merely "call out" words, they wanted to do a better job of promoting comprehension.

To promote comprehension, teachers began to rely on pictorial symbols. Some of them referred to this approach as the pictorial method; others referred to it as the natural or rebus method.

To implement the pictorial method, teachers substituted symbols for printed words. They relied on symbols that suggested the meanings of the omitted words. Suppose they had wished their students to read the following sentence: *Music made Mary happy*. They might have rewritten it in this manner: ♪ *made Mary* ☺.

Sentence Method

Proponents of the whole-word method were upset by critics who accused them of failing to develop comprehension. Stung by this criticism, they searched for distinct but philosophically compatible approaches. Although some of them turned to the pictorial method, others turned to the sentence method.

Teachers who employed the sentence method conversed with their students. They made transcriptions of the sentences that their students had spoken. They then used the transcribed sentences during instruction.

Enthusiasts claimed that the sentence method enabled children to recognize and comprehend printed samples of their own language. They reasoned that the children could recognize their own language more easily than that of textbook authors.

Experience Method

Critics alleged that the sentence method was far from perfect. They worried that children with limited English would have difficulties because the transcriptions that they were reading would not contain the novel language and concepts to which they would have been exposed in books.

In response to this criticism, proponents of the sentence method made changes to ensure that children would be exposed to novel language and concepts. They referred to their adaptation as the experience method.

Teachers who used the experience method continued to converse with students and transcribe their remarks. However, they arranged activities before the conversations. They made sure that the students discussed those activities during the conversations. They later used the transcriptions of those conversations during reading instruction.

The experience method was a hallmark of John Dewey's nineteenth-century "laboratory school" at the University of Chicago. The teachers at this school judged that it represented a creative alternative to textbook-centered instruction.

Children's Literature Method

The teachers at Dewey's school had confidence in the experience method; they also had confidence in the children's literature method. When they were employing the children's literature method, they surrounded students with books and encouraged them to select those that they found interesting. The teachers then used the books that students had selected for individualized literacy instruction.

Proponents predicted that the children's literature method would encourage students to read outside of the classroom. They also predicted that it would motivate them to read. Although they recognized that students who used the children's literature method might encounter advanced vocabulary, grammatical structures, and concepts in the books they selected, they believed that the advantages of this approach outweighed its disadvantages.

Bibliotherapy

Some teachers believed that the children's literature method could be adapted to make it even more effective. Instead of allowing students to select books, they wished to direct them to suitable volumes. They hoped to direct students to books with situations similar to those in which students were involved.

If the parents of their students were getting divorced, teachers might direct the students to books in which comparable events were transpiring. Advocates alleged that this approach could help children read and solve their emotional problems. Because they detected similarities between this instructional approach and psychological therapy, they referred to it as bibliotherapy.

Some teachers pointed out that they lacked the training to assess emotional health and recommend psychologically suitable books. However, proponents had an answer for them. They advised them to provide students with books that reflected the emotional problems that they were likely to encounter. For example, elementary-school teachers might give young students books about fear of the dark or separation from parents. High-school teachers might give adolescents books about loneliness or depression.

Technology-Based Approaches

Some early teachers began to incorporate educational technology into reading instruction. For example, they used candle-powered projectors to display letters, words, phrases, and sentences. As another example, they transformed primitive copying machines into classroom printing presses.

Even though most of the technological devices were impractical, they had advantages. They captured the interest of students, provided alternatives for learners who had failed with the traditional scholastic materials, and ensured that all of the students in a group had access to uniform learning materials.

Eclectic Approaches

The most popular way to teach reading at the beginning of the 1800s was the alphabet method. This simple and structured approach bolstered the confidence, and ultimately the effectiveness, of marginally prepared teachers. The phonic, phonetic, and kinesthetic methods were other simple and structured approaches that helped marginally prepared teachers.

The alphabet, phonic, phonetic, and kinesthetic approaches were examples of skills-based teaching methods. When teachers relied on two or more of them, they combined the elements within them eclectically.

The whole-word, pictorial, sentence, and experience methods were examples of language-based approaches. When teachers relied on two or more of them, they combined the elements within them eclectically.

The teachers who relied on the literature-based approaches or technology based approaches also had opportunities to use strategies eclectically.

Reading Textbooks

William H. McGuffey was a Protestant minister who began to write reading textbooks in 1836. Publishers sold almost 100,000,000 copies of his books during the next six decades.

McGuffey's textbooks sold well because of their positive attributes. They employed stimulating passages, beautiful illustrations, practical learning activities, and pedagogical tips for teachers. They also employed an eclectic approach to instruction; they included samples of language-based, literature-based, and skills-based learning activities.

Summary of the Early Approaches to Reading Education

Nineteenth-century approaches to literacy instruction fell into four categories.

Skills-Based Approaches

The skills-based approaches incorporated systematically developed instructional activities. They identified precise skills and then sequenced them according to the ease with which they could be mastered. The alphabet method was the most widely used skills-based approach at the beginning of the 1800s. The phonic method, the phonetic method, and the kinesthetic method emerged later.

Language-Based Approaches

The language-based approaches recognized the distinctive abilities of individual learners. Early language-based approaches included the whole-word method and the pictorial method; later approaches included the sentence method and the experience method.

Literature-Based Approaches

The literature-based approaches used meaningful materials to motivate learners. Some of them encouraged teachers to surround students with stimulating books. Others encouraged them to surround students with books corresponding to their emotional stages of development. Still others encouraged teachers to provide students with books addressing individual psychological needs.

Technology-Based Approaches

Technology-based approaches used mechanical or electrical devices to facilitate learning. They frequently were combined with the skills-based approaches.

Activity: Advantages and Limitations of Approaches

Diverse approaches to reading instruction appeared, gained support, and were implemented in the early schools. Some of them retained their advocates; others lost them. The popularity of the early approaches may have been affected by economic, social, cultural, and political factors. However, it also may have been affected by the pedagogical strengths and limitations of the approaches themselves.

What were some of the pedagogical strengths and limitations of the early approaches to literacy instruction? To answer this question, create a matrix.

Along the vertical axis of the matrix, place the four general categories of literacy instruction: skills-based, language-based, literature-based, and technology-based approaches.

Along the horizontal axis of the matrix, arrange a column for strengths and a column for weaknesses. In the appropriate cells, indicate pedagogical strengths and weaknesses for each approach. Focus your attention on practical features that were likely to catch the attention of teachers and school administrators.

Table 2.1. Nineteenth-Century Reading Education

Approach	*Strengths*	*Weaknesses*
Skills-Based		
Language-Based		
Literature-Based		
Technology-Based		

Your responses should be based on assumptions about the vested interests, values, and goals of teachers and school administrators. Although you can use the information in the case study to make some of these assumptions, you may wish to rely on a broader foundation of information.

You may gather additional information from the materials that are listed at the end of this chapter. You may gather it from lectures or discussions.

Case Study 2.2: Technological Innovations

Political liberals depicted the schools as cumbersome bureaucracies. Some of them, who were inspired by John Dewey and other university professors, referred to themselves as progressive educators. They called for extensive reforms during the late 1800s.

Political conservatives also were concerned about education. They provided their own distinctive advice. For example, they encouraged school administrators to adopt a business mentality. In fact, they encouraged them to form partnerships with businesses. They noted with pride that partnerships between the schools and businesses were responsible for the textbooks on which educators were relying.

The conservatives had additional advice. They advised school administrators to promote standardization. Unlike the progressive educators, they viewed standardization in the schools as a positive trend.

The conservatives supported standardized textbooks; they also supported standardized curricula, standardized testing, standardized credentialing of teachers, standardized vocational training, and standardized educational accountability. They alleged that these practices could reduce expenses and promote efficiency; they insisted that they were in the best interest of school administrators, teachers, students, employers, and taxpayers.

The conservatives had still more advice for the school administrators. They urged them to rely on innovative technology. They assured them that this technology would help the schools in the same ways that it had helped industry and commercial businesses. They even advised the school administrators to train students to operate the technologies that they were incorporating into their businesses.

Although they were pressured to use technology, nineteenth-century educators had limited funds with which to purchase it. Furthermore, they had a hard time locating devices that could improve learning. Although they had access to candle-powered projectors, these machines were expensive and impractical.

Eventually, educators did discover practical devices for the schools. For example, they discovered typewriters. Although they originally supplied typewriters only to their clerks, they later acceded to businesspersons who recommended that they supply them to students. Students used the typewriters to train for clerical jobs; they also used them to acquire literacy skills.

The early educators purchased copying machines. During the late 1800s, they relied on copying machines that employed waxed stencils. After writing on a waxed stencil with a stylus, they affixed the stencil to the copying machine. As the machine was cranked, ink passed through the stencil. The ink would seep through the portions of the wax stencil that had been removed with the stylus and make impressions on pieces of paper. At first, these machines produced only 20 copies before the stencil deteriorated. However, they later made more than 100 copies per stencil.

After the instructors had access to stencils on which they could type, they transformed the copying machines into inexpensive printing presses. They used them to make materials that appeared to be professionally typeset. They used them to reproduce and share student-generated materials.

Businesspersons continued to pressure educators to incorporate technology into the schools. They were persistent during the early 1900s. This was the era when Frederick Winslow Taylor was investigating the efficiency of commercial and industrial operations.

Taylor was a mechanical engineer who designed ingenious studies. In one of his studies, he observed workers shoveling coal. After analyzing their schedules, behaviors, muscular movements, and tools, he concluded that the workers were responsible for unnecessary expenses.

Taylor vowed that he would make workplace management more scientific. He referred to the persons who followed him as "scientific managers." In the popular press, reporters referred Taylor's disciples as "efficiency experts." They sometimes assigned a negative connotation to this phrase.

School administrators were adjured to rely on the principles of scientific management. Hoping that a highly visible use of technology would appease their critics, some of them purchased typewriters and copying machines. They would eventually expand their inventories to include film projectors, radios, phonographs, tape recorders, and televisions.

Entrepreneurs did develop some specialized equipment for the schools; they even developed some precisely for reading education. For example, they devised projectors that could display letters, words, sentences, and passages. They developed camera-like apertures with which teachers could control the amount of time that projectors displayed information to students. Some of them designed machines on which opaque wands progressively covered lines of print.

In spite of the enthusiasm that they generated among businesspersons, the early educational technologies did not inspire many teachers. Some skeptical educators began to question whether technology had substantive educational value.

Educators changed their attitudes toward technology after personal computers became available. Although they were disappointed by the educational programs that were available, they noted that computers were more adaptable than the earlier technologies. For example, they discovered that they could modify programs; they discovered that they could even create their own programs.

School administrators discerned the ways in which personal computers were transforming business, industry, commerce, and society and incorporated them into their schools. They accelerated their implementation after the World Wide Web was established.

The Web enabled students to communicate with an unlimited number of persons, agencies, institutions, and businesses. It had motivational value because it presented them with timely, novel, and relevant content. It also had pedagogical value because it gave them reasons to be verbally and technologically literate.

Activity: Emerging Classroom Technologies Affect Reading

Nineteenth- and twentieth-century educators experimented with diverse technologies in the schools. Some of them used these technologies to nurture vocational skills. Some of them used them to nurture academic skills. Some of them used them to nurture reading skills.

How do you think members of the general public felt about the use of technology to enhance reading instruction? To help answer this question, create a chart.

Table 2.2. Technological Innovations

Technology	*Support**	*Advantages*	*Disadvantages*
Typewriter			
Copying Machine			
Record Player			
Silent Film Projector			
Television			
Computer—No Web Access			
Computer—Web Access			

* (+) Supported
(-) Opposed
(+/-) Mixed Commitment

Along the vertical axis of the chart, place the following technological developments: typewriter, copying machine, record player, silent film projector, television, personal computer without access to the World Wide Web, and personal computer with access to the World Wide Web.

Along the horizontal axis of the chart, arrange several columns. In one column, use symbols to indicate whether the members of the general public primarily supported (+), opposed (-), or showed a mixed commitment (+/-) to the use of each technology to enhance the teaching of reading.

In a separate column of the chart, indicate advantages that the general public may have attributed to each type of technology. In still another column of the chart, indicate disadvantages that the general public may have attributed to each type of technology.

Your designations should be based on assumptions about the general public's vested interests, values, and goals. Although you can use the information in the case study to make some of these assumptions, you may wish to rely on a broader foundation of information.

You can gather additional information from the materials that are listed at the end of this chapter. You may gather it from lectures or discussions.

Case Study 2.3: Remedial Reading

Parents became concerned when teachers were unable to help children read. At the beginning of the 1800s, they were concerned about those teachers who knew about only one instructional approach—the alphabet method.

Teachers were aware that parents were distraught when their children could not read. Nonetheless, some of them assumed a Darwinian attitude. They judged that intellectually fit students would learn to read, attend high schools, and graduate from universities; they predicted that unfit students would fail in school, drop out, and work in menial jobs. Needless to say, some parents were upset by this attitude.

Parents were not only upset but also confused when they children did not become readers. They were confused because many of their children seemed to be as bright as the children who were succeeding. They wondered whether their children demonstrated some peculiar resistance to reading.

Unable to find help in the schools, parents went to physicians. They began their visits by asking the doctors why their children were not reading. After examining the children, the doctors concluded that disorders were interfering with learning. They hypothesized that the children had nervous system disorders.

The physicians cited neurological case studies to make their explanations of reading problems seem plausible. For example, they reviewed incidents in which bullets or shrapnel had damaged relatively small portions of soldiers' brains. The rehabilitating soldiers, who had preserved most of their abilities, had lost only certain skills. Sometimes they had lost the ability to read.

The physicians then made several assumptions. They assumed that neurological dysfunctions did not have to be the exclusive result of trauma. They assumed that neurological dysfunctions might be caused by congenital defects. They assumed that some neurological dysfunctions appeared at birth and others appeared developmentally.

The physicians who examined children with learning problems made another key assumption: they assumed that congenital and developmental neurological problems could be repaired. With the aid of a group of educators, they devised remedial reading instruction for the students that they had diagnosed.

During the first quarter of the twentieth century, a new generation of teachers could be observed. These were the remedial reading teachers who set up their businesses in private or university-affiliated clinics.

Although some parents sent their children to these businesses, others could not afford them. The poor parents demanded that school administrators offer remedial reading in the public schools.

The school administrators eventually acceded to the parents. However, they wished to control the amount of money spent on remedial instruction. Recognizing that the cost of remedial instruction increased with the level of specialization, they implemented it in progressive fashions. Some of them simply directed teachers to instruct students with severe reading problems in their classrooms. Some hired remedial teachers to provide instruction in separate classrooms. Still others paid for services at commercial facilities.

Just as resourceful school administrators adopted less expensive types of instruction, they also adopted economical practices for screening students with learning problems. Aware that they could not afford the types of screening that the commercial clinics were offering, they searched for trendy but inexpensive techniques. They were hopeful that assessments of eye movements would have these characteristics.

A group of educational professors had concluded that eye movements were reliable indicators of the neurological irregularities that interfered with reading. Even more remarkably, they concluded that altering eye movements could substantively improve reading.

The proponents of eye-movement-based remedial reading strategies relied on ingenious tracking devices. Some of them carefully positioned mirrors, placed themselves behind students, and then looked into the mirrors to track eye movements; others used cameras to make records of eye movements. They advised the school administrators to assign the responsibility for eliminating reading problems to highly trained specialists.

Even though school administrators tried to save money, the remedial reading programs were expensive. Fiscally conservative taxpayers questioned the cost of these programs. They accused educators of mimicking medical practices in order to increase the prestige of educators, the salaries of their staffs, and the funding for their schools.

In spite of criticism that was directed at them, school administrators and teachers expanded remedial reading in the schools. They claimed that the programs had successfully taught reading to children who otherwise would have failed and dropped out of school.

Professors supported the school administrators who implemented remedial reading programs. The professors were enthusiastic because the programs were generating positive publicity. This publicity was enhancing reading education; it also was enhancing the colleges of education and the entire educational field.

Parents supported the school administrators who implemented remedial reading programs. The parents of children who had been diagnosed with severe reading problems were understandably enthusiastic. After all, their children had received remedial services. However, the parents of children without severe reading problems also were enthusiastic; they may have hoped that their children eventually would receive some form of specialized instruction.

Activity: Students with Severe Reading Problems

Early-twentieth-century teachers developed highly original remedial reading programs. Although they initially offered these programs in private clinics, they eventually implemented them in the public schools.

How did different groups initially respond to implementation of remedial programs in the public schools? To help answer this question, create a chart.

Table 2.3. Remedial Reading

Group	*Support**	*Explanation*
Parents of Children with Severe Problems		
Parents of Children with Mild Problems		
Elementary School Teachers		
Elementary School Principals		
Professors of Education		
Politicians		

* (+) Supported
(-) Opposed
(+/-) Mixed Commitment

Along the vertical axis of the chart, place the following groups: parents of children with severe reading problems, parents of children with mild reading problems, elementary-school teachers, elementary-school principals, professors of education, and politicians.

Along the horizontal axis of the chart, arrange several columns. In one column, use symbols to indicate whether each group primarily supported (+), opposed (-), or showed a mixed commitment (+/-) to the novel reading programs.

Your indications about the responses of the groups should be based on assumptions about the vested interests, values, and goals of their members. Although you can use the information in the case study to make some of these assumptions, you may wish to rely on a broader foundation of information.

You can gather additional information from the materials that are listed at the end of this chapter. You may gather it from lectures or discussions.

On a separate page, summarize your assumptions about each group.

USING THE PAST TO UNDERSTAND THE PRESENT

Parents realized that children who could read would progress in school. They knew that they also would secure choice jobs. Pressured by parents, teachers made reading the focus of the schools.

Early teachers employed a type of instruction that was based on spelling. However, they searched for ways to improve that instruction. They eventually experimented with sophisticated pedagogies. They also experimented with specialized textbooks, standardized tests, diagnostic procedures, and remedial instruction.

During the 1800s and early 1900s, a literacy gap had separated financially established and financially struggling families. Children who were surrounded by books in their homes had advantages; children from impoverished backgrounds lacked those advantages. Aware of the damage that resulted from the literacy gap, a coalition took measures to close it. The coalition included governmental leaders, educators, and philanthropists.

Recently, another gap has opened between financially established and financially struggling families. Some educators (Buckingham, 2007) have noted that children with computers in their homes have opportunities that children without computers lack. They have asked whether this computer gap is effectively a literacy gap.

Parents historically have been concerned about the scholastic and career damage that illiteracy inflicted. When they were worried that their children did not have access to books, they recognized that school and public libraries represented solutions. Today parents are worried about the scholastic and career damage that their children sustain when they lack access to computers.

Although they approve of the placement of computers in schools and libraries, they still have questioned whether this represents an adequate solution.

Attempt to locate instances in which leaders in government, business, education, or philanthropy have referred to a computer gap. Did they suggest ways of closing that gap? Attempt to locate comments that were made by persons in your state or community.

CHAPTER SUMMARY

The early colonists prized reading's religious and utilitarian benefits; they made sure that teachers understood the importance of teaching children to read. The early teachers tried to nurture reading through spelling activities. Disappointed with this technique, they searched for alternatives. They tried techniques that relied on oral language, children's books, technology, and phonetic decoding. Later generations continued to be concerned about reading; they experimented with remedial and computer-based techniques.

ADDITIONAL READING

Introductory Passages

Friere, P. (1972). *Pedagogy of the oppressed.* New York: Herder & Herder.

Kliebard, H. M. (1999). *Schooled to work: Vocationalism and the American curriculum, 1876–1946.* New York: Teachers College Press.

Kliebard, H. M. (2004). *The struggle for the American curriculum, 1893–1958* (3rd ed.). New York: Routledge-Falmer.

Tyack, D. (2005). *The one best system: A history of American urban education.* Cambridge, MA: Harvard University Press.

Verhoeven, L. (Ed.). (1994). *Functional literacy: Theoretical issues and educational implications.* (Studies in Written Language and Literacy, Vol. 1). Philadelphia: Benjamins.

Case Study 2.1: Nineteenth-Century Reading Education

Adams, J. T. (1921). *The Founding of New England.* New York: Atlantic.

Anderson, V. D. (1993). *New England's generation: The Great Migration and the formation of society and culture in the 17th century.* New York: Cambridge University Press.

Bruce, P. A. (1896). *Economic history of Virginia in the seventeenth century: An inquiry into the material condition of the people, based on original and contemporaneous records.* New York: Macmillan.

Butts, R. F., & Cremin, L. A. (1953). *A history of education in American culture.* New York: Rinehart & Winston.

Cooke, J. E. (Ed.). (1993). *Encyclopedia of the North American colonies* (Vol. 1; Vol. 2; & Vol. 3). New York: Scribner's Sons.

Cremin, L. A. (1970). *American education: The colonial experience, 1607–1783.* New York: Harper & Row.

Giordano, G. (2000). *Twentieth-century reading education: Understanding practices of today in terms of patterns of the past.* New York: Elsevier.

Kaestle, C. F., & Damon-Moore, H. (1991). *Literacy in the United States: Readers and reading since 1880.* New Haven, CT: Yale University Press.

Morrison, S. E. (1956). *The intellectual life of colonial New England.* New York: New York University Press.

Noll, M. A., & Gaustad E. S. (2003). *A Documentary history of religion in America* (Vol. 1; Vol. 2). Grand Rapids, MI: Eerdmans.

Olmstead, C. E. (1960). *History of religion in the United States.* Englewood Cliffs, NJ: Prentice Hall.

Case Study 2.2: Technological Innovations

Allan, R. A. (2001). *A history of the personal computer: The people and the technology.* London, Ontario: Allan.

Cuban, L. (1986). *Teachers and machines: The classroom use of technology since 1920.* New York: Teachers College Press.

Kanigel, R. (1997). *The one best way: Frederick Winslow Taylor and the enigma of efficiency.* New York: Viking.

Nelson, D. (1980). *Frederick W. Taylor and the rise of scientific management.* Madison: University of Wisconsin Press.

Russo, T. A. (2002). *Mechanical typewriters: Their history, value, and legacy.* Atglen, PA: Schiffer.

Case Study 2.3: Remedial Reading

Fernald, G. (1943). *Remedial techniques in basic school subjects.* New York: McGraw-Hill.

Gates, A. I. (1927). *The improvement of reading: A program of diagnostic and remedial methods.* New York: Macmillan.

Giordano, G. (2000). *Twentieth-century reading education: Understanding practices of today in terms of patterns of the past.* New York: Elsevier.

Gray, W. S. (1922). *Remedial cases in reading: Their diagnosis and treatment.* Chicago: University of Chicago Press.

Harris, A. J. (1940). *How to increase reading ability: A guide to developmental and remedial methods.* New York: Longman-Greene.

Harris. A. J. (1968). Five decades of remedial reading. In J. A. Figurel (Ed.), *Forging ahead in reading* (pp. 25–34). Newark, DE: International Reading Association.

Kirk, S. A. (1940). *Teaching reading to slow-learning children.* Boston: Houghton Mifflin.

Monroe, M., & Backus, B. (1937). *Remedial reading.* Boston: Houghton Mifflin.

Smith, N. B. (1934). *American reading instruction: Its development and its significance in gaining a perspective on current practices in reading.* New York: Silver Burdett.

Chapter Three

Learners: Helping Urban and Immigrant Students

Many nineteenth-century Americans had become socially and financially secure; they were uneasy about the immigrants that were spilling into their country. Some of them were upset because the immigrants clustered in ethnic neighborhoods, did not speak English, ignored American traditions, and preserved loyalties to their former countries. Some were upset because the immigrants became social burdens. Some were upset because the immigrants competed with them for employment, property, and political power. As for the immigrants, they faced immediate financial problems and long-term social problems. They realized that the schools provided opportunities to solve both types of problems. Eventually, the established citizens realized that the schools could solve the problems about which they worried.

THE IMMIGRANT IN TODAY'S CLASSROOMS

A significant number of American citizens had become socially and financially established by the 1800s. Some of them were convinced that new immigrants were causing problems. Some of them became insecure. Some of them became hostile. Some of them became xenophobic.

Americans' attitudes toward immigrants were influenced by historical events. The attitudes of nineteenth-century Americans were influenced by the Mexican American War. The attitudes of twentieth-century Americans were influenced by the two world wars. The attitudes of twenty-first-century Americans were influenced by the events that transpired on September 11, 2001.

American citizens looked at Muslim Americans in a different fashion after 9/11. Some of them treated their Muslim American neighbors deplorably.

When these citizens were accused of behaving like xenophobes, they objected. They insisted that the opinions of xenophobes were influenced by features such as religion, dress, and appearance. They insisted that their opinions were influenced by a link between Muslim Americans and terrorism. They insisted that they had treated Muslim Americans in the same way that they would have treated any group that had been linked to terrorism.

The post-9/11 Americans who mistrusted Muslim American contended that they were not xenophobes. However, many of them were unaware that earlier generations had made similar retorts to comparable accusations. Had they been aware of those historical incidents, they might have been impressed by the immense suffering that was inflicted.

IMPACT OF IMMIGRANTS

At the beginning of the nineteenth century, many families had adapted to the United States; they had assumed a new culture, acquired land, and accumulated wealth. Some established families were positively disposed toward the new immigrants for idealistic reasons; they saw similarities between the immigrants and their own parents or grandparents.

Some Americans were positively disposed toward the new immigrants for pragmatic reasons. They recognized that they needed immigrants to build roads, bridges, tunnels, and dams. They needed them to erect residential and commercial facilities. They needed them to labor in mines and forests. They needed them to work on waterways and farms. They needed them to settle the frontiers, consume products, and invest in the economy.

Not all of the established families in the United States were happy about the new immigrants. Some of them were disconcerted by the large number of recent immigrants.

Large numbers of immigrants had enabled the United States to grow. The national population had been only 4,000,000 persons at the beginning of the nineteenth century. It increased to 24,000,000 persons by the middle of the century; it increased to 75,000,000 during the end. During the first quarter of the twentieth century, it increased to 125,000,000 persons.

Some of the immigrants resided in sparsely populated rural areas; others resided in densely populated urban neighborhoods. Irrespective of the locales in which they resided, they attracted attention. They attracted attention because they increased the cost of education, health care, and social services. They attracted attention because they affected the country's racial, ethnic, linguistic, religious, and cultural balance.

IMPACT OF URBANIZATION

Some immigrants settled in cities. They had several reasons for residing in these communities. A portion of those individuals who disembarked in New York City stayed there because it was economically expedient. Another portion traveled to nearby cities on the East Coast. As an example, they traveled to Boston, where the population grew from 65,000 to 350,000 persons in less than fifty years.

In the cities, immigrants might find helpful relatives. They might find persons who spoke their language, shared their culture, and sympathized with them. They might find employment.

Immigrants made compromises in order to ward off hunger and homelessness. They made compromises when they accepted unsavory jobs, labored for long hours, endured unsafe conditions, and settled for minimal wages. They made compromises when they required their children to work. They made compromises when they allowed their children to become malnourished, unhealthy, and ill.

COMBINING EDUCATION WITH SOCIAL WORK

Jane Addams was a social and educational reformer who helped urban immigrants. She predicted that teachers who attempted to educate immigrant children would fail if they were attentive only to their academic needs. She counseled the teachers to provide students with social and humanitarian services; she counseled them to provide the students with food, clothing, shelter, medical care, and security.

To demonstrate the approach that she had in mind, Addams opened a facility called Hull-House in 1889. She called her innovative facility a social settlement rather than a school. She initially provided services only for young children. However, she expanded those services over several decades. In addition to helping young children, she helped their older siblings, parents, and relatives.

To attract the older children, Addams organized music, art, and ceramic classes; she also established a gallery, theater, and a library. She offered the services of psychologists, youth protection personnel, and lawyers. She tutored children and their parents in English. She established an employment service for adults, introduced them to representatives from labor unions, and started a communal residence for women who had been abused.

Addams developed a distinctive approach to education. She changed the ways in which immigrant children and their families viewed their school, community, and country. In addition to influencing the children and their families, she influenced the many educators who visited Hull-House.

Case Study 3.1: The Johnstown Flood

Johnstown, Pennsylvania, is situated in a bucolic valley near Pittsburgh. Because it was served by a railway and a navigable waterway, in the nineteenth-century this community became the site of an iron factory. The employment opportunities at the factory assured that the town would prosper. By 1890, the town had grown to 30,000 residents. It comprised large groups from Germany and Great Britain and a very small group from Hungary.

Officials in the Pennsylvania government had engineered, constructed, and operated the waterway that flowed through Johnstown. They relied on a series of reservoirs to regulate it. They had situated one of these reservoirs in South Fork, only 15 miles from Johnstown. To expand the capacity of this reservoir, they erected a dam.

The Pennsylvania officials eventually decided that they did not need the South Fork reservoir. They sold it to a railroad company, which then sold it to a group of wealthy investors. These investors included Andrew Carnegie and Henry Clay Frick, of U.S. Steel; Andrew Mellon, a banking tycoon; Robert Pitcairn, a railroad executive; and Philander Knox, who later would serve as secretary of state.

The investors who purchased the South Fork reservoir established a private fishing and hunting club in 1879. During the years that followed, they turned their attention away from the reservoir's dam. When they were informed that it was deteriorating, the owners directed the managers to patch rather than renovate it. Even more regrettably, they allowed them to deactivate the mechanism for releasing excess water from the reservoir. Although several of the engineers had questioned these decisions, they did not prevail.

In May of 1889, several days of unusually heavy rain had caused the South Fork reservoir to swell. With hardly any warning, the dam collapsed. A colossal wall of water burst from the ruptured dam. It crushed the buildings, railroad cars, and trees on the valley floor. It swept up the shattered structures, transformed them into water-propelled missiles, and hurled them toward Johnstown.

Although a group of workers had observed the dam break, they were unable to warn the residents of Johnstown about the water that was heading for them. When the ferocious wave reached Johnstown, it obliterated homes, farms, churches, businesses, railroads, and neighborhoods. It swept away, crushed, or drowned two thousand persons.

Prior to the flood, the railway and the river were the routes by which most persons had traveled to Johnstown. After the flood, the railway was damaged. The river could not be used because of the piles of debris with which it was cluttered. The damage was so extensive that residents could not be reached by horseback or even telegraph.

On the evening after the flood, the residents of Johnstown were perilously isolated. Still feeling anguish over the family members, friends, and neighbors who had perished, they watched as another tragedy engulfed their community. As they listened to the cries for help that came from heaps of rubble, they realized that some persons had survived the flood but been trapped in the wreckage. They stood by helplessly as a fire started, roared into a conflagration, and threatened those individuals who were trapped. Scores of persons were burned alive in the fire.

Isolated, hungry, injured, and fearful, some of the Johnstown survivors resolved that they would defend themselves. They resolved to protect themselves and their community from criminals. They resolved to deal firmly with any miscreants who attempted to exploit their terrible situation.

Newspaper publishers were interested in the events in Johnstown. They sent enterprising reporters, artists, and photographers to hike through the cluttered valley that led to Johnstown. Undeterred by the damaged transportation routes, the reporters reached Johnstown, personally inspected the damage, interviewed the survivors, and asked them about ways in which they were coping.

In a *New York Times* article ("Desolated Valley," 1889) that was published just three days after the tragedy, reporters described the terrible scenes that they had observed. Not omitting any macabre details, they wrote that thousands of victims of the flood had been left homeless, starving, and terrorized by "robbers of the dead."

The reporters explained that robbers had been stealing wedding bands from corpses and they asserted that the criminals were members of Johnstown's small Hungarian community. The reporters assured readers that a group of Johnstown's vigilantes were apprehending and summarily executing these thieves. The reporters wrote sympathetically that the vigilantes had taken justice into their own hands because they were not willing to wait for "the tedious process of law."

The surviving adults at Johnstown were looking for some group on which to vent their frustration. They had two opportunities. They could have railed against the resort owners who had been responsible for maintaining the South Fork dam. Alternatively, they could have railed against the Hungarian immigrants who had not been assimilated into their community. They chose the Hungarians.

Many Johnstown residents had been suspicious of the Hungarian immigrants. The Hungarians spoke a distinct language and maintained distinct customs. They had taken jobs from local residents by agreeing to work for lower wages.

Although the Hungarians were aware that some residents of Johnstown looked down on them, they were startled when they were accused of robbing the dead. After the post-flood hysteria had passed, authorities investigated these accusations. During those inquests, only several persons claimed to have witnessed thefts from corpses. Most of the former witnesses conceded that their original allegations could have been erroneous.

As for the owners at the South Fork resort, they were not prosecuted for criminal acts. Although they were sued by the families that had survived, they insisted that the collapse of the dam had been an act of God for which they could not be held accountable. This logic enabled them to win the civil suits that were brought against them.

Activity: Lessons of the Johnstown Flood

The children who survived the 1889 flood in Johnstown were affected by that event. Some of them were affected by the loss of property. Some of them were affected by the loss of family. Some were affected by the ways in which their families and neighbors behaved in the aftermath of the flood.

The survivors were overwhelmed by physical and emotional suffering. They were confused about whom they should blame for that suffering. When they heard accusations that Hungarian immigrants had been robbing jewelry from corpses, a group of survivors were outraged. They pledged that they would arrest and hang the alleged criminals.

The attacks on the Hungarian immigrants may have been connected to actual events that survivors had witnessed. They may have been connected to the trauma that they had sustained. They may have been connected to social biases that they had formed before the tragedy had occurred.

Provide an example of a more recent event that has similarities to the Johnstown flood. In that event, were members of a minority groups involved? Did the recent event elicit emotional responses? Did those emotional responses threaten any of the participants' rights? Could those emotional responses have been based on feelings formed prior to the event?

To help answer these questions, create a chart. Place the names of two incidents along the vertical axis. Use the Johnstown flood for one of these incidents; use an event that transpired during the twentieth or the twenty-first century for the other incident.

Table 3.1. Johnstown Flood

Incident	*Details*	*Groups That Might Have Been Blamed*	*Group That Was Blamed*
Johnstown Flood, 1889			
Twentieth-Century- or Twenty-First-Century Event: ____________			

Along the horizontal axis of the chart, arrange several columns. In one of these columns, provide salient details about each incident. In another column of the chart, identify all of the groups that might have been blamed for each incident. In the final column of the chart, identify the group that actually was blamed for each incident.

Your example will be based on assumptions about the vested interests, values, and goals of the groups that were involved. Although you can use the information in the case study to make some of these assumptions, you may wish to rely on a broader foundation of information.

You can gather additional information from the materials that are listed at the end of this chapter. You may gather it from lectures or discussions.

Case Study 3.2: Italian Americans

Established residents in the United States became nervous when they observed large numbers of immigrants. They became nervous when they observed large numbers of immigrants from a single country. They became extremely nervous when they observed the large numbers of persons who were leaving Italy to enter the United States.

At the beginning of the 1800s, only several thousand Italians had moved to the United States. However, 1,000,000 Italians had moved by the end of that century. By 1920, a stunning 3,000,000 Italians had relocated to the United States.

Although established residents were upset with Italian Americans because of their numbers, they were upset with them for other reasons. They were upset because Italian Americans dressed in shoddy clothes, lived in dilapidated tenements, and labored in menial jobs. They were upset because the religion, language, foods, and festivals of the Italians were unfamiliar to them.

Italian Americans stood out because they had distinctive social, cultural, religious, political, and economic characteristics. They stood out for another reason: They were associated with organized crime. Realizing that Prohibition-era readers would be fascinated with the exploits of the Italian American criminals, reporters caricatured them to promote sales of newspapers. Filmmakers caricatured them to increase business in their industry.

During the twentieth century, Italian Americans were able to alter their public image. They benefited indirectly from respected public figures, such as Fiorello La Guardia. La Guardia, a three-term mayor of New York City from 1934 to 1945, effectively used populist rhetoric to appeal to poor laborers and their families.

Athletes, movie stars, and entertainers also increased the social standing of Italian Americans. Some Italian American celebrities had an enormous influence. This elite group included entertainers such as Frank Sinatra and Tony Bennett, sports figures such as Joe DiMaggio and Vince Lombardi, and filmmakers such as Francis Ford Coppola and Martin Scorsese.

Italian Americans competed with other minority groups for social and financial advantages. In the 1960s, they clashed with African Americans in Newark, New Jersey. African Americans were upset because they had been underrepresented on the local police force. They contrasted their own situation with that of Italian Americans, who were overrepresented. The frustration of Newark's African Americans was evident when riots resulted in extensive damage, injury, and death.

As their social status improved, Italian Americans noted that other aspects of their lives improved. They were able to move into new neighborhoods, receive large loans, and gain access to jobs, clubs, and social circles that were previously unavailable.

Italian Americans even profited from novels, films, and television programs that linked them to organized crime but that did so in a sympathetic manner. The *Godfather* films of Francis Ford Coppola became landmarks in cinema and popular culture.

Once they realized that members of the public had changed the ways in which they were viewing Italian culture, Italian Americans adults showed greater pride in their heritage. Like the adults, Italian American children also benefitted.

Activity: Integrating Italians into American Society

Italian American immigrants displayed a pattern of assimilation that had discernible milestones. Some of the milestones were economic; others were cultural, social, or political.

Has a more recently arrived group of immigrants exhibited a pattern of assimilation with discernible milestones? To answer this question, create a chart.

Table 3.2. Italian Americans

Group	*Milestone*	*Milestone*	*Educational Impact*
Italian American Immigrants			
Another Group of Immigrants: ________			

Along the vertical axis of the chart, arrange several rows. In one row, place Italian American immigrants. In another row, place a recently arrived immigrant group. Along the horizontal axis of the chart, arrange several columns. In two of those columns, identify milestones in the assimilation process. In the final column of the chart, describe a way in which the changes associated with those milestones affected the education of students from each of the two groups.

Your examples will be based on assumptions about the vested interests, values, and goals of Italian Americans and the other immigrant group that you have selected. Although you can use the information in the case study to make some of these assumptions about Italian Americans, you may wish to rely on a broader foundation of information. You will have to rely on a broader base of information to make assumptions about the other immigrant group that you select.

You can gather additional information from the materials that are listed at the end of this chapter. You may gather it from lectures or discussions.

Case Study 3.3: German Americans

Millions of Germans moved to the United States. Many of them had settled in the Midwest during the 1800s. They came to the United Sates to achieve goals that had eluded them in Europe. They came to work, own property, build homes, accumulate wealth, and acquire social status.

Germans quickly became the largest ethnic group in the United States. Although they influenced their new country because of their numbers, they also influenced it because of their ambition, resourcefulness, and community spirit.

German Americans attempted to replicate features of the communities that they had left in Europe. They attempted to maintain German culture, traditions, and language. They attempted to replicate features of German architecture, urban design, civil services, agriculture, manufacturing, and transportation.

German immigrants who valued their schools encouraged teachers to employ innovative German scholastic practices, such as those that Johann Herbart devised. Herbart had believed that children did not learn by simply repeating information. He dissuaded teachers from nurturing students' recitation skills; he adjured them to develop their intellectual, moral, and civic skills.

Herbart assured teachers that they needed to know about pedagogy in order to promote scholastic excellence. He envisaged pedagogy as a system for organizing and guiding instruction. He showed them how it could guide everyday classroom tasks, such as the ways in which they phrased their questions to students.

In addition to encouraging teachers to rely on the scholarly work of Herbart, German Americans encouraged them to rely on advice from Friedrich Froebel. Froebel noted that children learned differently at distinct developmental stages. Rather than assembling children of multiple ages in one-room schoolhouses, he sequestered very young children in kindergartens. Literally translated, the term *kindergarten* means a garden for children. Froebel depicted children as human plants that teachers could cultivate with patience, kindness, and affection.

Froebel encouraged teachers to use classroom activities in which their students employed multiple senses to explore, classify, and analyze items. He assured them that children who engaged in these types of creative learning activities would form deep insights.

The German Americans migrated from a country in which the citizens had regarded education highly. They transferred those attitudes to the United States. German Americans who lived in Ohio demonstrated their commitment to scholastic excellence when they insisted on building elementary schools and high schools in every community throughout their state.

Some of the German Americans who lived in Ohio set up schools that relied on German textbooks, German curricula, and German pedagogy. The instructors in these schools taught German history, German geography, German literature, German culture, and German traditions; they even taught exclusively in German.

Were the nineteenth-century German schools in Ohio segregated? The school administrators at the German schools did not designate which children were to attend; they did not exclude children. Nonetheless, the chances were low that non-Germanic parents would send their children to schools in which the students were taught in German, employed German textbooks, and learned about German traditions. As a result, the nineteenth-century schools in Ohio may have been de facto segregated.

Even though they may have been de facto segregated, the schools that German American children attended were different from those that American Indians and African Americans attended during this era. While the German schools may have been de facto segregated, the schools that American Indians and African Americans attended were de jure segregated—they were segregated by law.

German Americans voluntarily sent their children to schools in which they had confidence. American Indians and African Americans were forced to send their children to schools in which they did not have confidence. Although some contemporaries might have questioned whether the German schools were as superior as the German Americans maintained, they would not have characterized the German schools as inferior. In contrast, all contemporaries agreed that the schools for American Indians and those for African Americans were inferior schools.

During the course of World War I, American citizens changed their attitudes about the German schools in the Midwest. When combat commenced in Europe, most citizens urged the United States to remain neutral. Many immigrants from England, France, or one of the other Allied powers recommended neutrality, but many immigrants from Germany also recommended neutrality.

Although most American citizens favored neutrality, some of them did urge the United States to assist one of the warring coalitions. German Americans who were fiercely patriotic to the United States still maintained great loyalty to their ancestral country. Some of them demonstrated their loyalty by orchestrating public events. Some of them demonstrated their loyalty by raising funds. Some of them demonstrated their loyalty by sending their sons to fight in the German army.

After the United States entered the war on the side of the Allies, political activists reminded the public of the German Americans' rhetoric and fundraising. They warned the public to be suspicious about the genuine loyalties of German Americans.

Anti-German political activists were especially upset by the German schools. They pointed out that a significant number of the persons who had been drafted into the United States Army had not been able to communicate in English. They demanded that the educators in the German schools cease communicating in German; they also demanded that they cease instructing their students about German culture.

Over the course of just several months, the political activists forced school administrators to reorganize the German schools. They required the administrators to teach in English, purchase American textbooks, place a greater emphasis on American traditions, and inculcate American patriotism. The most extreme activists demanded the exclusion of German from high school foreign-language curricula.

During wartime Americans displayed irrational prejudices against German Americans. They revealed prejudices in their consumer habits. During the early part of the twentieth century, Americans had viewed lager beer, which was served cold, as a refreshing alternative to the tepid porters, stouts, and ales to which they had been accustomed. Because the commercial lager beers were associated with names such as Miller, Pabst, Schlitz, Anheuser, and Busch, American consumers could readily detect Germanic influences on those beverages. In spite of their fondness, Americans effectively boycotted lager beer during World War I.

After the war, Americans were less prejudiced toward Germany. German Americans contributed to this change. Popular German Americans who influenced culture, art, literature, science, academics, and government were able to lance the prejudices that had festered during World War I.

Activity: German-Language Schools versus Segregated Southern Schools

The German schools in the Midwest were instances of voluntary segregation. In contrast, the racially segregated schools in the South were instance of nonvoluntary segregation.

In addition to attendance policies, what were some of the differences between the German schools and the racially segregated schools in the South? What were some of the historical social conditions that contributed to these differences? To help answer these questions, create a chart.

Table 3.3. German Americans

System of Schooling	*Distinctive Features*	*Social Conditions*	*Explanation*
German Schools in Ohio			
Segregated Schools in the South			

Along the vertical axis of the chart, arrange several rows. In one of these rows place information about the German schools in the Midwest. In another row, place information about the segregated schools in the South.

Along the horizontal axis of the chart, arrange several columns. In one of these columns, identify the distinctive features of the two school systems. In another column, identify the historical social conditions that influenced the two school systems. In the final column of the chart, provide a brief explanation for the information that you have placed within the cells.

Your answers will be based on assumptions about the vested interests, values, and goals of the groups that were involved. Although you can use the information in the case study to make some of these assumptions, you may wish to rely on a broader foundation of information.

You can gather additional information from the materials that are listed at the end of this chapter. You may gather it from lectures or discussions.

USING THE PAST TO UNDERSTAND THE PRESENT

During the nineteenth and the twentieth centuries, the immigrants who arrived in the United States had to address major problems. They had to find residence and employment; they had to deal with a new language, culture, government, political system, and economy.

Although they faced pressing problems, the immigrants still preserved their distinctive aspirations. They aspired to preserve their linguistic, religious, educational, and cultural heritages.

To solve their problems and achieve their aspirations, the immigrants banded together in urban neighborhoods, rural settlements, farms, factories, synagogues, churches, social clubs, restaurants, stores, theaters, athletic fields, and parks.

The immigrants displayed remarkable qualities. They displayed the precise qualities that most established residents had hoped they would demonstrate. They displayed qualities that helped them survive; they displayed qualities that helped them succeed as workers, citizens, taxpayers, soldiers, and community members.

Although the qualities that the immigrants displayed evoked admiration from some, they evoked anxiety from others. The qualities evoked anxiety when the immigrants competed for property, political power, and social status.

The immigrants clashed with anxious residents. Some of them clashed with groups that were influential, wealthy, and socially established; others clashed with groups that had no greater social or financial status than they did.

Are there similarities between the historical clashes in which immigrants have been involved and the recent clashes in which they have been involved? To help answer this question, identify a recent clash. Identify the groups that were affected and the basis for the dispute. Was any group at a social or economic advantage? Did the dispute involve education? Did the groups find a short-term solution for their dispute? Did they find a long-term solution? Attempt to identify an incident that occurred in your own state or community.

CHAPTER SUMMARY

Immigrants who entered the United States faced immediate and long-term problems. They had to deal with housing, security, medical care, communication, and employment. They had to deal with assimilation into a new culture, society, and political system. They also had to deal with resentful and frightened residents. The immigrants and the established residents eventually realized that education could alleviate these problems.

ADDITIONAL READING

Introductory Passages

Bankston, C. L., & Hidalgo, D. A. (Eds.). (2006). *Immigration in U.S. history*. Pasadena, CA: Salem.

Diner, H. (2006) *The Jews of the United States, 1654–2000.* Berkeley: University of California Press.

Foner, N. (2000). *From Ellis Island to JFK: New York's two great waves of immigration.* New Haven, CT: Yale University.

Gabaccia, D. R. (2002). *Immigration and American diversity: A social and cultural history.* Oxford: Blackwell.

Glowacki, P., & Hendry, J. (2004). *Hull-House.* Chicago: Arcadia.

Hine, R. V., & Faragher, J. M. (2000). *The American West: A new interpretive history.* New Haven, CT: Yale University Press.

Howe, D. W. (2007). *What hath God wrought: The transformation of America, 1815–1848.* New York: Oxford University Press.

Kazin, M., & McCartin, J. A. (Eds.). (2006). *Americanism: New perspectives on the history of an ideal.* Greensboro: University of North Carolina Press.

Knight, L. W. (2006). *Citizen: Jane Addams and the struggle for democracy.* Chicago: University of Chicago Press.

Linn, J. (2000). *Jane Addams: A biography.* Champaign: University of Illinois Press. (Original work published in 1935.)

Nguyen, T. (2004). *We are all suspects now: Untold Stories from immigrant communities after 9/11.* Boston, MA: Beacon.

Pitti, S. J. (2004). *The devil in Silicon Valley: Northern California, race, and Mexican Americans.* Princeton, NJ: Princeton University Press.

Trelease, A. W. (1995). *White terror: The Ku Klux Klan conspiracy and Southern Reconstruction.* Baton Rouge: Louisiana State University Press.

Wade, W. C. (1987). *The fiery cross: The Ku Klux Klan in America.* New York: Simon & Schuster.

Case Study 3.1: Johnstown Flood

McCullough, D. G. (1968). *The Johnstown flood.* New York: Simon & Schuster.

O'Connor, R. (1957). *Johnstown: The day the dam broke.* Philadelphia: Lippincott.

Case Study 3.2: Italian Americans

Cosco, J. P. (2003). *Imagining Italians: The clash of romance and race in American perceptions, 1880–1910.* Albany: State University of New York Press.

Mangione, J. (1993). *La storia: Five centuries of the Italian American experience.* New York: Harper.

Puleo. S. (2007). *The Boston Italians: A story of pride, perseverance, and paesani, from the years of the great immigration to the present day.* Boston, MA: Beacon.

Riccio, A. V., Langdon, P., & Carolan, M. A. (2006). *The Italian American experience in New Haven: Images and oral histories.* Albany: State University of New York Press.

Vecchio, D. C. (2006). *Merchants, midwives, and laboring women: Italian migrants in urban America.* Champaign: University of Illinois Press.

Case Study 3.3: German Americans

Brosterman, N. (2002). *Inventing kindergarten.* New York: Abrams.

Conzen, K. N. (2003). *Germans in Minnesota.* St. Paul: Minnesota Historical Society Press.

De Garmo, C. (2001). *Herbart and the Herbartians.* Honolulu, HI: University Press of the Pacific.

Fogleman, A. S. (1996). *Hopeful journeys: German immigration, settlement, and political culture in Colonial America, 1717–1775.* Philadelphia: University of Pennsylvania Press.

Nolt, S. M. (2002). *Pennsylvania German history and culture.* University Park: Pennsylvania State University Press.

Reese, W. J. (2005). *America's public schools: From the common school to "No Child Left Behind."* Baltimore, MD: Johns Hopkins University Press.

Tolzmann, D. H. (2000). *The German-American experience.* Amherst, NY: Humanity.

Chapter Four

Learners: Demanding Opportunities for Minority Students

Groups that were part of the American majority had opportunities to acquire prestige, property, wealth, and political power; groups without this status had fewer opportunities. Some persons were separated from the majority because of their nationality, language, culture, or religion; some were separated because of their race. Children who were separated from the majority suffered socially and economically; they also suffered scholastically.

MINORITY LEARNERS IN TODAY'S SCHOOLS

In 1954, the United States Supreme Court reversed the decades-old decision that had provided the legal foundation for segregated education. However, the Court did not eliminate segregated education. While it forbade de jure segregation in the schools, it allowed de facto segregation to continue.

During the 1960s, the civil rights leader Malcolm X made a harrowing statement about the alienation that resulted from persistent racial discrimination:

> I'm not going to sit at your table and watch you eat, with nothing on my plate, and call myself a diner. Sitting at the table doesn't make you a diner, unless you eat some of what's on that plate. Being here in America doesn't make you an American [Malcolm X, 1964, as quoted by Breitman, 1994, pp. 136–137].

The discrimination that Malcolm X decried was evident in the segregated schools to which African American children sent their children. It influenced children while they were attending segregated schools, and it continued to influence them after they left the schools.

Does discrimination have an effect on African American children today? Does it have an effect on children from other minority groups? Some of the researchers who wished to answer these questions cast wide nets; they investigated the ways in which broad issues affected minority children. They investigated broad issues such as health, disease, access to medical care, poverty, community safety, employment, incarceration, and substance abuse.

Other researchers cast smaller nets; they investigated the ways in which narrower issues affected minority children. They investigated narrow issues such as special education participation rates, high school graduation rates, and college attendance rates.

Early researchers posed questions similar to those that recent researchers have posed. Like the recent researchers, they wondered whether they should cast wider or smaller investigative nets.

ORIGINS OF STEREOTYPES

Some American colonists supported slavery. They purchased slaves in order to gain wealth and social status. Some slaveholders who recognized that their actions were morally reprehensible released their slaves. Other slaveholders admitted that their actions were morally reprehensible and still retained their slaves. George Washington and Thomas Jefferson were among the slaveholders in the latter group.

To reduce their moral conflicts, Americans formed stereotypes about themselves and their slaves. They viewed themselves as the members of a race that was benevolent, superior, and predestined to rule society. Some of them viewed their slaves as children who required care; others viewed them as miscreants who required discipline.

Just as the wealthy individuals who owned slaves had reasons for forming stereotypes, so did poor white Southerners. Before the Civil War, these Southerners had reassured themselves that they were not on the bottom rung of the social and economic ladder. After all, slaves occupied that extremely low position. Even though they did not own slaves, poor white Southerners were not eager to see them released; they were not eager to compete for their meager social status. Therefore, they adopted the prevailing stereotypes about slaves.

Had seventeenth- and eighteenth-century American colonists decided to free their slaves, how many individuals would they have liberated? Because the colonists did not maintain a census, it is difficult to confirm the precise number of persons that they had enslaved.

After a national census was established, Americans could provide an accurate count of their slaves. In the early 1800s, the national population exceeded

5,000,000 persons, including more than 1,000,000 slaves. By the 1860s, the national population exceeded 30,000,000 persons and included more than 4,000,000 slaves (Gibson and Jung, 2002).

DAMAGE FROM STEREOTYPES

During the 1940s, two psychologists, Mamie Clark and Kenneth Bancroft Clark, tried to assess the impact of racial stereotypes. They conducted studies in which they gave children a chance to select a doll with which they would play. The children chose between two dolls. The features and skin color of one doll had been patterned after African American children; the features and skin color of the other had been copied from white children.

The psychologists assumed that white children would prefer white dolls. They were less sure about the type of dolls that African American children would choose. When they analyzed their results, they were struck by the frequency with which African American children had selected white dolls.

The Clarks concluded that children's selections of dolls had been influenced by racial stereotypes. When they published their conclusions, they did not attract a particularly attentive audience. However, in a 1954 U.S. Supreme Court case about racial discrimination in schools, Thurgood Marshall and a group of lawyers from the National Association for the Advancement of Colored People called the Clarks as expert witnesses.

That case was identified as *Brown v. Board of Education of Topeka*, 347 U.S. 483 (1954). The justices of the Supreme Court listened attentively to the Clarks; a national audience also listened to them.

In that 1954 case, the Supreme Court overturned segregation in the schools. For decades, lawyers, legislators, educators, and members of the public contemplated the decision and its implications (Ogletree, 2004; Patterson, 2001).

In spite of the limited scope of the issue on which they were ruling, the Supreme Court justices had attempted to influence the way in which segregated education was viewed. On the question of whether racial segregation in the public schools created educational inequalities, Chief Justice Earl Warren spoke for all of the justices; he stated that segregated education inevitably created inequalities.

POLITICAL TENSION IN THE SCHOOLS

At the end of the nineteenth century, the United States Supreme Court had heard another case about racial segregation. In that case, *Plessy v. Ferguson*,

163 U.S. 537 (1896), the members of the Court had validated racially segregated social policies and practices. For more than half a century, the justices stood by that decision.

The *Plessy v. Ferguson* decision was eventually reversed. The Supreme Court justices may not have anticipated the ways in which some citizens would react. Many citizens disagreed with the justices. Many of them resolved that they would resist. Many of them resolved that they would preserve segregated schools.

Three years after *Brown v. Board of Education* was decided, an incident in Arkansas attracted national attention. School administrators refused to admit African American students into a segregated high school. They were supported by school, community, and state leaders. The incidents in Arkansas demonstrated that attempts to racially integrate the schools would be complicated and confrontational.

In 1962, another event confirmed the difficulty of integrating schools in the South. School officials attempted to block an African American student from attending the University of Mississippi. President Kennedy dispatched federal marshals to protect the student. The student and the marshals were confronted by Governor Ross Barnett himself. One year later, the situation was virtually reenacted in Alabama by an African American college student, federal marshals, the president, and Governor George Wallace.

Brown v. Board of Education was a decision that affected public schools. It did not mark the end of de jure segregation in the public schools; it did not even mark the end of de facto segregation in them. It did not affect private schools; it did not affect housing, commerce, employment, or the many aspects of segregated society in the South. It did not mark the end of discrimination, racism, or racial stereotypes.

Even though its effects were limited, *Brown v. Board of Education* was a landmark decision. It indicated that American citizens were adopting new attitudes about their schools, race, and society. It revealed that many of them already had adopted these attitudes. It demonstrated that Americans were concerned about social justice. However, it was not the first time that they had demonstrated this concern.

Case Study 4.1: American Indian Education

Early Americans were concerned about security. They kept it in mind when they confronted the indigenous residents of the New World. They kept it in mind when they pondered whether their neighbors would help or threaten them.

The American Indians whom the settlers encountered were hardly uncivilized. They maintained distinctive and complex cultures, social organizations, and traditions. However, most colonists were unacquainted with the beliefs, practices, and institutions of their new neighbors.

When the colonists encountered Native Americans, they had to choose whether to collaborate with them or confront them. Some collaboration-minded colonists persuaded the American Indians to share food, clothing, arms, tools, and other resources. Some of them persuaded the Indians to support military campaigns against other colonists. Some of them persuaded the Indians to adopt Christianity.

When colonists had to deal with a large group of American Indians, collaboration had a clear advantage: It allowed them to survive. However, it also had a disadvantage: It restricted their opportunities to acquire more land.

Confrontation-minded settlers patrolled, fortified, and armed their communities. As they were joined by other settlers, they became more confident. They predicted that they eventually would be able to confront and expel the native inhabitants with ease. They were correct.

Although some colonists may have felt guilty about the way in which they treated the indigenous residents, they rationalized their own actions and demonized those of the American Indians. The pattern of praising one group and denigrating the other pervaded American popular culture for generations.

Entrepreneurial entertainers, such as Buffalo Bill, helped to perpetuate biased views of American Indians. William "Buffalo Bill" Cody, who had served as a scout on the frontier, developed a hugely popular "Wild West" show. He toured with his entourage throughout the United States and Europe. Cody assured audiences that his show recreated authentic frontier incidents.

The posters for Cody's show noted that genuine American Indians participated in his programs. The posters described features of the show, such as the reenactment of "weird war dances." They also described the highlight of the show, which was a scene in which a stagecoach full of peaceful travelers was attacked by ruthless savages. During that attack, a group of "rough riders" would appear to heroically suppress the assailants.

The publishers of newspapers, magazines, novels, and comic books reinforced the stereotypes about American Indians. Eventually, the creators of films and television programs reinforced them. They represented the American Indians as predators, the settlers as victims, and the cavalry troopers as heroes.

Textbook publishers were another group that validated the unflattering stereotypes of American Indians. They indirectly validated these stereotypes when they omitted American Indians from textual passages. These omissions reduced the chances for students to challenge the misleading images that the popular media promoted.

In addition to omitting American Indians from their books, most textbook publishers omitted them from illustrations. When they did include them, they did it in stereotypical fashions. Sometimes they included a picture of hostile American Indians sneaking up on peaceful settlers; sometimes they included one that showed soldiers pursuing a party of fleeing braves.

American Indians suffered severely from stereotypes; they suffered even more from the social and political policies that were linked to them. During the last quarter of the nineteenth century, these policies confined them to reservations. They dictated that those who resisted would be tracked down, imprisoned, or killed.

In the late 1870s, Captain Richard Pratt organized a prison camp in Carlisle, Pennsylvania. He established the camp for American Indians from the West. Pratt had wished to isolate intractable warriors from the environment, culture, and religion with which they were familiar.

Pratt had another reason for isolating American Indians. He wanted to suppress their spirit of independence and resistance. Once he had relocated them, he required them to cut their hair short, wear military uniforms, execute marching drills, speak in English, practice vocational trades, and profess Christianity. Pratt admitted that his program would "kill the Indian"; however, he bragged that it would "save the man."

Pratt had developed a model for rehabilitating hostile warriors, but he also believed that he could use it to educate and acculturate youths. He insisted that he could persuade American Indian youths to replace their traditional culture, tradition, and religion with his own.

Pratt requested that the federal government provide the funding to implement his plan. He pledged that he would use the funds to convert his prison into a residential vocational school. He then would gather children from distant reservations, ship them to Pennsylvania, and enroll them in his school. The males would engage in agriculture, printing, and carpentry. The females would engage in sewing, cooking, and cleaning.

The officials at the United States Bureau of Indian Affairs were impressed with Pratt's plan. They initially provided the money to set up the school, and they eventually provided enough money for ten thousand students to attend. They even extrapolated the philosophy at Pratt's school to other training institutions. By 1900, they had made his school the prototype for more than twenty other American Indian boarding schools.

Like the personnel at the Bureau of Indian Affairs, Christian missionaries were impressed with Pratt's model of discipline and training. The missionaries, who wished to promote their faith, also wished to promote education and acculturation. They resolved that they could achieve all their goals at boarding schools that were patterned after the one that Pratt had established.

American Indian parents were not enthusiastic about the boarding schools. They realized that the children living there would be separated from their families and communities. They predicted that the children would lose their language, religion, culture, and traditions—their identities.

Missionaries were aware that the American Indian parents were resisting the boarding schools; they placed psychological pressure on them. Federal bureaucrats also were aware of resistance; they forcibly separated children from their parents, transported them to boarding schools, and prevented them from leaving.

The boarding schools were operated during the latter part of the nineteenth century and the initial decades of the twentieth century. Eventually, members of the public learned about the suffering of the students at the boarding schools. They preferred models of education that did not require the removal of American Indian children from their families and communities.

Federal officials and missionaries gradually abandoned their coercive educational practices. As a result, enrollments at the boarding schools declined, and their budgets also declined. By the end of the 1930s, most of the schools had closed.

Activity: American Indian Boarding Schools

The American Indians who lived on reservations had to deal with numerous problems, including poverty, unemployment, mental health issues, inadequate medical care, and poor education. They had to deal with problems that threatened their culture; they had to deal with problems that threatened their lives.

Members of the American public were concerned about the American Indians. In an attempt to help them, they separated children from their parents, transported them to distant sites, and assigned them to boarding schools. The

Table 4.1. American Indians

Group	*Support**	*Explanation*
American Indian Parents		
Non-American Indian Parents		
Boarding Schools Teachers		
Boarding Schools Administrators		
Professors of Education		
Liberal Government Leaders		
Conservative Government Leaders		

* (+) Supported
(-) Opposed
(+/-) Mixed Commitment

supervisors and staffs at the boarding schools required the students to follow a strict regimen, assimilate a new culture, and profess Christianity.

How do you think different groups responded to the placement of American Indian children at boarding schools during the late nineteenth and early twentieth centuries? To help answer this question, create a chart.

Along the vertical axis of the chart, place the following groups: parents of American Indian children, parents of non–American Indian children, the teaching staff at boarding schools, the school administrators at boarding schools, professors of education, politically liberal government leaders, and politically conservative government leaders.

Along the horizontal axis of the chart, arrange several columns. In one column, use symbols to indicate whether each of the preceding groups primarily supported (+), opposed (-), or showed a mixed commitment (+/-) to the placement of American Indian children at boarding schools.

Your indications about the responses of the groups should be based on assumptions about the vested interests, values, and goals of their members. Although you can use the information in the case study to make some of these assumptions, you may wish to rely on a broader foundation of information.

You can gather additional information from the materials that are listed at the end of this chapter. You may gather it from lectures or discussions.

In a separate column of the chart, or possibly on a separate page, summarize your assumptions about each group.

Case Study 4.2: Post–Civil War African Americans

After the Civil War, Southerners confronted multiple issues, and they reacted to them in diverse ways. They felt relieved by the cessation of combat, appalled by the condition in which the war had left their communities, worried about the millions of slaves that had been freed, confused about ways to rebuild their economy, and flustered by a society in which former slaveholders and slaves now lived together.

Southerners also had to deal with radical abolitionists. They feared that the abolitionists would promote the freed slaves into positions of political and social equality. They became more apprehensive after President Lincoln was murdered and replaced by Andrew Johnson, a president who seemed less able to restrain the abolitionists.

Southerners were distraught about the terms of the Reconstruction. They were upset that Northern troops had been stationed in their communities. They were upset that agencies were providing freed slaves with housing, food, and clothing. They were upset that organizations were providing freed slaves with education.

Like their white neighbors, African Americans in the postwar South were upset. They were upset by laws that kept them from voting. They were upset by ordinances that prevented them from using public facilities. They were upset by the intimidation and violence of the Ku Klux Klan.

The Civil War had affected education in the North in a different way than it had affected education in the South. The war had not been waged on the North's territory; it had not destroyed its economy. It had not prevented most Northerners from sending their children to public schools throughout the conflict.

Southerners were upset because the war had interrupted public education in many of their communities. Given their post-bellum impoverishment, they questioned how they could rejuvenate public education. They also questioned how to deal with the African Americans who they previously had excluded from the schools.

Before the war, there were some literate slaves. Some of them had learned to read the Bible; others had learned to read while serving as caregivers for the children of their owners. However, most of the 4,000,000 slaves in the South were illiterate. Many of the white Southerners who labored in menial jobs also were illiterate.

Like the postwar Southerners, the Northerners were concerned about education. They recognized the social and economic benefits of educating all children in integrated classrooms. Nonetheless, they established Southern schools for African American children. They may have focused their efforts exclusively on African Americans because they suspected that Southerners would not tolerate integrated schools. They were correct. Southerners insisted on racially segregated education.

White Southerners had psychological, social, economic, and political reasons for insisting on racially segregated education; they also had a practical reason. They realized that segregated education would enable them to fund, equip, and staff the facilities to which they would send their own children more generously than those to which they would send African American children. They sent African American children to rundown buildings, gave them worn-out books, and transported them in dilapidated vehicles.

Although the teachers who were assigned to segregated African American schools may have demonstrated care and commitment, many of them lacked appropriate pedagogical training. To solve this problem, African American professors began to train teachers. Booker T. Washington, who had attended a normal school for African Americans in Hampton, Virginia, established a normal school at Tuskegee, Alabama.

African American scholars established normal schools and institutions of higher education throughout the South. By the early 1900s, they had set up Alabama State University, Morgan State University in Maryland, Alabama A&M, Prairie View A&M University in Texas, Southern University and A&M College in Louisiana, Florida A&M University, North Carolina A&T State University, North Carolina Central University, and Tennessee State University.

In addition to establishing public institutions, African Americans in the South established private colleges and universities. They established Fisk University in Tennessee, Howard University in Washington, D.C., Morehouse College in

Georgia, Hampton University in Virginia, Clark Atlanta University in Georgia, Spelman College in Georgia, Philander Smith College in Arkansas, and Tuskegee University in Alabama. By the second quarter of the twentieth century, African Americans had opportunities to attend more than one hundred privately funded or state-funded colleges and universities in the South.

Activity: Early Southern Education

African Americans in the South had lacked educational opportunities before the Civil War. They later had greater opportunities. However, their opportunities were restricted to segregated schools.

How do you think different groups responded to the establishment of segregated schools in the South? To help answer this question, create a chart.

Along the vertical axis of the chart, place the following groups: African American parents, non-African American parents, African American teachers, non-African American teachers, professors of education, Northern politicians, and Southern politicians.

Along the horizontal axis of the chart, arrange several columns. In one column, use symbols to indicate whether each group primarily supported (+), op-

Table 4.2. Post–Civil War African Americans

Group	*Support**	*Explanation*
African American Parents		
Non-African American Parents		
African American Teachers		
Non-African American Teachers		
Professors of Education		
Northern Politicians		
Southern Politicians		

* (+) Supported
(-) Opposed
(+/-) Mixed Commitment

posed (-), or showed a mixed commitment (+/-) to the post–Civil War segregated schools.

Your indications about the responses of the groups should be based on assumptions about the vested interests, values, and goals of their members. Although you can use the information in the case study to make some of these assumptions, you may wish to rely on a broader foundation of information.

You can gather additional information from the materials that are listed at the end of this chapter. You may gather it from lectures or discussions.

In a separate column of the chart, or possibly on a separate page, summarize your assumptions about each group.

Case Study 4.3: Twentieth-Century African American Students

Twentieth-century American citizens did not attempt to conceal their biases. They did not try to hide them in employment, housing, sports, entertainment, media, religion, and marketing. They allowed their biases to affect their own lives; they allowed them to affect the lives of African Americans.

Some African Americans hoped that the racial biases had begun to fall during the 1950s. They hoped that the Supreme Court's decision in *Brown v. Board of Education* had signaled an end to racial prejudice. During the decade and a half that followed, they realized that their hopes had been premature.

Battered by racial prejudice, African Americans fought back. They were inspired by remarkable leaders such as Martin Luther King and Malcolm X. They attacked racist legislation and litigation. They attacked discriminatory policies and practices. They even attacked racist stereotypes.

African Americans called attention to the racial stereotypes that permeated films, television programs, radio broadcasts, music, newspapers, magazines, and books. They detected connections between the stereotypes to which adults ascribed and the biases that they exhibited. They also detected connections between children's stereotypes and their biases.

African Americans recognized that classroom-fostered stereotypes were extraordinarily damaging. They pointed out that they affected children during the years that they were learning about their aptitudes, identities, and places in society. They reasoned that racial stereotypes were harming both African American and non-African American children. They decided to take steps to reduce the likelihood that school-age children would acquire racial stereotypes in the first place.

Although many social practices conveyed racial stereotypes, educational segregation was one of the primary channels. The Supreme Court had unanimously prohibited de jure educational segregation in 1954. Nonetheless, many Southerners had ignored the prohibition.

In those instances in which Southern officials had changed the ways in which they operated their schools, they had not respected the spirit of the Supreme Court decision. That spirit had been evident when the justices had decried even segregated schools in which the children were given adequate learning materials, assigned to adequately prepared instructors, and housed in adequate physical facilities.

In the case of *Brown v. Board of Education,* Chief Justice Warren expressed the opinion of the Supreme Court. He noted that he and his colleagues had attempted to view segregated schools through the eyes of African Americans. Warren explained that African Americans had refused to evaluate segregated schools solely on the basis of "buildings, curricula, qualifications and salaries of teachers, and other 'tangible' factors." They had insisted on examining "the effect of segregation itself on public education."

After Warren and his colleagues viewed segregated schools from the perspective of African Americans, they were disconcerted:

> [Education] is required in the performance of our most basic public responsibilities. . . . It is the very foundation of good citizenship. Today it is a principal instrument in awakening the child to cultural values, in preparing him for later professional training, and in helping him to adjust normally to his environment. In these days, it is doubtful that any child may reasonably be expected to succeed in life if he is denied the opportunity of an education. Such an opportunity, where the state has undertaken to provide it, is a right which must be made available to all on equal terms.
>
> We come then to the question presented: Does segregation of children in public schools solely on the basis of race, even though the physical facilities and other "tangible" factors may be equal, deprive the children of the minority group of equal educational opportunities? We believe that it does [*Brown v. Board of Education of Topeka,* 347 U.S. 483 (1954)].

Segregated schooling was a complex problem that entailed social, economic, and psychological forces. The difficulty of litigating a solution to this problem had been evident to some persons in 1954; it became evident to everyone three years later, when African American students tried to attend a segregated high school in Arkansas.

School administrators and city officials prevented nine African American students from entering a segregated high school in Little Rock. Governor Orval Faubus supported them. In fact, the governor ordered National Guard troops to bar the African American students from the school.

President Eisenhower responded decisively. He directed the governor to remand his order. When he realized that the governor would not back down, Eisenhower federalized the Arkansas National Guard troops, dismissed them from the high school, and replaced them with regular army soldiers. He ordered the newly arrived soldiers to reverse the situation: He directed them to protect the African American students and ensure that they had access to their school.

The photos that were taken in the Little Rock schools showed peers, neighbors, and community members bullying a small group of African American students. In spite of the hostility that greeted them, the African American students stayed in the school.

After a year of involuntary integrated education, the members of the school board closed the local high schools. As a result, the students of Little Rock had to make the best of their circumstances. Some of them commuted to nearby school districts or watched television-transmitted classes. Others stayed at home, dropped out of school, or took jobs.

Many citizens were shocked by the incidents in Little Rock. They were disillusioned and disheartened as they realized the limitations on the Supreme Court's ability to reduce stereotypes, bias, and discrimination in the schools.

Activity: Integrated Education during the 1960s

During the 1960s, Southern leaders attempted to sustain a racially segregated system of education. They were opposed by African Americans and their allies. The antidiscrimination alliance persuaded federal leaders to dismantle the segregated schools. As a result, African American and white children became classmates.

How do you think different groups in the South reacted to the federally mandated integration of their schools? To help answer this question, create a chart.

Along the vertical axis of the chart, place the following groups: parents of African American children, parents of non-African American children, African American teachers, non-African American teachers, professors of education, and state politicians.

Table 4.3. Twentieth-Century African American Students

Group	*Support**	*Explanation*
African American Parents		
Non-African American Parents		
African American Teachers		
Non-African American Teachers		
Professors of Education		
State Politicians		

* (+) Supported
(-) Opposed
(+/-) Mixed Commitment

Along the horizontal axis, arrange several columns. In one of these columns, use symbols to indicate whether each group primarily supported (+), opposed (-), or showed a mixed commitment (+/-) to racially integrated classes.

Your indications about the responses of the groups should be based on assumptions about the vested interests, values, and goals of their members. Although you can use the information in the case study to make some of these assumptions, you may wish to rely on a broader foundation of information.

You can gather additional information from materials that are listed at the end of this chapter. You may gather it from lectures or discussions.

In a separate column of the chart, or possibly on a separate page, summarize your assumptions about each group.

USING THE PAST TO UNDERSTAND THE PRESENT

The early teachers were confused by some of the problems that they faced. They especially were perplexed by community-wide problems. For example, they realized that poverty, which had a profound influence on learners, originated in circumstances that extended beyond the boundaries of their schools.

They recognized teenage pregnancy, neighborhood violence, alcoholism, substance abuse, and parentless homes as significant and community-wide problems. They recognized racial stereotypes as still another significant problem with a community-wide scope.

Attempting to solve community-wide problems, some teachers restricted their efforts to a few problems. Others ignored community-wide problems and focused exclusively on scholastic problems. Some teachers made these decisions on the basis of their philosophical principles; others made them on the basis of practical considerations.

Educators today confront problems that are similar to those of earlier colleagues; they also pose questions that are similar to those that their precursors posed. When they confront community-wide problems, such as those that are connected to stereotypes, they continue to struggle about appropriate ways to react. They ask themselves whether classroom activities can have an impact on these types of problems.

Can actions that are confined to the schools influence problems with society-wide scopes? To help answer this question, identify a recent incident in which students were depicted stereotypically. Describe the students that were involved. To what extent did they suffer because of the incident? Describe any school-wide steps that were taken to eliminate the stereotypes. Describe any community-wide steps that were taken to eliminate the stereotypes. Attempt to find an incident that transpired in your own state or community.

CHAPTER SUMMARY

Racial stereotypes were evident during the 1800s and the 1900s. They were evident in newspapers, magazines, novels, and the popular media; they were evident in the schools. They affected racial minority groups in multiple and complex ways. They affected their children while they attended segregated schools; they affected them long after they had left those schools.

ADDITIONAL READING

Introductory Passages

Berlin, I. (1998). *Many thousands gone: The first two centuries of slavery in North America.* Cambridge, MA: Harvard University Press.

Berlin, I. (2003). *Generations of captivity: A history of African American slaves.* Cambridge, MA: Harvard University Press.

Breitman, G. (Ed.). (1994). *Malcolm X speaks.* New York: Grove. (Original work published in 1965.)

Clark, K. B. (1957). *Prejudice and your child.* Boston: Beacon Press.

Clark, K. B. (1989). *Dark ghetto: Dilemmas of social power.* Middletown, CT: Wesleyan University Press.

Davis, D. B. (2006). *Inhuman bondage: The rise and fall of slavery in the New World.* New York: Oxford University Press.

Elkins, S. (1976). *Slavery: A problem in American institutional and intellectual life.* Chicago: University of Chicago Press.

Gallay, A. (2002). *The Indian slave trade: The rise of the English empire in the American South, 1670–1717.* New Haven, CT: Yale University Press.

Mason, M. (2006). *Slavery and politics in the early American republic.* Chapel Hill: University of North Carolina Press.

Malcolm X., and Haley, A. (1989). The autobiography of Malcolm X. New York: Ballentine. (Original work published in 1965.)

Schneider, D. J. (2005). *The psychology of stereotyping* (2nd ed.). New York: Guilford.

Case Study 4.1: American Indians

Adams, D. W. (1995). *Education for extinction: American Indians and the boarding school experience, 1875–1928.* Lawrence: University of Kansas Press.

Archuleta, M. L., Child, B. J., & Lomawaima, K. T. (Eds.). (2000). *Away from home: American Indian boarding school experiences.* Phoenix, AZ: Heard Museum Press.

Fixico, D. L. (Ed.). (1997). *Rethinking American Indian history.* Albuquerque: University of New Mexico Press.

Pratt, R. H. (2004). *Battlefield and classroom: Four decades with the American Indian, 1867–1904*. Norman: University of Oklahoma Press.
Shoemaker, N. (2006). *A strange likeness: Becoming red and white in eighteenth-century North America*. New York: Oxford University Press.
Smith, S. L. (2003). *Reimagining Indians: Native Americans through Anglo eyes, 1880–1940*. New York: Oxford University Press.

Case Study 4.2: Post–Civil War African Americans

Ayers, E. L. (1993). *The promise of the new South: Life after Reconstruction*. New York: Oxford University Press.
Bender, T. (1992). *The antislavery debate: Capitalism and abolitionism as a problem in historical interpretation*. Berkeley: University of California Press.
Blackmon, D. A. (2008). *Slavery by another name: The re-enslavement of black Americans from the Civil War to World War II*. New York: Doubleday.
Davis, D. B. (2006). *Inhuman bondage: The rise and fall of slavery in the New World*. New York: Oxford University Press.
Foner, E. (1988). *Reconstruction: America's unfinished revolution, 1863–1877*. New York: Harper & Row.
Franklin, J. H., & Moss, A. A. (2000). *From slavery to freedom: A history of African Americans*. New York: Knopf. (Original work published in 1947.)
Perman, M. (2003). *Emancipation and Reconstruction*. Wheeling, IL: Harlan Davidson.

Case Study 4.3: Twentieth-Century African American Students

Cortes, C. E. (2000). *The children are watching: How the media teach about diversity*. New York: Teachers College Press.
Holt, T. C., & Brown, E. B. (Eds.). (2000). *Major problems in African-American history: From freedom to "freedom now," 1865–1990s*. Boston: Houghton Mifflin.
Polite, V. C., & Davis, J. E. (Eds.). (1999). *African American males in school and society: Practices and policies for effective education*. New York: Teachers College Press.
Walker, V. S., & Snarey, J. (2004). *Race-ing moral formation: African American perspectives on care and justice*. New York: Teachers College Press.
Watkins, W. (2001). *The white architects of black education: Ideology and power in America, 1865–1954*. New York: Teachers College Press.

Chapter Five

Curriculum: Promoting Quality with Textbooks

Textbooks presented significant opportunities; they also presented significant challenges. Paying for textbooks was a significant challenge. Although teachers asked nineteenth-century families to purchase textbooks for their children, they realized that many of them were too poor to comply. Teachers had difficulty instructing students who came to school without learning materials; they also had difficulty instructing students who came to school with diverse learning materials. To resolve these problems, school administrators began to buy books and distribute them without charge. Commercial publishers prepared numerous products for a rapidly expanding market. However, critics complained about the expense of the new textbooks; they also complained about the pedagogy that they contained, the political content that they embodied, and the social biases that they reinforced.

TEXTBOOKS TODAY

Textbooks became popular during an era when school districts, teachers, and students faced critical problems. School districts lacked curricula, teachers lacked training, and students lacked learning materials. Textbooks addressed all of these problems.

Although small and large publishers created the textbooks, the large publishers flourished. They flourished because they had financial and personnel resources. They flourished because they used their resources creatively.

The large publishing companies continuously devised novel features for their books. They devised ingenious charts, tables, maps, photographs, and artwork for students. They devised useful lesson plans for teachers. They devised effective strategies to promote sales.

The cost of writing, editing, printing, storing, and distributing early textbooks was substantial. That cost escalated when the publishers introduced innovative features. It continued to escalate when they revised their books frequently.

Critics of textbook were upset with the publishers. They made multiple accusations. They accused them of ruthless profiteering. They accused them of demeaning females and the members of racial, ethnic, and religious groups. They accused them of promoting ineffective pedagogy. Some of them accused them of producing books that were excessively nationalistic; others accused them of producing books that were insufficiently nationalistic.

Because they did not wish to get caught in treacherous political currents, textbook publishers made adaptations cautiously. After all, they did not wish to jeopardize their products; they wanted to enhance them. Because they were convinced that pedagogy and visual aids had the greatest impact on sales, they prioritized these types of changes.

During the 1960s, many members of the public urged the publishers to present a balanced view of African Americans. They adjured them to eliminate stereotypes and to restore the important information that they had omitted from some of their books.

When critics detected textbooks that had not met their standards, they advised school boards to reject them. Faced with boycotts, the publishers made changes. When females, ethnic groups, and religious groups urged the publishers to make additional changes, they acceded to their advice as well.

Today critics continue to attack textbooks. Some of them decry them for promoting regimented instruction. Some claim that they enable publishers to earn unreasonably high profits. Some allege that they misrepresent minority groups. Some claim that they are excessively nationalistic; others claim that they are not sufficiently nationalistic.

Although current textbooks are criticized for reasons similar to those for which they were faulted in the past, they also are applauded for similar reasons. Proponents claim that textbooks help marginally qualified teachers provide effective instruction; they believe that they help marginal school administrators provide effective curricula.

MCGUFFEY READERS

When the McGuffey readers appeared in the 1830s, they immediately became popular. They remained popular throughout the century. Other than the Bible and Webster's dictionaries, they were the most frequently purchased books of that period. Although they had characteristics of other popular textbooks, they also had features that set them apart.

The McGuffey readers identified precise learning skills; they then arranged the skills in order of complexity, reinforced them with motivating passages, paired them with artistic illustrations, and complemented them with practical exercises. Each volume in the series dovetailed with the volumes that preceded and followed it.

Teachers appreciated many of the features of the McGuffey readers. They were gratified to find information about several different pedagogical approaches.

Parents also appreciated features of these readers. Some of them were reassured because the books were written by a Protestant minister and filled with information about morality. Others were reassured because the author had discussed morality in ways that were neither doctrinaire nor sectarian.

The publishers of the McGuffey readers were impressed by the educational progress that students made. They were impressed by the testimonials from teachers and parents. They also were impressed by the steady profits that these books earned.

Struck by the remarkable success of the McGuffey readers, competing publishers attempted to replicate them. In addition to publishing textbooks about reading, they produced books for many other subjects. In fact, they produced hundreds of textbooks during the last quarter of the nineteenth century.

Although their early achievements had been impressive, textbook publishers raised their performance to even higher levels during the early part of twentieth century. The national expenditure on textbooks provided an indication of their success; this expenditure doubled during the first ten years of the twentieth century (Giordano, 2003). The number of new books that academic publishers released provided another indication of their success; they released over one thousand new elementary and high-school textbooks during the first twenty-five years of the twentieth century (Giordano, 2003).

FREE TEXTBOOK MOVEMENT

The early school reformers believed that all American children should have access to public education. They encouraged states to develop free public schools. They suggested that all states copy the system of public education that had been implemented in New England. By the late 1800s, they realized that they were on their way to achieving their goal (Tash, 1888).

In spite of their progress, the reformers were disappointed. They realized that students had to purchase the textbooks on which they depended in school. They were sure that some of them were faltering because they could not afford textbooks. To solve this problem, they urged community leaders to purchase textbooks and provide them at no cost to the students.

The schools in Boston, New York, Philadelphia, and other East Coast cities had begun to distribute free textbooks during the 1800s. By the beginning of the next century, many other cities were following their lead. In fact, many states were distributing free textbooks. Delaware, Idaho, Maine, Maryland, Massachusetts, Nebraska, New Hampshire, New Jersey, Pennsylvania, Rhode Island, and Vermont were providing them to elementary school students (Cox, 1903). By World War I, some states had begun to provide free textbooks to high-school students (Hood, 1922).

The supporters of free textbooks were politically formidable. However, they had to deal with ardent opponents. Because of their ardor, the textbook opponents may have resorted to capricious arguments. For example, they argued that free textbooks should be avoided because they enabled germs to pass from student to student.

The opponents of free textbooks had additional arguments that today seem capricious. Some of their arguments concerned political and economic ideologies. They argued that the distribution of free textbooks was a socialist practice that eroded the foundation of a capitalistic economy.

Some of the arguments against free textbooks were based on practicality. For example, opponents claimed that free textbooks unfairly assisted students when they received books with the answers to problems already penciled in them.

Although the opponents of free textbooks may have resorted to capricious arguments, they had one argument that was difficult to refute. They contended that the distribution of free textbooks was expensive. The supporters of free textbooks had to agree.

Although they had admitted that their plan was expensive, the supporters of free textbooks contended that it still was prudent and even economical. They noted that school districts, which received discounts when they made high-volume purchases, could buy books for the lowest possible prices. As a result, books that school districts purchased were actually less expensive than those that parents purchased.

The supporters of free textbooks had another convincing rejoinder for their critics. They claimed tax-funded schools could not operate efficiently when students lacked appropriate learning materials. As a result, a good portion of the money spent on the public schools was being wasted. They claimed that free textbooks would eliminate this waste.

The supporters of free textbooks predicted that teaching would become more efficient once all students had textbooks; they predicted that their efficiency would increase even more once they had uniform textbooks. They insisted that school-wide purchases were the only practical means with which to achieve these two goals.

Members of the public, members of school boards, and civic leaders were persuaded by the argument in favor of uniform textbooks. Almost all school districts had begun to use them by the early years of the twentieth century; in most cases, they purchased them and then distributed them free to their students (Dexter, 1904).

Case Study 5.1: State-Published Textbooks

Many new schools were established during the late 1800s and early 1900s. They increased the demand for teachers; they also increased the demand for learning materials.

In most schools, textbooks were the primary learning materials; in many schools, they were the only learning materials. Teachers contended that they could provide better instruction if all of their students had textbooks. They contended that they could raise their instruction to even higher levels if all of their students had common textbooks.

School boards agreed with the teachers. Concerned about the scholastic success of the children in their districts, they wanted them to have textbooks; they also wanted them to have uniform textbooks. Therefore, they began to purchase textbooks and distribute them free.

The textbook publishers detected a lucrative market. However, they realized that they would have to take several steps to make profits. They would have to produce textbooks that were useful, appealing, and reasonably priced. They believed that they were prepared for these challenges. After all, they already had developed an immensely popular series of reading textbooks.

With the aid of William McGuffey, the publishers designed books with attractive features for students; they incorporated interesting stories, practical drills, and remarkable illustrations. They also included features for teachers. They adapted their series so that teachers could use sequentially arranged volumes as their students progressed through the grades. Because they produced these materials for a large audience, the publishers were able to sell them inexpensively.

Publishers were able to produce textbooks that were useful, appealing, and reasonably priced. However, they were aware that they still had to market them effectively. They experimented with several different strategies. They advertised their books in educational journals and even advertised future textbooks on the pages at the beginnings and ends of their current textbooks.

Publishers discovered that the best way to increase sales was to hire professional salespersons and award them bonuses. Some enterprising salespersons offered to split their bonuses with the school-board members, superintendents, or principals who were responsible for purchasing school materials. Unfortunately for the publishers, journalists discovered these practices and quickly disclosed them.

After they had read newspaper reports about the practices that the textbook salespersons were using, taxpayers were shocked. Politicians also were shocked. The politicians were prepared to suggest a remedy. They proposed that states publish their own textbooks.

The states that planned to publish their textbooks faced the same challenges as the commercial textbook companies. They had to produce textbooks that were useful, attractive, affordable, and effectively marketed. Producing books that were useful and attractive did not impress the politicians as difficult challenges. They thought that they would model their materials after those that already were on the market.

Producing books that were reasonably priced struck the politicians as another simple challenge. After all, they owned printing presses. Furthermore, they did not intend to make a profit. Some of them smugly noted that they would save additional money by refusing to pay bribes to school administrators.

The politicians realized that marketing their materials could pose a challenge. However, they had a foolproof plan. They proposed to enact legislation that would require all schools to adopt the state-published textbooks.

When members of the National Education Association heard about the politicians' plan, they had doubts about it. At their 1888 convention, they questioned whether the politicians who were behind state-published textbooks fully understood the magnitude of the commitment that they would have to make.

One ardent opponent of state-published books predicted that the politicians would fail. He noted that the states that wished to compete with commercial publishers had not paid sufficient attention to numerous practical issues. He explained that each state would have to "establish its own shops, gather material, construct its various machines, fix the prices thereof, and enforce their use throughout its jurisdiction—establishing its depots of supplies, and its numerous agents of distribution, and its collectors and accountants" (Cornell, 1888, p. 232).

In 1883, the members of the California State Teachers' Association had passed a resolution discouraging their state from publishing textbooks. They predicted that this venture would be plagued by practical problems and unanticipated expenses; they also predicted that California-published books would be less desirable than commercial books.

The legislators ignored the teachers' advice. In 1884, they wrote a bill authorizing California to publish textbooks. They presented the bill on the third day of the legislative session. They then shepherded it through both houses and forwarded it to the governor. The governor signed the bill only a week after it had been introduced.

The 1884 California legislature had authorized the state board of education to commission the writing, editing, printing, and selling of textbooks. However, the state board of education published only several books during the subsequent four years. It sold few of these.

The California State Board of Education could not sell its textbooks for several reasons. It could not attract the most talented textbook authors, artists, layout editors, and pedagogical experts, who already were employed by the commercial publishers.

The California State Board of Education could not sell its textbooks for another reason. Politicians had poorly estimated the cost of writing, illustrating, editing, printing, binding, marketing, storing, and shipping textbooks. As a result, the State Board of Education could not market its textbooks for the prices that politicians had promised.

The proponents of California-published textbooks recognized that they were facing a serious problem. They realized that school administrators, teachers, and parents did not wish to buy their textbooks. In 1888, they tried to solve their problem. They introduced legislation to prohibit the schools from purchasing commercial textbooks.

The large textbook publishers, which were located on the East Coast, received word of the California plan before it had been approved. One observer recounted that the publishers "sent special agents by fast express trains to Sacramento" (Chancellor, 1913, p. 218). When the agents met with influential legislators, they were directed to make payments to them. They were promised that these payments would assure that the textbook bills would be sent to committees, where they would "die of suffocation."

The textbook agents made the payments, assumed that they had eliminated the threat, and returned to the East Coast. To their dismay, they learned later that the textbook bills were released from their committees, approved by both houses, and signed by the governor.

The California experiment with state-published textbooks continued for two decades. In fact, the legislature and governor expanded the venture in 1913, when they required every school district not only to purchase state-published textbooks but also to distribute them free to all students.

The advocates of the California textbook initiative insisted that they were producing materials comparable to those of the commercial publishers. They also insisted that they were saving money.

The opponents of the California textbook initiative claimed that the state-published materials were inferior to commercial materials. They claimed that they also were more expensive. They accused their adversaries of submitting inaccurate financial records to mislead taxpayers about the true cost of their project.

Although several states debated whether to duplicate the California initiative, only Kansas copied it. Eventually succumbing to political and popular pressures, both Kansas and California returned to commercially published school materials.

Table 5.1. State-Published Textbooks

Group	*Support**	*Explanation*
Parents		
Teachers		
Principals		
Professors of Education		
Politicians		

* (+) Supported
(-) Opposed
(+/-) Mixed Commitment

Activity: Californians Use State-Published Textbooks

The nineteenth-century sponsors of state-published textbooks had to deal with complex issues. They had to create, edit, print, distribute, and update scholastic materials. The California legislators were not dismayed by these task; they resolved that they would produce their own books.

Initially, the California legislators decided to give school personnel the opportunity to purchase the books that the state had commissioned. After they realized that the school personnel were not interested in their books, the legislators required the schools to purchase them.

How do you think different groups in California responded to the requirement that their schools use state-published textbooks? To help answer this question, create a chart.

Along the vertical axis of the chart, place the following groups: parents, teachers, principals, professors of education, and politicians. Along the horizontal axis of the chart, arrange several columns. In one column, use symbols to indicate whether each group primarily supported (+), opposed (-), or showed a mixed commitment (+/-) to the California legislative mandate.

Your indications about the responses of the groups should be based on assumptions about the vested interests, values, and goals of their members. Although you can use the information in the case study to make some of these assumptions, you may wish to rely on a broader foundation of information.

You can gather additional information from the materials that are listed at the end of this chapter. You may gather it from lectures or discussions.

In a separate column of the chart, or possibly on a separate page, summarize your assumptions about each group.

Case Study 5.2: Nationalistic Propaganda

Many American citizens believed that textbooks influenced political attitudes. However, they disagreed about the precise nature of the influences. Their disagreements were apparent in the ways that they reacted to nationalistic textbooks. One faction condemned those books that promoted chauvinism; another faction examined the same books and praised them for promoting patriotism.

Partisan factions historically had argued about the political features of textbooks. They had argued during the late 1800s and early 1900s. They had become especially contentious during World War I. They had continued to squabble during the era that followed the war.

Post–World War I legislators were asked to take steps to prevent textbooks from eroding patriotism. Some of them were sympathetic to these requests. For example, legislators in New York sponsored a 1923 bill to address this issue. They tried to prohibit the use of any textbook that "ignores, omits, discounts, or in any manner belittles, ridicules, falsifies, distorts, questions, doubts, or denies the deeds and accomplishments of the noted American patriots, or questions the worthiness of their motives, or casts aspersions on their lives" ("New York Bill on History," 1923, p. 349).

Prominent liberals were upset by attitudes such as those that the New York state legislators had exhibited. They formed an organization to express their displeasure. John Dewey, Jane Addams, and more than sixty influential political activists formed the Save-Our-Schools Committee.

The members of the Save-Our-Schools Committee were censured by the conservatives for intruding into the schools. The liberals rejected this censure. In fact, they accused the conservatives of forcing their own political views onto the schools. They gave examples of conservative intrusions that had elicited their anger.

The liberals were especially angry about textbooks. They were angry about textbooks that characterized Americans as righteous and altruistic but characterized the residents of other nations as wrongheaded and selfish.

To substantiate their allegations about biased textbooks, the liberals found offensive passages in history, geography, political science, and social studies textbooks. Some of these passages denigrated Revolutionary-era British nationals; others denigrated persons from Central America, South America, Asia, Africa, the South Pacific, and Eastern Europe.

The following passage, which appeared in a popular textbook, is typical of those that the liberal critics found offensive:

> The low standards of living [of southern and eastern Europeans] tend to reduce wages and their congestion in the slums of the great cities makes breeding places

> for disease and offers the unscrupulous politician cheap votes with which to debauch the city government [Muzzey, 1911, pp. 621–622].

Prior to World War I, conservatives and liberals debated fiercely about the schools. However, the liberals became less confrontational as the war progressed. Those liberal critics who were alarmed about excessive textbook nationalism also may have been alarmed about the increasingly pro-war attitudes that the public was exhibiting. These attitudes became extremely evident once the United States entered the war and sustained combat casualties.

Worried about retribution, some liberal critics suppressed their true feelings during World War I. After the war, they expressed themselves freely. They rued America's participation in the war, its expenditures on the military, and its diversion from domestic problems. When the prospects of another world war became discernible, they demanded that the United States remain neutral.

In spite of their earlier opposition, the liberals tempered their dissent once the United States had entered World War II. The failure of liberals to criticize nationalistic textbooks during this period could have stemmed from fear of an aroused public. It could have stemmed from a change of heart. However, it might have resulted from still another factor.

The failure of liberals to criticize nationalistic textbooks during World War II might have resulted from reluctance to confront the U.S. Office of Censorship. Although it was a politically potent office, this agency modulated its authority. It demonstrated discretion in the way that it interacted with authors and publishers. It encouraged them to self-assess whether materials promoted the interests of the Axis powers. It then advised them to self-edit these materials.

Even though many persons expressed confidence in the self-censorship and self-editing policy, some were skeptical. To demonstrate that self-censorship was ineffective, one prewar critic cited examples of flagrantly offensive passages in scholastic materials. He extracted the following passage from the teacher's guide to a popular textbook.

> The United States is not a land of opportunity for all our people; for one-fifth of the people do not earn any money at all. There are great differences in the standards of living of the different classes of the people. The majority do not have any real security [passage from the teacher's guide to a textbook by Harold Rugg, as quoted by Armstrong, 1940, p. 51].

The critic who located the preceding passage claimed that authors of subversive educational materials had been collaborating with the Soviet Union. In fact, he claimed that the Soviet Union had published copies of seditious books so that these could be placed in America's school libraries. The critic entreated American citizens to purge the schools of these materials.

Some conservative critics entreated American citizens to confront the persons and businesses that were responsible for seditious textbooks. They identified authors who had written controversial textbooks and the companies that had published them. Because many of the authors were professors, they also identified the universities at which the professors were employed.

After World War II, liberals protested against the wartime restrictions. For example, they attempted to organize opposition to the community-enforced censorship programs. A special issue of the *New Republic* in 1953 documented instances in which the conservatives had restricted or suppressed publications ("Special Report on Book Burnings," 1953). It described one censorship program that initially was voluntary but that had been transformed into a mandatory ordinance. The ordinance prohibited the sale of any publication that endorsed unsavory, dangerous, or un-American activities.

Activity: Debating Nationalism in Textbooks

Some critics of textbooks alleged that commercial publishers were more concerned about selling products than educating students. They accused them of producing excessively nationalistic books because they recognized that many school districts would be eager to purchase them.

Table 5.2. Nationalistic Propaganda

Group	*Support Prior to World War I**	*Support during World War I**	*Support during the Early 1930s**	*Rationale*
Parents				
Teachers				
School Administrators				
School Board Members				
Professors of Education				
Liberal Politicians				
Conservative Politicians				
Textbook Publishers				

* (+) Supported
(-) Opposed
(+/-) Mixed Commitment

How did different groups respond to the allegations that textbooks were excessively nationalistic? Do you think their responses changed during different eras? To help answer these questions, create a chart.

Along the vertical axis of the chart, place the following groups: parents, teachers, school administrators, members of local school boards, professors of education, liberal politicians, conservative politicians, and textbook publishers.

Along the horizontal axis of the chart, arrange several columns. In one column, indicate whether each group primarily supported (+), opposed (-), or showed a mixed commitment (+/-) to nationalistic history and social studies textbooks during the pre–World War I era. In another column of the chart, indicate the reactions of each group to nationalistic history and social studies textbooks during World War I. In still another column, indicate the reactions of each group to nationalistic history and social studies textbooks during the Great Depression.

Your indications about the responses of the groups should be based on assumptions about the vested interests, values, and goals of their members. Although you can use the information in the case study to make some of these assumptions, you may wish to rely on a broader foundation of information.

You can gather additional information from the materials that are listed at the end of this chapter. You may gather it from lectures or discussions.

In a separate column of the chart, or possibly on a separate page, summarize your assumptions about each group.

Case Study 5.3: Sources of Stereotypes

During the 1960s, scholastic publishers listened to accusations that textbooks were racially biased. They already had heard these allegations. In fact, they had heard them on numerous occasions.

During the 1920s and the 1930s, educators, political activists, and members of the public had asked publishers to remove offensive passages from scholastic materials. They had highlighted passages such as the following one, printed in a post–World War I history textbook:

> [The African American slaves] were not only far beneath their masters in all civilized ways of living but they were divided from them also by a great gulf of race differences which to this day keeps white people and black people from living together upon a footing of perfect equality [Burnham, 1920, pp. 547–548].

Like history textbooks, geography textbooks were replete with racist passages. The author of a 1920s geography textbook informed students that Africans and South Americans "would, of themselves, scarcely rise above barbarism" because "the climate, always sultry and depressing, robs man of ambition" (Whitbeck, 1922, p. 311). This author added that the Africans and South Americans rarely demonstrated "thrift and forethought" because these traits were unnecessary in the tropics.

African Americans suffered because of the explicitly racist misinformation in textbooks; they also suffered because of information that was omitted. These omissions were evident in a Freeland, Walker, and Williams's popular American history textbook, published in 1937. This book contained a chapter titled "Working Together." In spite of the chapter's topic, African Americans were excluded from the text and the illustrations.

Some authors and publishers tailored the content in their textbooks to appeal to customers in southern states. The authors of one textbook explained that the Ku Klux Klan "sought to control the Negroes by playing upon their ignorance and superstition" (Coleman and Wesley, 1939, p. 388). They added that the Klan "frightened the Negroes into better behavior . . . made the carpetbaggers more careful; and it showed the nation that the southern people would not quietly endure outrages" (pp. 389–390).

During the 1930s, the members of the National Association for the Advancement of Colored People were upset about racially biased textbooks. They documented inaccurate passages within popular textbooks (National Association for the Advancement of Colored People, 1939). They also listed critical information about African Americans that had been omitted. As an example of an omission, they noted that the African American revolts against slavery had been left out of all of the popular history textbooks.

Although publishers did revise textbooks from the 1930s to the 1960s, they did not make comprehensive revisions until the 1960s. During that decade, they did overhaul their textbooks. In fact, journalists remarked about the dramatic changes that textbook publishers had made even before the decade had ended (e.g., "Integrating the Texts," 1966).

Those textbook publishers who changed their depictions of African Americans still had to deal with criticism for failing to revise the ways in which they depicted other minority groups. During the 1970s, critics of gender-biased school materials noted that few females were identified in textbooks. They added that those who were depicted were represented in domestic roles and described with sexist language.

Just as the 1960s reformers had discussed the rights of racial minority groups, the 1970s reformers discussed the rights of women. Concerned about the immediate and long-term impact of gender-biased materials, they demanded that the publishers make modifications. They urged them to implement changes aggressively; they urged them to replicate their responses to racially biased books.

Aware that their customers and members of the public were demanding revisions of gender-biased school materials, publishers responded quickly. In the early 1970s, they developed guidelines for detecting and eliminating gender biases. They then applied those guidelines to their textbooks.

Some critics were disappointed with the publishers' voluntary efforts; they developed their own textbook guidelines. For example, Californians developed a highly distinctive set of guidelines. Because they purchased such a large number of books, the Californians influenced the ways in which the entire textbook publishing industry depicted males and females.

Lerner and Rothman (1990) summarized some of the provisions of the California guidelines for reducing gender biases in textbooks.

> (1) Illustrations must contain approximately equal proportions of men and women; (2) in the representation of each profession, including parent, men and women must be shown in equal numbers; (3) the contributions of men and women to developments in history or achievements in art or science must appear in equal numbers; (4) mentally and physically active, creative, problem-solving roles, and success or failure in these roles, must be divided evenly between males and females; (5) the number of traditional and non-traditional activities engaged in by characters of both sexes must be approximately even; (6) the gamut of emotions must occur randomly among characters, regardless of gender; and (7) both sexes must be portrayed in nurturing roles with their families [p. 55].

Californians developed prescriptive measures to ensure that publishers produced bias-free scholastic materials. They then asked publishers to implement those measures. The publishers acceded to their requests.

Activity: Eliminating Textbook Stereotypes

Some critics protested about the ways in which textbooks depicted racial minority groups. They adduced multiple examples of biased passages in history, geography, political science, and social studies textbooks. Although the textbook publishers initially ignored their critics, they eventually made changes.

When textbook publishers were making decisions about the ways in which they would depict African Americans, what types of events influenced them? To help answer this question, create a chart.

Table 5.3. Sources of Stereotypes

Event	*Reason That the Event Influenced Textbook Publishers*

Along the horizontal axis of the chart, place a column in which you identify three events that influenced the publishers. In another column of the chart, provide a short explanation of the reason that each event was influential.

Your examples will be based on assumptions about the vested interests, values, and goals of the textbook publishers. Although you can use the information in the case study to make some of these assumptions, you may wish to rely on a broader foundation of information.

You can gather additional information from the materials that are listed at the end of this chapter. You may gather it from lectures or discussions.

USING THE PAST TO UNDERSTAND THE PRESENT

The textbook enthusiasts of the 1800s highlighted multiple reasons to use commercial learning materials. They contended that textbooks helped teachers who were weak in pedagogy; they alleged that textbooks helped school administrators who were unsophisticated about curriculum. Some of them claimed that they helped immigrants learn English and assimilate a new culture.

Some persons disagreed with the textbook enthusiasts; they contended that textbooks could be harmful. They explained that textbooks were harmful when school administrators, teachers, and students depended on them excessively. Because they detected numerous instances of overdependence, they discouraged the use of textbooks.

Critics had additional reasons for rejecting textbooks. They rejected them for promoting cultural homogeneity. They rejected them for promoting the interests of ruthless businesspersons. They rejected them for demeaning females and the members of racial, religious, and ethnic minority groups.

From the middle of the nineteenth century to the present, textbooks have guided American classroom instruction. Nonetheless, they have been objects of contention. Can you think of a recent instance in which critics have questioned the use of textbooks?

You may choose an incident in which critics questioned the cost of textbooks. You may choose an incident in which they questioned the political, religious, racial, ethnic, or social content in textbooks. You may choose an incident in which they questioned the ways in which females or persons with alternative sexual orientations were represented. If you identify an incident that was contentious because of textbook content, indicate whether the critics accused publishers of including offensive content or excluding critical content. Attempt to locate an incident that occurred in your own state or community.

CHAPTER SUMMARY

Advocates promoted the use of textbooks. They claimed that textbooks helped students who required specialized learning materials, teachers who were weak in pedagogy, and school administrators who needed assistance with curricula.

Critics of textbooks discouraged their use. They claimed that textbooks were designed primarily to generate profits. They alleged that textbooks restrained the creativity of teachers and students. They alleged that textbooks promoted biased views of international relations, domestic politics, economics, race, ethnicity, religion, and women.

ADDITIONAL READING

Introductory Passages

Barnard, H. (1863a). American textbooks. *American Journal of Education, 13*, 210–222, 401–408, 626–640.

Barnard, H. (1864a). American textbooks. *American Journal of Education, 14*, 539–575, 601–607, 753–778.

Beechold, H. F. (1971). *The creative classroom: Teaching without textbooks.* New York: Scribner's Sons.

Burnham, W. H., Small, W. S., & Standish, M. (1911). Report of the committee on the standardization of school books, etc. *American Physical Education Review, 16*, 254–257.

Giordano, G. (2000). *Twentieth-century reading education: Understanding practices of today in terms of patterns of the past.* New York: Elsevier.

Higbee, E. E. (1888). Discussion—State uniformity of textbooks. *Addresses and Proceedings of the National Education Association, 28*, 229–233.

Hilton, H. H. (1913). Cost of textbooks per pupil. *Journal of Education, 77*, 369.

Lehmann-Haupt, H., Wroth, L. C., & Silver, R. G. (1951). *The book in America* (2nd ed.). New York: Bowker.

Madison, C. A. (1966). *Book publishing in America.* New York: McGraw Hill.

Marshall, W. I. (1895). *Should the public schools furnish text-books free to all pupils?* Chicago: Illinois State Teachers' Association.

McGregor, F. H. (1908, April). Free textbooks. *American School Board Journal, 36*, 27.

McNeal, T. A. (1915). Discussion and correspondence: The state publication of school books. *School and Society, 2*, 669–670.

Monahan, J. (1915). *Free textbooks and state uniformity* (U.S. Bureau of Education Bulletin No. 36). Washington, DC: Government Printing Office.

Reid, J. M. (1969). *An adventure in textbooks: 1924–1960.* New York: Bowker.

Sabin, H. (1908). Is state uniformity of text-books desirable? *Journal of Education, 68*, 359–360.

Sanders, T. E. (1914). Renting school books. *American School Board Journal, 48*, 28.

Shawkey, M. P. (1918). The adoption of textbooks by state, county or district. *American Education, 21*, 402–404.

Sprague, H. B. (1888). Discussion. State uniformity of textbooks. *Addresses and Proceedings of the National Education Association, 28*, 233–237.

State distribution of textbooks. (1914, January 22). *Nation, 98*, 73.

State-wide uniformity in high school text-books. *Journal of Education, 82*, 119–120.

Stevenson, R. W. (1888). Should the state furnish books and appliances free? *Addresses and Proceedings of the National Education Association, 28*, 211–220.

Summary of the situation in various states regarding textbooks. (1928). *Elementary School Journal, 28*, 404–405.

Swett, J. (1888). The general function of the state in relation to school-books and appliances. *Addresses and Proceedings of the National Education Association, 28*, 198–201.

Textbook industry. (1918). *School and Society, 8*, 380–382.

Textbooks and the state. (1915, September 9). *Nation, 101*, 321–322.

Three types of textbook troubles. (1922). *School Review, 30*, 85–87.

Townsend, E. J. (1891). The text-book question. *Education, 11*, 556–565.

Waterman, S. D. (1903). The advantages and disadvantages of a free text-book system. *Western Journal of Education, 8*, 362–366.

Whipple, G. M. (1929). The modern textbook and the school. *Journal of Education, 109*, 637–638.

Winship, A. E. (1908). State uniformity in text-books. *Journal of Education, 67*, 339–342.

Case Study 5.1: State-Published Textbooks

Avery, L. B. (1919). State-printed textbooks in California. *Elementary School Journal, 19*, 628–633.

Brown, G. E. (1915). Should the state publish its own textbooks? *Journal of Education, 81*, 566–567.

Brown, J. F. (1915). *State publication of school books*. New York: Macmillan.

Bruce, W. G., & Bruce, W. C. (1925). The state publication of school books. *American School Board Journal, 71* (3), 67.

Criticism of Kansas textbook publication. (1917). *Elementary School Journal, 17*, 537–541.

Davis, P. R. (1930). *State Publication of Textbooks in California*. Berkeley: California Society of Secondary Education.

Evans, L. B. (1914). State publication of textbooks. *School and Home, 6* (6), 7–10.

Faulkner, R. D. (1900). The California state text-book system. *Educational Review, 20*, 44–60.

Kansas decision on textbooks. (1913). *Elementary School Teacher, 13*, 414–415.

McNeal, T. A. (1915). Discussion and correspondence: The state publication of school books. *School and Society, 2*, 669–670.

Shirer, H. S. (1919). Experiments in state publication. *Proceedings of the National Education Association, 57*, 465–468.

Smith, C. H. (1929). California's state printing office: Million dollars invested in bureau. *Tax Digest, 7*, 380–383.

Winship, A. E. (1909). The California text-book plan: Its history and results. *Journal of Education, 69*, 173–180.

Case Study 5.2: Nationalistic Propaganda

American Council on Education. (1944a). *Intergroup relations in teaching materials* (Report of the Committee on the Study of Teaching Materials on Intergroup Relations). Washington, DC: Author.

American Council on Education. (1944b). *Latin America in school and college teaching materials* (Report of the Committee on the Study of Teaching Materials on Inter-American Subjects). Washington, DC: Author.

American Council on Education. (Ed.). (1946). *Treatment of Asia in American textbooks.* New York: American Council, Institute of Pacific Relations.

American Federation of Teachers. (1987). *Democracy's untold story: What world history textbooks neglect.* Washington, DC: Author.

Armstrong, O. K. (1940, September). Treason in the textbooks. *American Legion Magazine, 20* (3), 8–9, 51, 70–72.

Bainbridge, J. (1952, October). Danger's ahead in the public schools. *McCall's*, 56, 92–94, 98, 108, 110, 112, 116, 120, 122.

Beale, H. K. (1936). *Are American teachers free? An analysis of restraints upon the freedom of teaching in American schools* (Report of the Commission on the Social Studies, Part 12). New York: Scribner's Sons.

Burkhardt, R. W. (1946). The Far East in modern problems and civics tests. In American Council on Education (Ed.), *Treatment of Asia in American textbooks* (pp. 79–104). New York: American Council, Institute of Pacific Relations.

Bushnell, A. (1911). *School books and international prejudices* (Monograph No. 38). New York: American Association for International Conciliation.

Chase, W. L., & Cornforth, M. C. (1932). The world war in junior high school history textbooks. *Education, 53*, 224–228.

Cole. C. E. (1939). The war content of American history textbooks. *Social Studies, 30*, 195–197.

Counts, G. S. (1946). Soviet version of American history. *Public Opinion Quarterly, 10*, 321–328.

Eagleton, C. (1918). Discussion: The attitude of our textbooks toward England. *Education Review, 56*, 424–429.

Elliott, D. L. (1990). Textbooks and the curriculum in the postwar era: 1950–1980. In D. L. Elliott & A. Woodward (Eds.), *Textbooks and schooling in the United*

States (89th Yearbook of the National Society for the Study of Education, Part I, pp. 42–55). Chicago, IL: University of Chicago Press.

England, J. M. (1963). England and America in the schoolbooks of the Republic, 1783—1861. *University of Birmingham Historical Journal, 9,* 92–111.

Griffen, W., & Marciano, J. (1980). Vietnam: The textbook version. *Social Science Record, 17,* 16–20.

Harbourt, J. (1931). The world war in French, German, English, and American secondary school textbooks (*Yearbook of the National Council for the Social Studies,* Vol. 1, pp. 54–117). Arlington, VA: National Council for the Social Studies.

Harding, S. B. (1919). What the war should do for our history methods. *Historical Outlook, 10,* 189–190.

Hart, D. V. (1944). What do our school books say about Latin America? *Harvard Educational Review, 14,* 210–220.

Hayes, C. J. H. (1923). Nationalism and the social studies. *Historical Outlook, 14,* 247–250.

Kendig-Gill, I. (1923). *War and peace in United States history text-books* [pamphlet]. Washington, DC: National Council for Prevention of War.

Kretman, K. P., & Parker, B. (1986). New U.S. history texts: Good news and bad. *Social Education, 50,* 61–63.

Krug, M. M. (1960). "Safe" textbooks and citizenship education. *School Review, 68,* 463–480.

Krug, M. M. (1963). The distant cousins: A comparative study of selected history textbooks in England and the United States. *School Review, 71,* 425–441.

Lew, T. T. (1923). *China in American school text-books: A problem of education in international understanding and worldwide brotherhood* (Special Supplement of the Chinese Social and Political Science Review). Peking, China: Chinese Social and Political Science Association.

Lutz, P. E. (1929). Nationalism in German history textbooks after the war. *Historical Outlook, 20,* 273–279.

New York bill on history text-books. (1923, March 31). *School and Society, 17,* p. 349.

O'Brien, S. (1988). The reshaping of history: Marketers vs. authors—Who wins? Who loses? *Curriculum Review, 28* (1), 11–14.

Palmer, J. R. (1961). History textbooks and social change. *Social Education, 25,* 135–136.

Perpiñan, J. E. (1934). The Philippine Islands in American school textbooks. *Journal of Experimental Education, 2,* 366–393.

Pierce, B. L. (1926). *Public opinion and the teaching of history in the United States.* New York: Knopf.

Pierce, B. L. (1930). *Civic attitudes in American school textbooks.* Chicago: University of Chicago Press.

Prescott, D. A. (1930). *Education and international relations: A study of the social forces that determine the influence of Education.* Cambridge, MA: Harvard University Press.

Ravitch, D., & Finn, C. E. (1987). *What do our 17-year-olds know?* (Report on the First National Assessment of History and Literature). New York: Harper & Row.

Robbins, J. (1961). The new Asia and American education. *Teachers College Record, 62*, 339–347.

Root, E. M. (1959). *Brainwashing in the high school: An examination of eleven American history textbooks.* New York: Deven-Adair.

Schuyler, R. L. (1918). History and public opinion: The nationalist interpretation of history and Anglo-American antagonism, *Educational Review, 55*, 181–190.

Scott, J. F. (1926). *The menace of nationalism in education.* London: Allen & Unwin.

Stephens, H. M. (1916). Nationality and history. *American Historical Review, 21*, 225–236.

Turner, R. (1922). Are American school histories now too pro-British? *Landmark, 4*, 251–255.

Wallace, W. S. (1919). The text-book poison in Canadian-American friendship, *Bookman, 48*, 680–684.

Walworth, A. (1938). *School histories at war: A study of the treatment of our wars in the secondary school history books of the United States and in those of its former enemies.* Cambridge, MA: Harvard University Press.

Wellington, E. E. (1929). Ridding the schools of propaganda. *Journal of the American Association of University Women, 22* (3), 157.

Wood, H. J. (1951). The Far East in world history. *Social Education, 15*, 155–159.

Zimmern, A. (1930, April). The League of Nations and the teaching for history. *New Era, 11*, 71–72.

Case Study 5.3: Sources of Stereotypes

American Association of University Women. (1929). *Report of the committee on U.S. history textbooks used in the U.S. schools.* Washington, DC: Author.

Carpenter, M. E. (1941). *The treatment of the Negro in American history school textbook: A comparison of changing textbook content, 1826 to 1839, with developing scholarship in the history of the Negro in the United States.* Menasha, WI: Banta.

Glazer, N., & Ueda, R. (1983). *Ethnic groups in history textbooks.* Washington, DC: Ethics and Public Policy Center.

Graebner, D. B. (1972). A decade of sexism in readers. *Reading Teacher, 26*, 52–58.

Hahn, C. L., & Blankenship, G. (1983). Women and economics textbooks. *Theory and Research in Social Education, 11* (3), 67–76.

Janis, J. (1970). Textbook revisions in the sixties. *Teachers College Record, 72*, 289–301.

Kane, M. B. (1970). *Minorities in textbooks: A study of their treatment in social studies texts.* Chicago: Anti-Defamation League of B'nai Brith.

Kealey, R. J. (1980). The image of the family in second-grade readers. *Momentum, 11* (9), 16–19.

Kirp, D. L., (1991). Textbooks and tribalism in California. *Public Interest, 104*, 20–36.

Knight, E. W. (1949). Southern opposition to northern education. *Educational Forum, 14*, 47–58.

Lerner, R., Nagai, A. K., & Rothman, S. (1989). Filler feminism in high school history. *Academic Questions, 5* (1), 28–40.

Levine, M. (1937). Social problems in American history textbooks. *Social Studies, 28*, 161–166.

Marcus, L. (1961). *The treatment of minorities in secondary school textbooks*. New York: B'nai B'rith.

Marten, L. A., & Matlin, M. W. (1976). Does sexism in elementary readers still exist? *Reading Teacher, 29*, 764–767.

McLaurin, M. (1971). Images of Negroes in Deep South public school state history texts. *Phylon, 32*, 237–246.

National Association for the Advancement of Colored People. (1939). *Anti-Negro propaganda in school textbooks*. New York: Author.

National Project on Women in Education. (1978). *Taking sexism out of education*. Washington, DC: U.S. Department of Health, Education, and Welfare.

Nolen, E. W. (1942). The colored child in contemporary literature. *Horn Book, 18*, 348–355.

Pate, G. S. (1981). Research on prejudice reduction. *Educational Leadership, 38*, 288–291.

Purcell, P., & Stewart, L. (1990). Dick and Jane in 1989. *Sex Roles, 22*, 177–185.

Reddick, L. K. (1934). Racial attitudes in American history: Textbooks of the South. *Journal of Negro History, 19*, 225–265.

Reynolds, C. J. (1952). Textbooks and immigrants. *Phi Delta Kappan,* 33, 295–296.

Rosenberg, M. (1973). Evaluate your textbooks for racism, sexism! *Educational Leadership, 31*, 107–109.

Saveth, E. N. (1949). Good stocks and lesser breeds: The immigrant in American textbooks. *Commentary, 7*, 494–498.

Schenck, J. P. (1976). Sexism in textbooks: A guide to detection. *American Vocational Journal, 51*, 42–45.

Scott Foresman. (1972). *Guidelines for improving the image of women in textbooks*. Glenview, IL: Author.

Stewart, C. E. (1964). Correcting the image of Negroes in textbooks. *Negro History Bulletin, 28* (2), 29–30, 42–44.

Stewart, M. S. (1950). *Prejudice in textbooks* (Public Affairs Pamphlet No. 160). New York: Public Affairs Committee.

Stewig, J., & Higgs, M. (1973). Girls grow up to be mommies: A study of sexism in children's literature. *Library Journal, 98*, 236–241.

Trecker, J. L. (1971). Women in U.S. history high school textbooks. *Social Education, 35*, 249–260, 268.

Vogel, V. J. (1968). The Indian in American history textbooks. *Integrated Education, 6* (3), 16–32.

Wargny, F. O. (1963). The good life in modern readers. *Reading Teacher, 17*, 88–93.

Wiik, S. L. (1973). The sexual bias of textbook literature. *English Journal, 62*, 224–229.

Wilson, H. E. (1947). Intergroup relations in teaching materials. *Educational Record, 28*, 114–121.

Zinet, S. G. (1972a). Males and females in American primers from colonial days to the present. In S. G. Zinet (Ed.), *What children read in school: A critical analysis of primary reading textbooks* (pp. 79–86). New York: Grune & Stratton.

Zinet, S. G. (1972b). Values and attitudes in American primers. In S. G. Zinet (Ed.), *What children read in school: A critical analysis of primary reading textbooks* (pp. 87–97). New York: Grune & Stratton.

Chapter Six

Learners: Dealing with Gender and Religious Biases

America has always been socially and economically stratified. Some groups benefitted because of the strata that they occupied; others suffered. Some groups were able to progress to new strata; others were not. Females were one of the groups that historically were assigned to disadvantageous strata. The members of certain religions also were confined to these strata. These groups suffered in numerous ways; their children suffered in the schools.

GENDER AND RELIGIOUS BIASES IN CURRENT CLASSROOMS

American women were victims of discrimination. They were not able to change their situation at the beginning of the twentieth century. Even after they had called attention to the numerous injustices to which they were subjected, they were not able to improve their situation.

During World War I, women were entreated to assume unprecedented wartime responsibilities. They were assured that their contributions were needed to protect or regain the rights of citizens in foreign countries.

Women responded enthusiastically to the wartime calls. They labored as volunteers, teachers, clerks, salespersons, nurses, and doctors. They took on many of the agricultural and industrial jobs that males had vacated.

While they labored to protect the rights of citizens in foreign countries, women pointed to their own situations; they pointed out that women were denied those rights in the United States. Although they were able to identify numerous examples of rights that women had been denied, they focused attention on voting rights. They adjured members of the public to support the national women's suffrage movement. They adjured them to ratify the Nineteenth Amendment to the United States Constitution.

Women had expected President Wilson to provide leadership for the women's suffrage movement. They had expected leadership from him because of his public statements. They reminded Wilson that he had campaigned on a promise to promote women's suffrage. They also reminded him of their heroic participation in the homefront campaign.

Although they detected some presidential support for the Nineteenth Amendment, women still were disappointed with Wilson. They believed that he had not brought the passion and commitment to women's suffrage that he had brought to international affairs. Although they conceded that his extraordinary concern about international affairs may have been justified during the war, they became disenchanted with him when he later continued to focus his efforts almost exclusively on international affairs.

The advocates for women's suffrage eventually prevailed. In 1920, they secured the ratification of the Nineteenth Amendment. During subsequent decades, they expanded women's political, legal, economic, and social rights. Their goal was to create a nation where women and men had the same rights and where they were treated in the same fashion.

Twentieth-century world events highlighted the historical discrimination to which women were subjected; they later highlighted the discrimination to which other minority groups were subjected. European anti-Semitism, the anti-Semitic pogroms, and the Diaspora were world events that highlighted the discrimination to which Jews were subjected.

At the end of World War II, American soldiers entered European concentration camps. They were shocked by the scenes that they encountered. As Americans at the homefront learned about this tragedy, they also were stunned. Even the civilian residents in the countries where these crimes had been perpetrated alleged that they had not understood the nature, severity, and scope of those crimes until later.

Although American anti-Semitism never disappeared, it declined after World War II. Professing sympathy for the Jews who had survived the Holocaust, many American citizens supported the designation of a site at which they would be safe. They supported the creation of a Jewish state in the Middle East: Israel.

Recent discriminatory practices against females and Jews have replicated historical patterns. With regard to females, some harmful societal practices have been analyzed. For example, researchers have indicated that female workers earn salaries lower than those of males with comparable training and experience (e.g., Babcock and Laschever, 2003; Dey and Hill, 2007).

Although analyses of salary patterns were relatively easy to execute, some analyses were more difficult, among them analyses of sexual harassment in workplaces and classrooms. Because victims were reluctant to speak out, even the prevalence of sexual harassment was difficult to ascertain.

When school administrators and teachers attempted to combat social problems, they sometimes became frustrated. They were frustrated because these problems were encumbered by bureaucratic processes; they also were frustrated because the problems extended beyond the domain of the schools. They became frustrated with combatting sexual harassment for both of these reasons.

Like sexual harassment and gender discrimination, anti-Semitism is a problem with a complex origin. Students who have been the victims of sexual harassment or gender discrimination hoped that their teachers and school administrators would help them; students who have been the victims of anti-Semitism also hoped that they would help. Students had similar hopes during earlier eras.

GENDER BIAS

The historically unfair treatment of American women was evident. It was evident in the difficulties that women encountered while securing the right to vote. It was evident in the unfair laws, workplace restrictions, government policies, and social practices against which they subsequently protested.

Although reformers campaigned for the elimination of gender biases throughout society, they focused a great deal of attention on the schools. They questioned whether teacher practices, school policies, and curricular patterns had contributed to social biases. They questioned whether textbooks had contributed to them.

Reformers found multiple examples in which females were denigrated in textbooks. They noted that they were omitted from many books. In the few instances in which they were mentioned, they were portrayed as legally, politically, financially, socially, and psychologically dependent on males. Biased depictions of females in newspapers and novels reinforced those in the textbooks.

Reformers demanded revisions of gender-biased textbooks. They even gave the publishers practical suggestions. They encouraged them to ensure that textual references accurately depicted the historical roles of females. They adjured them to exclude passages or illustrations that demeaned females. They urged them to include information about the cultural, social, and intellectual achievements of women. They also counseled them to represent females and males interacting in integrated groups.

RELIGIOUS BIAS

During the 1800s, textbooks publishers frequently referred to the historical contributions of Protestants. They occasionally referred to the contributions of non-Protestant Christians. They rarely referred to the contributions of Jewish Americans.

In those instances in which textbook publishers referred to Jewish Americans, they represented them as shrewd, avaricious, and generally out of step with the values and ideals of their Christian neighbors. These representations were reinforced by biased depictions in newspapers, novels, and the popular media.

Jewish Americans objected to their unfair treatment. They especially were concerned about the harm that was inflicted on children in the schools. To protect their children, some Jewish Americans sent them to private religious schools.

The teachers and administrators at the Jewish schools set high academic standards, relied on sophisticated instructional techniques, and expanded the curriculum to encompass the arts. At the private schools, they ensured that children studied a full academic curriculum; they also ensured that they studied the Hebrew language, Judaism, and the history of the Jewish people.

Not all Jewish families sent their children to private schools. Because these schools depended on tuition, some families could not afford them. Because many of the Jewish schools were situated in urban areas, rural families lacked access. Some families had another reason for not sending their children to Jewish schools.

Some families worried that the sequestering of children in private schools would not solve the anti-Semitic problems in society. They reasoned that religiously biased practices and textbooks were harming non-Jewish students as well as Jewish students. Although the removal of Jewish children from the public schools might shield those children from discrimination, this practice might inadvertently nurture anti-Semitism. Jewish advocacy groups such as B'nai B'rith and the Anti-Defamation League stated this argument with passion and eloquence.

Some persons ignored the demands to reduce anti-Semitism in the schools. They claimed that the impact of anti-Semitism was exaggerated. They claimed that it might not be greater than that which Catholics, Mormons, Muslims, Hindus, and the members of some Protestant sects had sustained.

Jews retorted that the historical prejudice directed at them had been linked to violence; they feared that this violence would reemerge.

During World War II, more and more Americans learned about anti-Semitic atrocities in Europe and the Soviet Union. Nonetheless, some of them did not realize the depths of these atrocities until the war had ended. Americans listened in disbelief to the stories of persons who had survived the Holocaust. They wept as they read the tragic diary of Anne Frank, a 13-year-old-girl who had failed to evade her Nazi persecutors.

After the horrors of the Holocaust were publicized, Jewish Americans reminded the textbook publishers of their earlier warnings. They again requested that the publishers adapt educational materials. As an example of the changes they had in mind, they suggested that the publishers include information about the Holocaust in social studies textbooks.

Jewish Americans suggested multiple changes. They recommended the exclusion of caricatures from textbooks. They recommended the inclusion of textual passages that accurately reflected historical records. They endorsed the inclusion of passages that recounted the cultural, social, and intellectual achievements of Jewish Americans. They endorsed the inclusion of illustrations containing integrated groups of Jewish Americans and non-Jewish Americans.

Prior to World War II, many publishers ignored the adjurations to reduce religious biases in textbooks. After the war, they did make some revisions. In addition to including information about the Holocaust in their history textbooks, they excised deprecatory passages and illustrations. Nonetheless, few of them accurately and fully chronicled the contributions of American Jews.

Jewish Americans continued to press for textbook revisions; they implored their non-Jewish neighbors to assist them. Although they had been able to elicit strong support after World War II, they later detected an ebb and flow to the support.

The movement to revise religiously biased textbooks continued to be influenced by the memory of the Holocaust and the other persecutions to which Jews had been subjected. However, it also was influenced by emerging international events. These events included the establishment of Israel, the feuds between Israelis and Arabs, and terrorism in the Middle East and around the globe.

Case Study 6.1: Females

During the nineteenth and early twentieth centuries, discrimination against females could be detected. It sometimes was explicit and intentional. Discriminatory laws were explicit and intentional. Discriminatory laws recognized that unmarried women had some civil and financial rights; however, they specified that women would lose many of those rights should they marry (McElroy, 2006).

Although the discrimination revealed in laws was overt, other forms of discrimination were subtle. Late nineteenth-century and early twentieth-century political cartoonists may have demonstrated a more subtle form of discrimination (Camhi, 1994; National Women's History Museum, 2007). When those cartoonists were accused of infusing venomous content into their graphics, they rejoined that they had only intended to be witty.

The Nineteenth Amendment to the United States Constitution specified that women had the right to vote. Once this amendment was ratified, women realized that their political power had increased. Even though they were able to improve some aspects of their lives, they continued to confront discrimination. They confronted it in workplaces, courts, newspapers, novels and films, schools and textbooks.

Textbooks were replete with stereotypical images of females. The passages in them depicted males as athletic, brave, and self-confident; they depicted females as noncompetitive, demure, and deferential. They depicted male workers as professional, executives, and entrepreneurs; they depicted female workers as clerks, assistants, and homemakers.

Textbooks conveyed stereotypes when they contained inaccurate information; they also conveyed stereotypes when they selectively omitted information. Prior to the 1970s, publishers had omitted females from the illustrations and photographs in most history textbooks. In those rare instances where they had included them, they had represented them in stereotypical manners and situations.

During the 1920s and the 1930s, publishers were asked to edit gender-biased textbooks. In response, some of them did produce nondiscriminatory textbooks. However, the publishers who made the revisions did not find a profitable market (Giordano, 2003).

Equating profits with success, the publishers judged that nondiscriminatory textbooks were unsuccessful. The publishers who made the revisions and their competitors concluded that they did not need to be concerned about gender-biased materials. They interpreted the continued high sales of traditional textbooks as a validation of their conclusion.

The critics of discriminatory textbooks eventually did gain the attention of the publishers. However, they did not get publishers' full attention until the 1970s. They warned the publishers that the political mood in America was changing. They advised them to align their textbooks with feminism, a national movement that was altering economic, employment, social, and educational practices.

During the 1970s, women were concerned that students were developing gender-biased attitudes in elementary and high schools. They detected biases in school policies and practices. They also detected them in textbooks. They demanded that the publishers eliminate the biases from textbooks.

The reformers pointed to the textbook changes that publishers had made a decade earlier. They noted that the publishers had made those changes to eliminate biased depictions of African Americans. They asked the publishers to demonstrate similar zeal and alacrity in eliminating biased depictions of females.

The publishers had listened to the opponents of racially biased textbooks. They had listened because the opponents had assembled a broad and supportive coalition. Their coalition had included school administrators, teachers, members of boards of education, community activists, politicians, and parents. After the publishers listened to these groups, they acted quickly and decisively to make the suggested changes.

The opponents of gender-biased textbooks followed the same strategy that African Americans had employed. After assembling a powerful and supportive coalition, they threatened to boycott biased learning materials.

Fearful that their products would be rejected, publishers again made changes to them. They included more females in textual passages and illustrations. They ensured that males and females were depicted non-stereotypically. They eliminated sexist language. They collaborated with political, governmental, and educational groups to develop guidelines for bias-free learning materials.

School administrators and teachers who previously had purchased biased textbooks, films, and auxiliary learning materials began to select materials that were less biased. Moreover, they began to employ procedures and practices to foster bias-free learning environments.

Even though school administrators and teachers had taken steps to reduce gender bias in the schools, educational reformers questioned whether those steps were effective. To demonstrate the basis for their skepticism, they conducted research about the ways in which teachers were treating female and male students.

The researchers examined the types of questions that elementary-school and high-school teachers posed to female and male students (American Association of University Women, 1992). After documenting that teachers directed different types of questions to the males and females in their classes, they concluded that these actions had affected the students' attitudes about women.

The reformers advised school administrators and teachers to continue their efforts to eliminate gender-biased practices. They also advised them about the complex etiology of those practices.

Activity: The Depiction of Females in Textbooks

Publishers traditionally had left females out of most history textbooks. When they included them, they depicted them stereotypically. However, they eventually made revisions.

What types of events influenced the publishers when they made decisions to reduce or eliminate gender biases from history textbooks? To help answer this question, create a chart.

Table 6.1. Females

Event	*Reason That the Event Was Influential*

Along the horizontal axis of the chart, create a column in which you identify three events that influenced the publishers. In another column of the chart, provide a short explanation of the reason that each event was influential.

Your examples will be based on assumptions about the vested interests, values, and goals of the textbook publishers. Although you can use the information in the case study to make some of these assumptions, you may wish to rely on a broader foundation of information.

You can gather additional information from the materials that are listed at the end of this chapter. You may gather it from lectures or discussions.

Case Study 6.2: Jewish Americans

Americans were aware of the pitiless persecution of the Jews during the 1930s and the 1940s. Feeling sympathy, they may have reduced instances of anti-Semitism during this era (e.g., Katz and Braly, 1933; Gilbert, 1951).

Postwar Americans listened carefully to the Zionists. The Zionists were historical scholars, religious leaders, and political activists who were committed to solving religious and nationalist problems. They argued that the Jewish people, like Italian Catholics and German Lutherans, had mingled religious and nationalist goals. They advocated for a nation in which religion and nationalism could prosper. They advocated for a nation in the Middle East. They advocated for Israel.

Many American citizens agreed with the Zionists about the need to establish Israel (Ruby, 2007). Some of them agreed because they feared that Jews would never be safe until they had their own nation. Others agreed because they believed that a strategic alliance with this new nation could enhance the security of their own country.

Israel was established in 1948. The event was preceded by many decades of feuding; it was followed by additional decades of feuding. Those Americans who initially were unconcerned about the Middle East eventually changed their minds. Many of them changed their minds in 1967, when the Israelis and Palestinians formally engaged in war.

The 1967 war was fought for only several days. However, it altered national boundaries; it also altered Palestinian attitudes. The hostile attitudes of Palestinians became apparent in 1972, when a group of terrorists massacred Israeli athletes at the Munich Olympics. Their hostile attitudes became apparent in 1973, when they engaged in another war with Israel. The hostility remained evident during the subsequent decades.

The United States had provided financial, political, and military support to Israel from the time of its founding. Some American citizens may have been unaware of the degree to which this support antagonized Arabs in the Middle East. But they may have become aware on September 11, 2001, the date on which Arab terrorists killed American civilians in New York City.

After the events of September 11, some Americans questioned their nation's multi-decade commitment to Israel. Drawing a distinction between Jewish national interests and Jewish religious interests, these Americans alleged that they were not committed to Israeli nationalism or Zionism. Many Jewish Americans objected. Some of them even questioned whether the anti-Israel critics were not truly anti-Semitic. Like the conflict between the Israelis and the Arabs, the disagreements between American supporters and opponents of Israel became a complex dispute.

Activity: Stereotypes of Jewish Americans in the Schools

Textbook publishers traditionally depicted Jewish Americans in unflattering ways. However, they reduced those depictions during the eras that followed World War II.

What types of events influenced publishers when they made changes to textbooks that were biased against Jewish Americans? To help answer this question, create a chart.

Along the horizontal axis of the chart, create a column in which you identify three events that influenced the publishers. Identify events that occurred during World War II or afterwards.

Table 6.2. Jewish Americans

Event	*Reason That the Event Was Influential*

The events that you identify may have persuaded the publishers to be less biased in the ways that they depicted Jews in the United States or those in other countries. They also may be events that persuaded them to be less biased in the ways that they depicted Zionism or Israel.

In another column of the chart, provide a short explanation of the reason that each event was influential. Your examples will be based on assumptions about the vested interests, values, and goals of the textbook publishers. Although you can use the information in the case study to make some of these assumptions, you may wish to rely on a broader foundation of information.

You can gather additional information from the materials that are listed at the end of this chapter. You may gather it from lectures or discussions.

Case Study 6.3: Unsympathetic Critics

Reformers objected to the ways in which textbook publishers depicted females and the members of some racial, ethnic, and religious groups. However, they had difficulty persuading the publishers to make changes. They eventually decided to adopt a strategy that African Americans had used during the Civil Rights era.

The reformers persuaded parents, school board members, and school district staffs to boycott biased learning materials. Some of them were able to persuade state politicians to enact bans against biased materials.

Aware that the threats that had been made against them were genuine, the publishers made adaptations. For example, they expanded the coverage of women and other minority groups in history textbooks.

Not everyone was impressed by the adaptations that the publishers made to their textbooks. Critics alleged that the publishers had made too many concessions to the reformers; they alleged that they had misrepresented the genuine history of the United States.

A *Washington Post* columnist agreed with the critics. She worried that the teaching of American history had been distorted by "the spirit of equal outcomes." To demonstrate the basis for her concern, she recounted a series of incidents that had transpired in New Jersey.

> Once ubiquitous in American classrooms, Washington's portrait has all but disappeared from schools. When . . . a New Jersey businessman noticed the first president was missing from his daughter's classroom, he set out to correct the oversight. . . . He began producing high-quality prints of Washington. . . . [and] lobbied for state legislation proposing that at least one Washington portrait be placed in each school district. Although a bill passed the House several years ago, it died in a Senate committee after the New Jersey Education Association (NJEA) objected. [A] spokeswoman for the NJEA summed up the general sentiment to *USA Today*: "Requiring legislation to honor one person does a disservice to many individuals," she said. "There are so many others who were also instrumental in securing our country's freedom" [Parker, 2007, p.1].

Although this columnist conceded that "both sexes and all races should be included in history books," she asserted that "not all participants in history are equal." She accused the members of the New Jersey Education Association of substituting "silly sensitivity" for "intellectual honesty." To highlight the damage that she felt this juxtaposition had caused, she pointed to the multiple errors that recent college students had made on factual tests about American history.

The *Washington Post* columnist was not the sole critic to call attention to the ways in which politics and special interests had influenced education. In fact, the expansion of "talk radio" and highly editorialized television programs increased the opportunities for critics to publicize these types of allegations (Barker, 2002; Hutchby, 1996). Politically conservative personalities such as Rush Limbaugh, Bill O'Reilly, Sean Hannity, and Anne Coulter made acerbic oral commentaries; they then paired them with equally acerbic publications. Scores of regional spokespersons and commentators mimicked their pronouncements.

Liberal editorialists also wished to highlight the ways in which politics had influenced education. Personalities such as Michael Moore, Al Franken, Jon Stewart, and Stephen Colbert followed the leads of the conservatives. They were applauded by like-minded ideologues and booed by their opponents.

Activity: Backlash against Efforts to Eliminate Stereotypes

Imagine that you are about to analyze a recent edition of a history textbook. You wish to determine the benefits and the drawbacks of this book. As you prepare to make your analysis, you notice that the publishers have expanded the new book's coverage of females and Jewish Americans.

The publishers have listed the new book for the same price as the previous edition. In order to add new material to the book without raising its price, they have reduced its total length. They have eliminated several types of information, including passages that were biased against females and Jewish Americans.

After you have completed your analysis of the new textbook, you intend to present the results to an audience that will include critics and supporters of

Table 6.3. Unsympathetic Critics

Benefits of Revised American History Textbooks	*Drawbacks of Revised American History Textbooks*

revised history textbooks. Wishing to make a balanced presentation, you decide that you will create a chart.

Create two columns in your chart. In one column, arrange three cells. In each of these cells, list a reason for being enthusiastic about history textbooks with expanded coverage of females or Jewish Americans. In a separate column of your chart, create three additional cells. In these cells, list reasons for being cautious about textbooks with expanded coverage of females or Jewish Americans.

When you are specifying reasons for being enthusiastic or cautious about revised history textbooks, you may focus on educational issues. However, you also can consider the broader economic, social, and political issues to which textbooks are connected.

Your chart will be based on assumptions about the vested interests, values, and goals of the groups that respectively support and oppose textbooks with expanded coverage of females or Jewish Americans. Although you can use the information in the case study to make some of these assumptions, you may wish to rely on a broader foundation of information.

You can gather additional information from the materials that are listed at the end of this chapter. You may gather it from lectures or discussions.

USING THE PAST TO UNDERSTAND THE PRESENT

Community leaders sometimes made educational decisions out of expediency. Out of expediency, they built one-room schoolhouses. Out of expediency, they organized students without regard to their academic levels or ages.

Once they had sufficient resources, community leaders were able to make decisions more cautiously. They replaced the one-room schoolhouses with larger facilities. They also hired administrators to manage the new facilities.

When school administrators had to organize students, some sorted them on the basis of their ages. Some sorted them on the basis of their academic abilities. Some sorted them on the basis of other factors.

Many school administrators sorted students into neighborhood schools. Although they made the assignments on the basis of neighborhoods, they realized that persons of a single race sometimes lived in one neighborhood. In these cases, the school administrators effectively relied on race. In the South, school administrators were required by state lawmakers to pay attention to race whenever they assigned students to schools.

Some school administrators paid attention to gender when they grouped students. They may have been restricted by law. For example, they may have been constrained by legal charters that limited the enrollments in certain schools to males.

Sometimes social norms and traditions restricted school administrators. These factors may have influenced them when they directed males to vocational schools in which they would learn woodworking, mechanics, or masonry. These factors may have influenced them when they directed females away from these programs.

Like their counterparts in public schools, administrators in private schools restricted enrollments. Even though Catholic parents could send their children to Jewish schools, they rarely did. Even though Jewish parents could send their children to Catholic schools, they rarely did. As a result, their schools were effectively segregated.

Some schools adopted admission policies to ensure that only minority students would attend them. Were there advantages to schools that admitted only minority students? For example, did students who attended all-female schools have opportunities to develop in atmospheres that were free of bias and discrimination? Did students who attended private religious schools have these opportunities?

During earlier eras, some citizens extolled the benefits of voluntarily segregated schools. However, others questioned their effectiveness. The proponents and opponents of voluntarily segregated schools continue to debate these issues.

To better understand the debate, analyze a recent incident in which critics raised questions about a voluntarily segregated, all-minority-student school. Find a school that used gender, religion, or some other characteristic of students in its admission policies. About which groups of students did the critics express concerns? Did they question whether segregated environments harmed the students who enrolled? Did they question whether they harmed the students who were unable to enroll? Ideally, find an incident that transpired in your own state or community.

CHAPTER SUMMARY

Americans demonstrated discrimination during all eras. They discriminated against some groups because of religion. They treated Jews especially cruelly. Many Americans changed their attitudes after they learned of the suffering of European and Soviet Jews during World War II. They continued to change their attitudes as they observed the founding of Israel, fighting in the Middle East, and the rise of terrorism.

Like Jewish Americans, American females were the victims of historical and long-lived discrimination. They campaigned for changes in employment, property rights, social practices, and voting rights. They documented discrimination in the schools and proposed ways to reduce it.

ADDITIONAL READING

Introductory Passages

Diller, A., Ayim, M., & Morgan, K. (1996). *The gender question in education: Theory, pedagogy, and politics*. Boulder, CO: Westview.

Kaplan, M. A. (1999). *Between dignity and despair: Jewish life in Nazi Germany*. New York: Oxford University Press.

Laqueur, W. (2006). *The changing face of anti-Semitism: From ancient times to the present day*. New York: Oxford University Press.

Netherlands Institute for War Documentation. (2003). *The Diary of Anne Frank: The revised critical edition*. (A. J. Pomerans, Trans.) New York: Doubleday.

Sadker, M., & Sadker, D. (1996). *Failing at fairness: How our schools cheat girls*. New York: Scribner. (Original work published in 1994.)

Salomone, R. C. (2005). *Same, different, equal: Rethinking single-sex schooling*. New Haven, CT: Yale University Press.

Case Study 6.1: Females

Brownmiller, S. (2000). *Our time: Memoir of a revolution*. New York: Dial.

Hunter College Women's Studies Collective. (1995). *Women's realities, women's choices: An introduction to women's studies* (2nd ed.). New York: Oxford University Press.

Kerber, L. K., & De Hart, J. S. (2003). *Women's America: Refocusing the past*. (6th ed.). New York: Oxford University Press.

Meehan, D. (2007). *Learning like a girl: Educating our daughters in schools of their own*. Cambridge, MA: Public Affairs.

Norton, M. B., & Alexander, R. M. (Eds.). (2006). *Major problems in American women's history: Documents and essays* (4th ed.). Boston: Houghton Mifflin.

Orenstein, P. (1994). *Schoolgirls: Young women, self-esteem, and the confidence gap*. New York: Anchor.

Stabiner, K. (2003). *All girls: Single-sex education and why it matters*. New York: Riverhead.

Sternberg, S. R., & Kincheloe, J. L. (Eds.). (2004). *Kinderculture: The corporate construction of childhood* (2nd ed.). Boulder, CO: Westview.

Ware, S. (2001). *Modern American women: A documentary history* (2nd ed.). New York: McGraw-Hill.

Woloch, N. (2005). *Women and the American experience: A concise history* (4th ed.). New York: McGraw-Hill.

Case Study 6.2: Jewish Americans

Carr, S. A. (2001). *Hollywood and anti-Semitism: A cultural history up to World War II*. Cambridge, UK: Cambridge University Press.

Lewis, B. (1999). *Semites and anti-Semites: An inquiry into conflict and prejudice*. New York: Norton.

Lipstadt, D. (1994). *Denying the Holocaust: The growing assault on truth and memory*. London: Penguin.

Perry, M., & Schweitzer, F. (2002). *Anti-Semitism: Myth and hate from antiquity to the present*. New York: Palgrave Macmillan.

Steinweis, A. E. (2006). *Studying the Jew: Scholarly Antisemitism in Nazi Germany*. Cambridge, MA: Harvard University Press.

Urofsky, M. I. (1995). *American Zionism from Herzl to the Holocaust*. Omaha: University of Nebraska Press.

Case Study 6.3: Unsympathetic Critics

Colbert, S. (2007). *I am America (and so can you!)*. New York: Grand Central.

Coulter, A. (2007). *If Democrats had any brains, they'd be Republicans*. New York: Crown Forum.

Franken, A. (2003). *Lies and the lying liars who tell them: A fair and balanced look at the right*. New York: Dutton.

Hannity, S. (2002). *Let freedom ring: Winning the war of liberty over liberalism*. New York: Morrow.

Limbaugh, R. (1992). *The way things ought to be*. New York: Pocket.

Moore, M. (2002). *Stupid white men . . . and other sorry excuses for the state of the nation*! New York: Regan Books.

O'Reilly, B. (2007). *Culture warrior*. New York: Broadway.

Stewart, J. (2006). The *Daily Show with Jon Stewart presents America (the book)*. New York: Grand Central.

Chapter Seven

Politics: Dealing with Domestic Problems

Americans faced serious problems after World War I. Veterans could not find jobs because of an economic recession and competition from homefront civilians. Like other returning veterans, African Americans were upset when they could not find jobs; they also were upset about their peers' racial attitudes, which were less tolerant than those of the Europeans that they had met abroad. Although some Americans hoped that their lives would improve, they changed their minds after the Great Depression devastated the country. During this crisis, liberal extremists exhorted teachers to prepare students for a socialist economy and government; conservative activists urged them to prepare students to deal with the threats from European fascism, Japanese imperialism, and Soviet communism.

EDUCATION AND DOMESTIC PROBLEMS TODAY

Communities are affected by economic conditions. Education is affected by economic conditions. When communities are not prospering, educators have difficulty helping students, faced with overcrowded classrooms or rundown buildings. They have difficulty in purchasing textbooks, equipment, and technology, and in hiring and retaining talented teachers.

Some children are affected directly by economic conditions. They suffer when their parents become unemployed. They suffer even more if unemployed parents become ill, depressed, violent, alcoholic, or addicted to drugs.

Do economic conditions affect some children indirectly? Do they affect how they view their teachers and peers? Do they affect how they view alcohol, drugs, and sex? Do they affect how they learn, how much they learn, and whether they learn?

Some sociologists (Berger and Luckmann, 1967) have argued that a complex web of social interactions influences the ways in which children view themselves, their peers, their schools, and society. Calling themselves social constructionists, these sociologists have alleged that the ways in which persons interact with others affect whether they feel socially enfranchised or disenfranchised.

Socially disenfranchised persons are evident today as they have been during all eras. They were strikingly evident during the economic and social turbulence of the 1920s and the 1930s.

THE 1920s

When World War I ended, most citizens were surprised by the problems that ensued. They then were disappointed by the ways that government officials reacted to those problems. They especially were disappointed in President Wilson's reactions.

Ignoring the counsel from Congress and from many of his own advisors, Wilson decided to personally represent the United States at a postwar peace conference. He resolved that he would leave the United States, travel to Europe, and then remain overseas for an extended stay.

Wilson had been elected on a pledge to keep America out of World War I. After his reelection, he reversed his stance. He explained that he had changed his mind because he realized that American intervention could end combat forever. Wilson later indicated that his attendance at the European conference was another step in the journey toward world peace.

Motivated by idealism, political opportunism, and vanity, Wilson announced that he would spend six months abroad at the postwar conference. Some critics protested that he would be physically removed from America's domestic problems; some protested that he might be mentally removed as well.

After he returned to the United States, Wilson focused his attention almost exclusively on foreign affairs. He expended most of his energy trying to persuade the American public to support the League of Nations, which he characterized as still one more step along the road to world peace.

Wilson disappointed the many Americans who were battling domestic problems. He disappointed American women who were battling gender discrimination. He disappointed African Americans who were battling racial discrimination. He disappointed American workers who were battling economic injustice.

While attempting to convince the American public to adopt his views, Wilson's physical health began to decline; his mental health also deteriorated.

Eventually, he had a debilitating stroke. For more than a year, his wife and a handful of close associates concealed the president's condition from the public, Congress, and even his own cabinet.

Wilson had failed to attend to the domestic problems that already had arrived. He also had failed to prepare the country for the international crises that were approaching. The three presidents who followed him—Harding, Coolidge, and Hoover—had little more success.

Harding became ill and died before he even had completed a single term. His vice president, Calvin Coolidge, finished Harding's term and then one of his own. Herbert Hoover then succeeded Coolidge.

Because of their personal dispositions, political philosophies, or limited abilities, Harding, Coolidge, and Hoover ignored approaching international problems. They did not discern the dangers associated with the growth of the German Nazi party, Hitler's emergence as the Nazi leader, the formation of a Fascist government in Italy, Stalin's acquisition of political power in the Soviet Union, and Hirohito's appointment as regent and then Emperor of Japan.

The three presidents who followed Wilson failed to address international perils. They also failed to address domestic perils. Some domestic perils were revealed by fighting, rioting, and lynching; others were revealed by economic omens.

Economic omens of pending economic calamity were evident. However, they evaded the attention of many contemporaries. Excessive reliance on credit was one of the omens. Consumers relied on credit to purchase the new products that had appeared on the market; they used it to purchase steam irons, vacuum cleaners, refrigerators, gas stoves, radios, and automobiles.

Consumers also used credit to make investments. They borrowed money without collateral, bought stocks, and resolved that they would use profits to pay off their original loans.

Sharing consumers' economic euphoria, entrepreneurs used credit to purchase factories, farms, businesses, and real estate. Like the consumers, they intended to pay off their debts with the profits that they made.

THE 1930s

During most of the 1920s, American citizens viewed the stock market as an inexhaustible source of wealth. However, they watched it wither in 1929. They subsequently witnessed the collapse of the real estate market, the failure of banking, a devastating drought, and a worldwide depression.

The damages from financial troubles and natural disasters were severe; they were aggravated by the federal government's injudicious monetary practices.

Many investors, entrepreneurs, industrialists, and business owners suffered. Some were financially destroyed. Even persons with modest incomes lost their small farms, small businesses, jobs, savings, and homes.

Some contemporaries had praised presidents Harding and Coolidge because the country had seemed to prosper during their terms. They were less kind to Hoover. Some blamed Hoover for damaging the economy; others blamed him for failing to repair it.

After he was unable to meet the expectations of citizens, Hoover lost their confidence; he then lost his own confidence. He eventually realized that the public wanted a charismatic, articulate, and activist president.

President Franklin Roosevelt accurately diagnosed the nation's mood. After he took office in 1933, he immediately commenced an ambitious program to regenerate the economy. He won the affection of blue-collar laborers when he established social security and strengthened the legal rights of labor unions. He earned the gratitude of investors and industrialists when he established the Securities and Exchange Commission, which reduced the chances of future financial disasters.

Although Roosevelt placated liberals with his domestic programs, he angered them with his foreign policies. Lobbied by industrialists and political conservatives, he prepared the country for war. He reinstated the draft, expanded the armed forces, and sent war matériel to combating nations. He renovated the ships, planes, artillery, and equipment on which the American military depended. He disseminated domestic propaganda and established school-based military readiness programs.

Political liberals and conservatives disagreed about the military benefits of Roosevelt's foreign policies. However, they agreed about their economic benefits. As they watched factories hire workers and the armed forces conscript soldiers, they realized that the economy of the United States was revitalizing.

Case Study 7.1: Domestic Unrest

With the signing of an armistice, most Americans assumed that World War I had ended. They eventually realized that world leaders did not share their assumption. The leaders of the victorious Allied nations wished to resolve economic, political, and territorial issues. Because these issues were partisan, parochial, and divisive, the leaders chose to confront them at a postwar conference.

President Woodrow Wilson wanted to personally represent the United States at this conference, which was scheduled to convene in Europe during 1919. His advisors warned him that his departure would reduce his opportunities to manage America's domestic problems. Wilson ignored their warnings and went overseas.

While in Europe, Wilson focused his attention on world affairs. After his return, he retained this focus. He failed to detect the degree to which Americans were upset about the economic recession, unemployment, racism, and ethnic conflict.

Americans also were concerned about a deadly epidemic. Early in 1918, a new strain of flu had been detected at a military base in Kansas. Even though it initially was detected at a military facility, it was not related to the war. It seemed to originate in the United States, yet it was referred to as the Spanish flu.

The Spanish flu was distinctive because of its severe symptoms. It caused victims to drown in their own pulmonary secretions. It was distinctive because of the speed of infection. It struck victims so quickly that they sometimes died less than two days after they had shown symptoms. It was distinctive because of its high mortality rate. In an eighteen-month period, it infected hundreds of millions of individuals around the world and killed twenty percent of them. It killed even healthy young adults.

One out of every four residents in the United States contracted the Spanish flu. Five hundred thousand of them died. Astonished reporters calculated that more Americans had perished from the flu than from wartime battles.

The epidemic created a panic; severe economic problems increased that panic. During the war, industrialists had turned to minority groups to fill the jobs that servicemen had vacated. They recruited females, African Americans, older adults, disabled veterans, and even high school students. The new workforce members responded to the wartime urgings to propel the nation's "total war" effort. They benefited financially and socially from opportunities previously unavailable to them.

After the war, homefront workers expected to keep their jobs. However, the owners of factories, businesses, and farms fired many of them. Some of the owners fired workers because of an economic recession. Some of them fired their workers to make room for returning veterans. The dismissed workers were distressed; those veterans who were unemployed also were distressed.

Many African American veterans were disconcerted when they could not find jobs. They also were disconcerted by the ways in which their neighbors were treating them. They were struck by the different ways in which the Europeans had interacted with them during the war. They contrasted the egalitarian attitudes of Europeans with the discriminatory attitudes of their American peers. They questioned why they had risked their lives liberating politically oppressed persons overseas when they had to endure political oppression in their own country.

African American veterans realized that their postwar employment and racial problems were intermingled. Discharged and unemployed, many of them took extraordinary steps to procure jobs.

African Americans moved to parts of the country where the employment opportunities were the greatest. To increase their prospects of being hired, they agreed to work for wages that were lower than those which other job applicants would accept. The workers against whom they competed became resentful and hostile.

The postwar struggles for employment became infused with racism and violence. During the summer of 1919, racial riots erupted. They erupted in the District of Columbia and in Arkansas, Illinois, Nebraska, South Carolina, Tennessee, and Texas.

James Weldon Johnson was an African American writer who was affected by the bloodshed that characterized a five-month period in 1919; he referred to that period as the Red Summer. Johnson's contemporaries acknowledged the aptness of this phrase.

Activity: Health, Race, and Employment Problems

Post–World War I Americans had to deal with a deadly flu epidemic, racism, and unemployment. How do you think different groups responded? To help answer this question, create a chart.

Table 7.1. Domestic Unrest

Group	*Flu**	*Race**	*Work**	*Rationale*
Non-African American Veterans				
African American Veterans				
Women in Wartime Factories				
Teachers				
Local School Boards				
Liberal Politicians				
Conservative Politicians				

* (+) Supported
(-) Opposed
(+/-) Mixed Commitment

Along the vertical axis of the chart, arrange the following groups: non-African American veterans, African American veterans, women who had been working in wartime factories, teachers, members of local school boards, liberal politicians, and conservative politicians.

Along the horizontal axis of the chart, arrange several columns. In one of these columns, indicate the importance that each group assigned to the flu epidemic of 1919. Select the value *1* if they viewed it as a matter of low importance, *2* if they viewed it as a matter of moderate importance, and *3* if they viewed it as a matter of great importance.

In another column of the chart, indicate the importance that each group assigned to racial problems during the summer of 1919. To indicate the importance assigned to these problems, use the same system that you employed in the previous task.

In another column, indicate the importance that each group assigned to post-war unemployment. To indicate the importance assigned to these problems, use the same system that you employed in the previous tasks.

Your responses should be based on assumptions about the vested interests, values, and goals of each group. Although you can use the information in the case study to make some of these assumptions, you may wish to rely on a broader foundation of information.

You can gather additional information from the materials that are listed at the end of this chapter. You may gather it from lectures or discussions.

In a separate column, or possibly on a separate page, summarize your assumptions about each group.

Case Study 7.2: The Era from 1920 to 1940

During the 1920s and the 1930s, conservative and liberal politicians disagreed about the best way to respond to international problems. They disagreed about the best ways to respond to economic problems. They disagreed about the best ways to respond to social problems. They disagreed about the best way to respond to educational problems.

Attitudes toward education were connected to attitudes toward foreign and domestic issues. These connections were evident when the conservatives and the liberals recommended ways to prepare schoolchildren for critical challenges. The attitudes of the conservatives were connected to their views of America's participation in the war.

American conservatives were proud of the achievements of the Allied forces during World War I. They recognized that they had won a decisive victory. Nonetheless, they maintained that the Central Powers had been formidable adversaries who could have been the victors. They warned that Germany, which was aware of its military prowess, might engage in still another war. They detected portents of war in Germany; they detected portents in Japan, Italy, and the Soviet Union as well.

The conservatives were pleased that the United States had lost relatively few soldiers in World War I. Nonetheless, they argued that too many of them had died because of the hurried manner in which the American forces had been assembled, trained, and equipped.

The conservatives advised government leaders to take measures that would deter a military tragedy. They urged them to prepare youths as well as adults immediately for another war.

The liberals agreed with the conservatives that educators should prepare America's youths for the serious challenges that their country faced. However, they were preoccupied with domestic rather than military challenges.

Many of the liberals had opposed the American entry into World War I. They had exhorted President Wilson to preserve his prewar commitment to neutrality, reduce the national defense budget, and redirect military funding to domestic agencies. They were dismayed when Wilson ignored their advice and led the nation into war.

Once the United States entered World War I, many liberals became less vocal. They succumbed to intense public pressure and temporarily hid their true sentiments.

However, the liberals became vocal again after the war. They berated President Wilson and the presidents who followed him for failing to deal with racism, ethnic conflict, unemployment, child labor, and other domestic problems. They insisted that educators prepare youths to alleviate these problems.

Many post–World War I political liberals admired John Dewey. They respected his academic prominence, commitment to education, and social philosophy. They also respected his political attitudes, which mirrored their own. Those liberals who had joined the Progressive Education Association were particularly inspired by Dewey

The Progressive Education Association was a modestly sized organization in the early 1920s. During that era, it had attracted little more than one hundred participants. However, it mushroomed into an organization of ten thousand members during the subsequent decade (Nusser, 1996). It attracted teachers, school administrators, and professors of education.

Beginning in 1934, a group of professors began to publish a journal in which they combined educational and political writing. They called it the *Social Frontier.* Although they did not rely on funding from the Progressive Education Association, they made it clear that their journal was linked to this organization. They highlighted the political messages of the Progressive Education Association (Bowers, 1964; O'Neill, 1988). They enjoined teachers and school administrators to form unions, join political groups, and lobby for social reforms.

Although the editors and authors of the *Social Frontier* endorsed the political aspirations of the Progressive Education Association, some of them were extremists. The extremists, who were more impressed by the philosophy of Karl Marx than that of John Dewey, urged teachers to promote communism. They claimed that the suffering of the American people during the Great Depression demonstrated the need for social and economic revolution.

The *Social Frontier* attracted six thousand subscribers during the initial year of publication. However, it quickly lost most of them. Although the subscribers may have tired of the rhetoric in the *Social Frontier*, conservative critics did not. The conservatives perused the journal for controversial statements. They had decided that they could use these statements to discredit their political adversaries.

The members of the Progressive Education Association were protected from the *Social Frontier*. After all, they did not own this controversial journal, which was published by a group of professors at a New York City university. By maintaining their separation from the journal, they could have disclaimed the inflammatory articles in it. However, instead of maintaining the wall between them and the *Social Frontier*, the members of the Progressive Education Association decided to eliminate that wall. They decided that they would directly manage, fund, and publish the journal.

The members of the Progressive Education Association soon realized the danger of their actions. They realized they were in danger when they were grilled about their motives for opposing high school military preparedness programs. Their critics accused them of opposing these programs because they had greater loyalty to the Soviet Union than to the United States.

The liberals readily admitted that they disapproved of high school programs in which students wore uniforms, drilled with rifles, and learned about tactical skills. However, they objected to the ulterior motives that the conservatives attributed to them. They insisted that they disapproved of these programs because they did not belong in the schools.

The members of the Progressive Education Association tried to reduce their political peril. They attempted to disavow already-published pro-communist articles. They also decided to give the *Social Frontier* a new and more patriotic name; they rechristened it *Frontiers of Democracy*. However, this legerdemain did not subdue the political storm that was raging about them.

Eventually the members of the Progressive Education Association decided to cease publishing their controversial journal. They made this decision in the early 1940s. During the subsequent decade, they disbanded their organization altogether. Even though the liberal educators were dispirited by the loss of their journal and their organization, they immediately began to reframe their arguments, attract new supporters, and establish fresh political alliances.

Activity: School-Based Military Preparedness Programs

During the 1930s, students participated in school-based programs. They learned about military equipment, policies, and procedures; they wore uniforms, carried rifles, marched, and participated in patriotic assemblies.

How do you think groups responded to the school-based military preparedness programs? To help answer this question, create a chart.

Along the vertical axis of the chart, arrange the following groups: parents, teachers, school administrators, members of local school boards, and professors

Table 7.2. The Era from 1920–1940

Group	*Support**	*Explanation*
Parents		
Teachers		
School Administrators		
School Board Members		
Professors of Education		

* (+) Supported
(-) Opposed
(+/-) Mixed Commitment

of education. Along the horizontal axis of the chart, arrange several columns. In one column, indicate whether each group primarily supported (+), opposed (-), or showed a mixed commitment (+/-) to the school-based military preparedness programs.

Your indications about the responses of the groups should be based on assumptions about the vested interests, values, and goals of their members. Although you can use the information in the case study to make some of these assumptions, you may wish to rely on a broader foundation of information.

You can gather additional information from the materials that are listed at the end of this chapter. You may gather it from lectures or discussions.

In a separate column, or possibly on a separate page, summarize your assumptions about each group.

Case Study 7.3: Social Engineering in the Tennessee Valley

While campaigning to become president, Franklin Roosevelt had articulated his intentions clearly. He had pledged to take aggressive steps to extract the United States economy from the depression into which it had slumped. When he assumed office in 1933, he validated his pledge by releasing a torrent of legislative proposals.

Liberals and conservatives reacted differently to the new president's proposals. While the liberals generally were pleased, the conservatives were dismayed. The conservatives chastised Roosevelt for attempting to create a new social order. They warned him that many of his initiatives were incompatible with the United States Constitution. They predicted that the Supreme Court would side with them.

The conservatives were correct; they initially won many of their legal challenges. Nonetheless, they continued to fret. They were upset with the way that Roosevelt had reacted to the legal decisions; they were shocked when he proposed to expand the number of justices on the Supreme Court. They alleged that Roosevelt wanted to pack the Court with political allies in order to undermine the constitutional system of checks and balances.

Roosevelt's critics complained that his programs were too radical. They also complained that his political style was too divisive. Although they may have been troubled by the president's programs and his political style, they were more troubled by the political philosophy that they attributed to him.

Roosevelt's critics claimed that the president's philosophy had been revealed in the Tennessee Valley Authority. This federal initiative, which was referred to as the TVA, was authorized in 1933. It was created to develop a defined area. In addition to the state of Tennessee, that area included portions of Alabama, Georgia, Kentucky, Mississippi, North Carolina, and Virginia.

The TVA was distinctive because of the massive geographical area for which it was responsible; it also was distinctive because of its management system. The TVA was run by a group of directors. The directors were nominated by the president, confirmed by the Senate, and then invested with unprecedented responsibilities.

Some of the responsibilities of the TVA directors had been identified in the Tennessee Valley Authority Act. This legislation stated that the directors should attend to "reforestation . . . flood control . . . proper use of marginal lands . . . agricultural and industrial development . . . and national defense" (Tennessee Valley Authority Act, 1933, p. 1). However, the bill also authorized them to commence initiatives "for other purposes" (p. 1).

The directors of the TVA were ambitious. Leaders such as Arthur Morgan and David Lilienthal recognized that they had to address complicated problems. They began by searching for solutions. They erected a complex bureaucracy to assist them in discovering and implementing solutions.

Many of the problems that the directors faced were somewhat conventional. Although they faced conventional problems, they did not hesitate to try unconventional solutions. For example, they had to make electricity available and affordable for rural residents. To generate affordable electricity, the directors could have subsidized privately owned power stations. However, they chose a different tactic. They erected utility stations, then insisted that the federal government operate and maintain ownership of the stations.

The directors of the TVA demonstrated ingenuity while trying to solve electricity problems. They again demonstrated ingenuity when they promoted the use of scientific agricultural methods. After they educated farmers about the benefits of fertilizers, they needed significant quantities of low-cost chemicals. They therefore created regional fertilizer factories to supply the farmers. They showed the same type of ingenuity when they erected dams and reclaimed flooded areas.

Although they commenced ambitious projects in engineering, construction, and agriculture, the TVA directors extended their vision further. They wished to conduct social and educational experiments. They even had the perfect sites at which to conduct them.

When they designed their multiyear projects in engineering, construction, and agriculture, the TVA directors built towns for the persons who would work on the projects. They resolved that they would use these towns for social and educational experiments.

The TVA directors designed towns around the lifestyles that they wished to promote. They designed towns that accommodated and promoted retail sales, professional services, banking, and religious worship. They built low-cost houses that the workers could rent and then eventually purchase. They built and managed cafeterias where the workers could obtain wholesome and reasonably priced meals. They built and managed libraries, schools, parks, and health clinics. Refusing to treat workers differently on the basis of their race, gender, or ethnicity, they allocated equal wages and benefits.

Conservative critics were upset with President Roosevelt and the New Deal administrators. They argued that the federal government's ownership of utilities was a socialist practice that had suppressed private competition in the Tennessee Valley. They asked the Supreme Court to halt the practice. The Supreme Court declined.

After they had lost their court challenge, Roosevelt's critics continued to stew. They were convinced that the president and his administrators wished to strengthen the executive branch of government, assemble a massive bureaucracy, and engage in social engineering. Some of them claimed that the Roosevelt administration was laying the foundation for socialism; others claimed that it was building the foundation for communism.

The proponents of the TVA acknowledged that their efforts had expanded governmental bureaucracy, strengthened presidential power, and buttressed social engineering. However, they insisted that they were neither socialists nor communists.

Proponents pointed out that their goal had been to raise the quality of life for the residents of the Tennessee Valley. They explained that the modification of land, the extension of utilities, and the provision of jobs would not, by themselves, improve the quality of life. They claimed that these improvements required unconventional educational measures.

Proponents of the TVA had pointed to the similarities between their initiatives and those that political liberals historically had championed. They claimed that they had continued to broaden the scope of public education to affect adults as well as children, encompassing not only academics but also health, hygiene, nutrition, personal finance, safety, vocational training, and community membership.

Activity: Tennessee Valley Authority Projects Involving Education

The directors of the Tennessee Valley Authority engaged in civil and agricultural engineering; they also engaged in social engineering. They designed educational programs to bring about social change. They designed them for adults as well as children.

How do you think groups responded to the innovative educational programs of the Tennessee Valley Authority? To help answer this question, create a chart.

Along the vertical axis of the chart, arrange the following groups: parents, teachers, school administrators, members of local school boards, community members, professors of education, liberal politicians, and conservative politicians.

Along the horizontal axis of the chart, arrange several columns. In one of these columns, indicate whether each group primarily supported (+), opposed (-), or showed a mixed commitment (+/-) to the innovative educational programs of the TVA.

Table 7.3. Social Engineering in the Tennessee Valley

Group	*Support**	*Explanation*
Parents		
Teachers		
School Administrators		
School Board Members		
Community Members		
Professors of Education		
Liberal Politicians		
Conservative Politicians		

* (+) Supported
(-) Opposed
(+/-) Mixed Commitment

Your indications about the responses of the groups should be based on assumptions about the vested interests, values, and goals of their members. Although you can use the information in the case study to make some of these assumptions, you may wish to rely on a broader foundation of information.

You can gather additional information from the materials that are listed at the end of this chapter. You may gather it from lectures or discussions.

In a separate column, or possibly on a separate page, summarize your assumptions about each group.

USING THE PAST TO UNDERSTAND THE PRESENT

During the 1920s and the 1930s, political liberals and conservatives engaged in fierce disputes. They disagreed about domestic problems. They disagreed about international problems. They disagreed about effective ways to solve domestic and international problems. They even disagreed about the relative priority that they should assign to the two types of problems.

The liberals had detected serious domestic problems immediately after World War I. They discerned even greater problems during the 1930s. Some of the liberals focused their attention on solving the problems at hand. However, some of them used economic and social crises as pretexts for addressing political issues about which they had been concerned for decades. Some of them used current crises to advance socialism or communism.

While the liberals had directed their attention to domestic issues, the conservatives had directed a great deal of their attention to international issues. The conservatives had detected serious international problems immediately after the war. They had watched those problems intensify during the 1930s.

Some of the conservatives restricted their attention to the looming international problems. However, some of them used international threats as pretexts for addressing political issues about which they had been concerned for decades. Some of them used the international crises to advance their own financial interests.

The pre–World War II liberals and conservatives engaged in high-stakes political gamesmanship. The conservatives called the liberals communists or the dupes of communists. The liberals called the conservatives jingoists or ruthless capitalists. Has this type of high-stakes political gamesmanship endured?

To help answer the preceding question, identify a school-based initiative that was advanced by one political group but opposed by another. How did the supporters and the opponents characterize that initiative? Provide examples of the strategies on which they relied. Try to find a recent incident in your own state or community.

CHAPTER SUMMARY

After World War I, severe domestic problems emerged. The problems involved workers. Some workers suffered when their jobs were reassigned to returning veterans; other workers suffered when their jobs were eliminated because of an economic recession. Health and racial problems compounded the employment problems.

Domestic problems intensified during the Great Depression. Political liberals recommended that the federal government use domestic programs to stimulate the economy and help individual citizens. Conservatives recommended spending on defense programs; they pointed out that this type of spending would stimulate the economy and prepare the country for war. In addition to differing on social, economic, and military matters, the two groups differed about education.

ADDITIONAL READING

Introductory Passages

Ballantine, J. H. (2001). *The sociology of education: A systematic analysis* (5th ed.). Englewood Cliffs, NJ: Prentice Hall.

Boemeke, M. F., Feldman, G. D., & Glaser, E. (Eds.). (1998). *The Treaty of Versailles: A reassessment after 75 years.* Cambridge, UK: Cambridge University Press.

Cooper, J. M. (2001). *Breaking the heart of the world: Woodrow Wilson and the fight for the League of Nations.* Cambridge, MA: Cambridge University Press.

Hallinan, M. T. (Ed.). (2006). *Handbook of the sociology of education.* New York: Springer.

Levin, P. L. (2001). *Edith and Woodrow: The Wilson White House.* New York: Simon & Schuster.

Loan, R. W. (1997). *The betrayal of the Negro: From Rutherford B. Hayes to Woodrow Wilson.* New York: Da Capo.

Moore, R. (2004). *Education and society: Issues and explanations in the sociology of education.* Cambridge, UK: Polity.

Sadovnik, A. R. (Ed.). (2007). *Sociology of education: A critical reader.* New York: Routledge.

Case Study 7.1: Domestic Unrest

Barry, J. M. (2004). *The great influenza: The epic story of the greatest plague in history.* London: Penguin

Best, G. D. (2003). *The dollar decade: Mammon and the machine in 1920s America.* Westport, CT: Praeger.
Cohen, L. (1990). *Making a New Deal: Industrial workers in Chicago, 1919–1939.* Cambridge, UK: Cambridge University Press.
Conor, L. (2004). *The spectacular modern woman: Feminine visibility in the 1920s.* Bloomington: Indiana University Press.
Crosby, A. W. (1990). *America's forgotten pandemic: The Influenza of 1918.* Cambridge, UK: Cambridge University Press
Dray, P. (2002). *At the hands of persons unknown: The lynching of Black America.* New York: Random House.
Kyvig, D. E. (2002). *Daily life in the United States, 1920–1939: Decades of promise and pain.* Westport, CT: Greenwood.
Starr, K. (1996). *Material dreams: Southern California through the 1920s.* New York: Oxford University Press.
Tolnay, S. E., & Beck, E. M. (1995). *A festival of violence: An analysis of Southern lynchings, 1882–1930.* Champagne: University of Illinois Press.
Tuttle, W. M. (1996). *Race RIOT: Chicago in the Red Summer of 1919.* Champagne: University of Illinois Press.

Case Study 7.2: The Era from 1920–1940

Bowers, C. A. (1969). *The progressive educator and the Depression: The radical years.* New York: Random House.
Cremin, L. A. (1961). *The transformation of the school: Progressivism in American education, 1876–1957.* New York: Knopf.
Graham. P. A. (1967). *Progressive education: From Arcady to academe—A history of the Progressive Education Association, 1919–1955.* New York: Teachers College Press.
Greenberg, C. L. (1997). *Or does it explode? Black Harlem in the Great Depression.* New York: Oxford University Press.
Kennedy, D. M. (1999). *Freedom from fear: The American people in depression and war, 1929–1945.* New York: Oxford University Press.
Liebovich, L. W. (1994). *Bylines in despair: Herbert Hoover, the Great Depression, and the U.S. news media.* Westport, CT: Praeger.
McMahon, K. J. (2004). *Reconsidering Roosevelt on race: How the presidency paved the road to Brown.* Chicago: University of Chicago Press.
Ravitch, D. (2000). *Left back: A century of battles over school reform.* New York: Simon & Schuster.
Willard, C. A. (1992). *Liberalism and the social grounds of knowledge.* Chicago: University of Chicago Press.

Case Study 7.3: Social Engineering in the Tennessee Valley

Colignon, R. A. (1997). *Power plays: Critical events in the institutionalization of the Tennessee Valley Authority.* Albany: State University of New York Press.

Hargrove, E. C. (2002). *Prisoners of myth: The leadership of the Tennessee Valley Authority, 1933–1990*. Knoxville: University of Tennessee Press.

Himmelberg, R. R. (2001). *The Great Depression and the New Deal*. Westport, CT: Greenwood.

McGovern, J. R. (2000). *And a time for hope: Americans in the Great Depression*. Westport, CT: Praeger.

Rosen, E. A. (2005). *Roosevelt, the Great Depression, and the economics of recovery*. Charlottesville: University Press of Virginia.

Schulman, B. J. (1991). *From Cotton Belt to Sunbelt: Federal policy, economic development, and the transformation of the South, 1938–1980*. New York: Oxford University Press.

Tennessee Valley Authority Act. Pub. L. No. 73-17. (1933). (Retrieved on 25 September 2007 from: http://www.tva.gov/abouttva/pdf/TVA_Act.pdf.)

Tindall, G. B. (1967). *The Emergence of the New South, 1913–1945*. Baton Rouge: Louisiana State University Press.

Chapter Eight

Politics: Responding to War

Although they were criticized for the historically slow pace at which they made reforms in the schools, educators made changes quickly in wartime. They provided elementary school students with opportunities to recycle, purchase bonds, and garden; they provided high school students with vocational training, military drilling, and critical academic instruction. They expeditiously made changes during World War I, World War II, and the Cold War.

WAR'S IMPACT ON TODAY'S CLASSROOMS

The combat in World War I and World War II was widespread, complicated, and deadly. It influenced millions of persons at the battlefront; it influenced millions on the homefront. It affected societies, economies, and governments; it affected the ways in which citizens viewed the world.

In contrast to the combat during world wars, combat in mid- and late twentieth-century wars was relatively restricted. Nonetheless, it still influenced innumerable persons. It affected many of them profoundly. It directly affected those persons who lived on or adjacent to a battlefront; it indirectly affected those who lived on the homefront.

Some schoolchildren were affected by war indirectly when they learned about it from parents, relatives, or acquaintances. They may have learned about it from newspapers, magazines, or websites. They may have learned about it from images or photographs. They may have learned about it from radio, film, or television.

Sometimes war directly affected the lives of children. It directly affected their lives when it ripped through their homes, schools, villages, cities, or countries. It affected the lives of children in New York City on September

11, 2001. On that date, children observed terrorists crash planes into their community. Some children observed the actual events; others observed images of them.

The events of 9/11disconcerted children; the events that followed also disconcerted them. The ensuing events included the invasion of Afghanistan, the invasion of Iraq, the imposition of security measures throughout the United States, and the imposition of security measures in many countries.

In addition to influencing children, the incidents of 9/11 influenced teachers. The incidents influenced teachers when they created problems that the teachers had not anticipated (Hoff, 2002; Reynolds and Smith, 2002). As just one example, teachers did not anticipate that persons would begin to mistrust their Muslim American peers and neighbors.

Some of the persons who distrusted Muslim Americans after 9/11 knew little about them. They could not make reasonable estimates about the number of Muslim Americans, the religious beliefs to which they subscribed, or the political attitudes that they maintained (Pew Research Center, 2007). In spite of a lack of information, they wished to limit their civil rights ("Polls Show," 2004).

At the beginning of the twenty-first century, war intruded on the lives of American schoolchildren and educators. It affected them in profound and complex ways. When war had intruded into the lives of schoolchildren during earlier eras, it had remarkably similar effects.

WORLD WAR I

World War I combat commenced in 1914. Countries had diverse motives for participating in it. Some of them participated because they were allies of other nations. Some participated because they had been invaded. Some participated because they wished to increase trade, expand boundaries, grab economic resources, or resolve ethnic feuds.

The countries that went to war had been squabbling for decades. For this reason, observers were not surprised when they commenced military maneuvers. However, the observers were surprised by the rapid escalation of those maneuvers.

Some of the belligerent nations formed the Allied powers. These included France, England, czarist Russia, and many of the countries and colonies that these nations ruled. After the war commenced, Italy and the United States joined the Allied powers; Russia withdrew. The Allied nations were opposed by the Central Powers, which comprised Germany, the Ottoman Empire, Austria-Hungary, and many of the areas that they ruled.

The combat in World War I was different from that in prior wars. It was different because of its geographic scope. During its four-year course, battles were waged in western, central, and eastern Europe. Other clashes also took place in Serbia, the Mediterranean, the Middle East, Africa, and the Pacific regions.

The combat in World War I also was distinct because of the size of the fighting forces. Some of the armies swelled to millions of soldiers.

In addition, the combat in World War I was distinguished by its martial technology. The new generation of conventional weapons encompassed handguns, rifles, machine guns, mortars, and artillery. The conventional weapons were augmented by revolutionary inventions, such as airplanes, blimps, dreadnaught vessels, naval mines, tanks, and poison gases.

The combat in World War I was so distinctive that it changed the dynamics of combat. These changes ensured a high number of battlefield deaths. France alone sustained 1,368,000 military deaths; Germany sustained significantly more.

DEBATING NEUTRALITY

Americans had been reading newspaper reports about the accelerating pace at which European countries were replenishing their arsenals and expanding their armies. Even though European politicians had assured them that these steps were designed to deter aggressive neighbors, they were not convincing. As a result, Americans were not shocked when fighting commenced in 1914.

Americans originally referred to World War I as the "Great War." Even though they were relatively insulated from it, many of them prodded their government to get involved. Some of them urged the United States to participate because they were worried about relatives who resided in Europe. They hoped that American soldiers could protect their relatives. They attempted to influence not only politicians but those neighbors and citizens who had not made up their minds about the war.

Businesspersons also urged the United States to join the Great War. Some of them had idealistic motives; they hoped that American involvement would preserve balance among the world's powers. Some of them had practical reasons; they hoped that war would create financial opportunities for them. They attempted to influence those members of the public who had not made up their minds about the war.

Some of the persons who supported American intervention may have been influenced by the arguments from pro-war citizens or businesspersons.

Others may have been influenced by propaganda. They were moved by propaganda that depicted the war as a clash between good and evil. They were moved by propaganda that depicted valiant soldiers, bereaving families, and orphaned children. They were moved by propaganda that depicted innocent civilians who perished in submarine attacks.

Although some Americans advocated war, others opposed it. German Americans opposed American entry into the war because they admired Germany. They revealed their admiration by sending their children to German-language schools, providing them with German textbooks, and teaching them about Germanic culture and traditions. Aware that most of the pro-war factions blamed the war on the Central Powers, they dreaded the prospect of the United States battling with Germany.

President Wilson had run for reelection in 1916 on a platform affirming America's neutrality. After winning reelection by a narrow margin, he changed his mind; he decided that he would seek a declaration of war.

President Wilson proceeded carefully with his war campaign. He began by explaining the reason for his change of mind. He pointed out that his original commitment to neutrality had been based on a misconception that America should steer clear of wars that would continue indefinitely. He relinquished that misconception after arriving at the belief that the Great War was a singular opportunity to prevent all future wars. He believed that the cessation of future wars would transpire only if the United States joined the Allied powers. In 1917, he asked Congress to declare war against Germany and the Central Powers.

POLITICAL TENSION IN THE SCHOOLS

President Wilson benefitted from the "war-to-end-all-war" rhetorical strategy, and he also benefitted from another rhetorical strategy. He asserted that wartime nations would win conflicts only if they were fully committed to winning them. He explained that the United States would not prevail if it merely raised an army, equipped it, and sent it overseas. He stipulated that it could win only if every man, woman, and child joined a "total war" effort.

Wilson established the Committee on Public Information to create and circulate the domestic propaganda that was required for total warfare. He appointed George Creel, a journalist, to manage this committee. Creel was confident that the marketing strategies that had been used to promote commercial products could be used to promote the president's policies.

Creel's unabashed reliance on commercial marketing techniques was apparent when he selected a title for his autobiography, *How We Advertised*

America (Creel, 1920). In that memoir, he wrote unapologetically that the American government's "recognition of Public Opinion as a major force" in crafting foreign policy was the feature on the basis of which "the Great War differed most essentially from all previous conflicts" (p. 4).

Creel released information about the war in ways that would promote national unity. He placed propaganda in newspapers, magazines, and films. He wove it into songs and art. In one of his most inventive initiatives, he recruited thousands of "four-minute-men" to give short, patriotic speeches at plays, concerts, movies, and public gatherings.

Creel placed propaganda in posters. He created posters to influence battlefront soldiers and homefront laborers. In addition to producing posters for adults, he designed them for children. He created posters that encouraged elementary school students to purchase savings stamps, recycle metals, and cultivate gardens. He created posters that encouraged high school students to prepare for military service.

The architects of the World War I propaganda campaign explicitly targeted students. They also targeted the school administrators and teachers who supervised them. They filled educational journals with pro-war rhetoric, illustrations, and lessons. They encouraged businesspersons to incorporate pro-war themes into the advertisements that they placed in these journals.

WORLD WAR II

During World War I, members of the American public demonstrated national unity. They responded ardently to a propaganda campaign that highlighted the impressive contributions of soldiers on the battlefront and families on the homefront. Their unity was especially remarkable because of the earlier opposition to the war.

Twenty years after World War I, the citizens of the United States faced the possibility of another massive conflict. Similar to that former instance, they were divided about the benefits and risks of American intervention. However, they detected additional points of similarity between the two conflicts.

During World War I, the Central Powers, which had been anchored by Germany, had been opposed by the Allied powers, which had been anchored by England and France. In World War II, Germany emerged as a leading force behind the Axis powers. The World War II Axis powers were opposed by the Allied powers, which again included England and France.

During the eras that preceded America's entry into World War I and World War II, a president had just commenced his second term. Even though

President Roosevelt had won election to a second term by a much larger margin than had Wilson, he decided to copy Wilson's strategies.

Roosevelt argued that the United States should preserve its neutrality; he simultaneously argued that it should take actions to deter aggressors. Therefore, he modernized the armed services, commenced a military draft, and stockpiled supplies. He also commenced an ambitious domestic propaganda campaign.

Before America's entry into World War I, many liberals had urged the United States to remain neutral. During the era that that preceded America's entry into World War II, liberals again advocated neutrality.

The liberals were upset with Roosevelt when he began to send wartime matériel to the Allied powers. However, they were in a politically awkward position. They realized that many Americans supported the president because they were upset over the Axis nations' insatiable aggression and their anti-Semitic persecutions. After the Japanese attacked Pearl Harbor, the liberals recognized that the public would provide Roosevelt with robust pro-war support.

THE POSTWAR ERA

American leaders emerged from World War II with enormous political, economic, and military power. Nonetheless, they were anxious. They were anxious about a military confrontation with the Soviet Union. They also were anxious about subversion. They worried that subversive factions in the United States were planning a revolution similar to that which they had executed in Russia.

Well before World War II, citizens had been terrified about communist subversion. During the financial hardships of the 1930s, they had listened to antiestablishment critics call for a revolution to displace America's government, economy, military, and way of life. They listened again to these remarks when post–World War II political conservatives used them as evidence that the communists were plotting to overthrow the United States. These accusations created fear. They profoundly influenced American society and with it the schools.

Case Study 8.1: World War I and World War II

Prior to World War I, the Americans had seen multiple instances of domestic propaganda. During the Civil War, they had seen propaganda designed to create support for slavery; they also saw propaganda intended to create abhorrence of slavery. They later had observed propaganda about westward expansion, the Spanish-American War, the women's suffrage movement, the labor movement, immigration, and eugenics. In spite of their experiences, they were unprepared for the propaganda of World War I.

Specialists in the federal government distributed propaganda to a wide audience. They distributed it through newspapers, magazines, films, music, posters, speeches, public events, and testimonials. They even distributed it through comic books.

The propaganda specialists wished to achieve multiple goals. They wished to raise enthusiasm for conscription, bolster enlistments, create sympathy for the Allied nations, promote President Wilson's wartime agenda, enhance the president's political image, and convince citizens to assume vital homefront jobs.

Some of the wartime propaganda initiatives were aimed at the schools. For example, they were designed to persuade school administrators to adapt vocational curricula. Even though educators had established vocational programs prior to World War I, they had not emphasized the precise career fields on which the wartime economy depended. They were asked to adapt their programs to the current needs of the nation.

Businesspersons supported the use of propaganda to promote vocational programs. They hoped that these programs would train workers to take the places of the millions of men who were serving in the armed forces. Although employers applauded those school administrators who promoted vocational learning, many of them could not wait for students to graduate; they needed workers immediately.

Employers urged school administrators to allow high school students to take jobs even before they graduated. However, the school administrators feared a backlash from political liberals who were pressuring the federal government to protect child laborers. Although the liberals did persuade the government to impose restrictions, they were disappointed when these restrictions applied only to children who were thirteen years old or younger.

School administrators reacted differently to the wartime pressures. Some of them devised cooperative solutions for employment problems. For example, they allowed students to substitute the activities that they were performing in the factories for the academic activities they were missing in school. In this way, they were able to argue that child laborers actually were students.

Although school administrators were pleased that the substitution of occupational work for academic work solved one of their problems, they still worried about the many students who were quitting school to enlist in the armed services. To solve this second problem, they began to substitute military activities for academic activities.

Opponents of wartime school programs questioned the use of propaganda to promote these programs; they also questioned the benefits of the programs. They focused a great deal of their criticism on those high school programs that prepared students for military service. Some of them claimed that these programs were similar to those that had predisposed a generation of fascist youths toward war.

The supporters of wartime school programs had convincing retorts for their critics. They claimed that wartime school programs promoted physical conditioning, career interests, personal discipline, patriotism, and citizenship. They added that they were transforming students into the fighting forces that the United States might someday need to repel an invading army. In view of these benefits, they insisted that the federal government had the right to market the programs.

Some of the wartime school programs were subsidized by local governments or civic organizations; others were subsidized by the federal government. Critics were especially concerned about the programs that were supported by the federal government. They warned that the programs created immediate dangers because they distracted students from academic learning. The critics added that they created long-term dangers because they might endure in the schools long after the Great War was over.

Progressive educators opposed the wartime school programs. Almost a decade after the Great War had ended, John Dewey, who was the most famous spokesperson for progressive education, attested that he still could detect the vestiges of the wartime pre-induction training programs. He wrote that he discerned "a well-organized movement to militarize the tone and temper of our national life" and an effort by the "vested interest to militarize the country . . . deliberately and knowingly through the medium of the schools" (Dewey, 1927, p. 3).

Although the wartime programs in the high schools were designed to prepare children for homefront jobs or military service, those in the elementary schools had a distinct character. The elementary school programs were designed to predispose youngsters toward the war effort. Because the elementary school initiatives required the participation of school administrators, teachers, and family members, they affected many more persons than the students.

The elementary school initiatives fostered supportive attitudes. President Wilson had made the "Garden Army" into one of the most publicized elementary school initiatives of World War I. He encouraged school administrators and teachers to use the Garden Army to bolster patriotism. He urged them to convince students that home gardening was "just as real and patriotic an effort as the building of ships or the firing of cannon" (Wilson, quoted in "Gardening: A Patriotic Duty," 1918, p. 643). He praised home gardening for raising morale; he also lauded it for raising significant amounts of produce.

During the Second World War, President Roosevelt and his advisers replicated the propaganda campaigns of World War I. In fact, they enlarged their scope (Giordano, 2004). For example, they made the Garden Army the prototype for the ubiquitous victory gardens. To encourage the cultivation of victory gardens, officials turned the lawns next to government buildings into gardening plots. As a result, they were able to provide urban children with opportunities to grow crops.

Supporters claimed that the victory gardens had indirect benefits. They alleged that they taught children about the agriculture sciences, nurtured patriotism, and even raised academic performance. In addition to their indirect benefits, supporters claimed that the victory gardens made substantive contributions to the war. They maintained that they produced more than twenty-five percent of the fresh vegetables that wartime Americans consumed.

Although personnel in the federal government designed educational programs around agriculture, they also developed programs with overtly military characters. They hoped that World War II programs such as the Junior Salvage Army and the Civil Air Patrol Cadets would engage students in homefront service and prepare them for battlefront responsibilities.

The High School Victory Corps was the most successful military school program. It was so popular that it was even offered through correspondence courses. Reporters for a popular magazine described the activities in which the participants engaged. They wrote that they spent "an hour a day in military drill and calisthenics" as well as "intensive courses for boys and girls in metal work, blueprint reading, airplane riveting, and drafting" ("Victory Corps," 1942, p. 53).

Participants in the High School Victory Corps developed military attitudes through distinctive drills; they also developed them through distinctive reading. The authors of one Victory Corps book (United States Office of Education, 1943) advised the participants to prepare for military duty. They advised them to enroll in those high school courses "from which military men tell us spring the most important of all qualifications for success and usefulness in the Army and Navy" (p. 101). They explained that these were courses in physical education, mathematics, science, vocational education, business, communication, and civics.

Although some of the wartime high school programs prepared students for military service, others prepared them for employment in agriculture or industry. Because of the severe shortage of workers, some managers had begun to recruit students. School administrators who were upset at the number of students who were dropping out of school to take jobs began to schedule classes so that the students could work and attend school. For example, urban school administrators scheduled high school classes at times that did not interfere with factory shifts. Rural school administrators made similar adaptations to accommodate seasonal farming schedules.

Flexibly scheduled academic programs were extremely popular. Their popularity in urban areas was indicated by student employment records. These records indicated that one third of Chicago's high school students participated in some type of wartime employment (Jessen, 1945).

The popularity of flexibly scheduled programs in rural areas is revealed by the number of farmwork permits issued to children. Permits issued to children who were fifteen years old or younger increased by more than one hundred fifty percent during the first three years of the war (Magee, 1944).

Politically liberal educators who opposed the World War II educational initiatives had problems finding allies. Conservative critics created some of their problems. Conservative critics claimed that the liberals' resistance to national defense had been one of the factors that had contributed to a second global war. They also claimed that romanticizing of communism had fostered subversion.

Liberal educators hoped that President Roosevelt would take their side. However, their hopes evaporated after the president restricted free speech, detained Japanese Americans, and authorized the use of propaganda in the schools.

Activity: Pro-War Marketing Materials in the Schools

Government officials organized a campaign to foster support for American participation in World War I. They urged students to enroll in critical academic courses, such as those in mathematics, the sciences, and physical education. They also urged them to prepare for wartime employment, gather recyclable materials, promote savings, participate in patriotic community activities, and volunteer for school-based military training. Although they used propaganda to popularize these initiatives, the programs themselves were instances of propaganda.

Table 8.1. World War I and World War II

Group	*Support During WWI**	*Support During WWII**	*Explanation*
Parents			
Politically Conservative Teachers			
Politically Liberal Teachers			
School Board Members			
Professors of Education			
Liberal Politicians			
Conservative Politicians			

* (+) Supported
(-) Opposed
(+/-) Mixed Commitment

Two decades after World War I, federal officials wished to foster support for another war. They decided that they would duplicate and expand the school programs that had been successful during the earlier war.

How do you think groups responded to school-based propaganda during World War I? How do you think they responded to it during World War II? To help answer these questions, create a chart.

Along the vertical axis of the chart, place the following groups: parents, politically conservative teachers, politically liberal teachers, members of local school boards, professors of education, liberal politicians, and conservative politicians.

Along the horizontal axis of the chart, arrange several columns. In one column, indicate whether each group primarily supported (+), opposed (-), or showed a mixed commitment (+/-) to school-based propaganda during World War I. In another column of the chart, indicate each group's reaction to school-based propaganda during World War II.

Your indications about the responses of the groups should be based on assumptions about the vested interests, values, and goals of their members. Although you can use the information in the case study to make some of these assumptions, you may wish to rely on a broader foundation of information.

You can gather additional information from the materials that are listed at the end of this chapter. You may gather it from lectures or discussions.

In a separate column of the chart, or possibly on a separate page, summarize your assumptions about each group.

Case Study 8.2: Japanese Americans

During World War II, federal bureaucrats advised American educators to prepare their students for wartime attacks. Although their advice was practical, it was unnerving. For example, they advised school personnel to rehearse evacuations into bomb shelters. Once they had shepherded children into these areas, the educators were to gather their eyeglasses; they were assured that this precaution would protect the children from the shards of shattering lenses.

Other pieces of advice were equally unnerving. For example, bureaucrats advised educators to prepare for the disfigurement that incendiary bombs would cause. After pointing out the importance of accurately identifying bodies, they discouraged the school administrators from issuing metal identification tags, which might melt during an attack. Instead, they suggested that they tattoo identification numbers onto students. They assured the educators that the tattoos would be legible even on charred corpses.

Americans were concerned about the damage that enemy combatants might inflict; they also were concerned about the damage that subversive forces might inflict. Journalists were one of the groups that fanned these fears. They continually called attention to what they viewed as the subversive threat from Japanese Americans.

Alarmist journalists predicted that Japanese Americans would help invading forces. They urged the government to arrest Japanese Americans who resided on the West Coast, remove them from this area, and confine them in special camps. They insisted that these camps be situated in remote areas, surrounded with barbed wire, and policed by armed guards.

The concern over Japanese Americans was in some ways surprising. After all, most Japanese Americans had been born in the United States. Furthermore, they were not a large group. They were overshadowed by some of the other groups that had relatives fighting for enemy armies. The several hundred thousand Japanese Americans were eclipsed by the millions of German Americans and Italian Americans. In spite of these circumstances, many persons concentrated their distrust and hostility on Japanese Americans.

Walter Lippmann was one of the journalists who did not conceal his distrust of Japanese Americans. Weeks after the attack on Pearl Harbor, he warned that "the Pacific coast is in imminent danger of a combined attack from within and from without." He lectured readers that "the Japanese navy has been reconnoitering the Pacific coast more or less continually" and "communication takes place between the enemy at sea and enemy agents on land." He added portentously that the "Pacific coast is officially a combat zone" and that it "may at any moment be a battlefield" (Lippmann, February, 1942, quoted by United States Department of the Interior, 1946, pp. 12–13).

President Roosevelt agreed with the political extremists. He signed Executive Order 9066 on February 19, 1942. This order gave military commanders the power to remove potentially dangerous American citizens from any areas that the commanders judged to be vulnerable to military assaults. It enabled them to arrest more than 110,000 Japanese Americans on the West Coast, relocate them, and confine them in detention camps. Even Japanese Americans who did not live on the West Coast were affected; they lived in fear that they and their children eventually would be singled out for arrest, relocation, and detention.

Government bureaucrats attempted to disassociate the American detention camps from the concentration camps in Europe. They referred to the American camps as "assembly centers" and insisted that they were not stark, uncomfortable, or repressive. They portrayed them as places in which the residents were "guaranteed security and protection, a common measure of food, shelter, clothing, medical attention, and schooling, and opportunity to work for a small fixed wage" ("War Relocation Centers: Education Program," 1942, p. 7).

The American government and military leaders arrested and confined Japanese Americans in 1942. They took these actions in order to prevent them from providing assistance to an invading army. Three years later, they recognized that the Japanese army had become too weak to mount a military attack on the United States. Therefore they released the imprisoned Japanese Americans.

Although Japanese Americans were permitted to return to their communities, they had lost their jobs, professional practices, and careers. Unable to make loan payments, they had lost their homes, stores, offices, businesses, and farms.

Several years after the war ended, the federal government wished to rectify the injustices for which it had been responsible. It paid some of the detained Japanese Americans for a portion of the property that they had lost. Forty years later, it paid flat fees of $20,000 to surviving detainees.

Although they were compensated for some of their financial losses, Japanese Americans were not compensated for their emotional suffering. They had been publicly humiliated. They had watched as their children were torn away from their classmates and teachers. They had been forced out of their neighborhoods, stripped of civil rights, deprived of freedom, and depicted as traitors. They had

Table 8.2. Japanese Americans

Group	*Support**	*Explanation*
Non-Japanese American Students		
Non-Japanese American Parents		
Teachers		
School Administrators		
School Board Members		
Professors of Education		
Liberal Politicians		
Conservative Politicians		

* (+) Supported
(-) Opposed
(+/-) Mixed Commitment

lost their identities as successful, responsible, proud, and valued members of their communities.

Activity: Detention of Japanese Americans

World War II government officials feared that the Japanese forces would invade the United States. They feared that Japanese Americans would assist the invading forces. Because they suspected that an attack would come from the Pacific Ocean, they arrested, relocated, and detained Japanese Americans on the West Coast.

How did different groups react to this massive arrest and detention? To help answer this question, create a chart.

Along the vertical axis of the chart, place the following groups: non-Japanese American students in West Coast schools, non-Japanese American parents in West Coast communities, teachers in West Coast schools, school administrators in West Coast schools, members of West Coast school boards, professors of education, liberal politicians, and conservative politicians.

Along the horizontal axis of the chart, arrange several columns. In the first column, indicate whether each group primarily supported (+), opposed (-), or showed a mixed commitment (+/-) to the ways in which Japanese Americans citizens were treated.

Your indications about the responses of the groups should be based on assumptions about the vested interests, values, and goals of their members. Although you can use the information in the case study to make some of these assumptions, you may wish to rely on a broader foundation of information.

You can gather additional information from the materials that are listed at the end of this chapter. You may gather it from lectures or discussions.

In a separate column of the chart, or possibly on a separate page, summarize your assumptions about each group.

Case Study 8.3: The Cold War and Its Aftermath

Even though they opposed the wartime educational initiatives, political liberals succumbed to public pressure. They had repressed their true feelings and been quiet about the wartime educational programs. After the war, the liberals were ready to confront the conservatives.

The conservatives also were ready. Major Augustin Rudd was one of the many conservatives who relished opportunities to clash with the liberals. Rudd was the chairman of the Guardians of American Education. He assured the liberals that he was not intimidated by them.

Rudd characterized the liberals as naïve idealists who had underestimated the danger from hostile countries. He added that they also underestimated the danger from subversive agents in their own country. He claimed that communist agents were undermining America's military, economy, and government. As chairman of the Guardians of American Education, Rudd was especially concerned about communist attempts to undermine the schools.

The conservatives had strong allies in the federal government. Officials in the federal Office of Education (United States Department of Health, Education, and Welfare, 1956) revealed their sympathetic attitudes when they entitled a post-war book *Education for National Survival.* In that book, they encouraged school personnel to prepare children for war with the communists. They advised them to continue the evacuation drills that they had been practicing throughout the war. In fact, they advised them to expand the drills and prepare for new threats from biological, chemical, and nuclear attacks.

Some conservative critics worried about communists who resided in foreign countries; others worried about those who resided in the United States. Still others worried about American citizens who were not communists but who sympathized with them. The critics believed that the members of all three groups posed dangers.

The conservative critics claimed that the events surrounding Whittaker Chambers had validated their fears. Whittaker Chambers, a Soviet spy, had been captured during the late 1940s. He then identified Alger Hiss, a high-ranking officer in the U.S. State Department, as another Soviet spy. The conservatives speculated that many other spies had infiltrated the government during the long administration of President Roosevelt.

The conservative critics were upset about several famous communists, including Julius and Ethel Rosenberg. They were accused of stealing secret information about the atomic bomb and giving it to the Soviet Union. The conservatives alleged that this incident revealed the damage that Soviet agents had inflicted. They explained that the Soviet Union already had gained access to information that was critical to the military security of the United States.

Congressional hearings amplified the sensational trials of alleged communists. Senator Joseph McCarthy arranged some of these hearings. In a campaign that he christened the "fight for America," McCarthy entreated Americans to help ferret out communists who had infiltrated the government and the military.

Some conservatives feared that communists were taking control of the schools. They warned that subversive teachers were enervating America's military, economy, and government. Legislatures who were impressed by these warnings required teachers to take oaths of national loyalty. The number of states that required these oaths increased from twenty-one to thirty-two during the 1940s.

Although some conservatives scrutinized schoolteachers, others examined professors. Writing in the *American Legion Magazine,* one analyst claimed that liberal professors were spreading the philosophy of "spiritual darkness"—communism—among their students (Root, 1952). Another analyst accused them of turning college students into political acolytes (Kuhn, 1952).

The conservatives claimed that liberal professors were undermining the patriotism of schoolchildren as well as college students. They alleged that they were reaching the schoolchildren through the subversive textbooks that they had written. They explained that these books made the schoolchildren doubt America's economy and system of government.

The conservatives scolded the liberal professors for the damage that they had inflicted on America's youths. They explained that they especially were upset because the professors were weakening the national loyalty of youths in the United States at the same time that Soviet communists had been strengthening that of their own youths.

During the 1940s and the 1950s, conservatives repeatedly voiced concern about the inadequacies of American education. Although they detected ideological weaknesses, they also detected academic weaknesses. These critics became more distraught about the academic weaknesses in the fall of 1957. This was the season during which the Soviets launched the *Sputnik* satellite.

Critics fretted because the Soviet Union had achieved this impressive scientific achievement. They were sure that the development placed the United States at a military disadvantage. A former U.S. Commissioner of Education wrote that Americans worried that the Soviets would use the new technology to drop hydrogen bombs onto their cities (McGrath, 1958).

Vice Admiral Hyman Rickover berated American teachers. Insisting that Soviet educators were superior, Rickover blamed the teachers for the limited number of students who were pursuing critical military careers. Just as conservatives had used Pearl Harbor to their political advantage, Rickover and like-minded ideologues used the launch of *Sputnik* to their advantage.

During the initial half of the twentieth century, the United States had fought two expensive, deadly, and controversial wars. During the first war, President Wilson employed a homefront propaganda campaign with gratifying results. When President Roosevelt replicated that campaign, he also was gratified with the results.

Post–World War II Americans continued to engage in conflicts. They were involved in the Korean War from 1950 to 1953; they were involved in the Vietnam War from the early 1960s until 1975. These conflicts were expensive, deadly, and controversial.

During the Korean War, President Truman attempted to duplicate the homefront propaganda campaigns that had been so effective during earlier wars. However, he was not successful. When presidents Johnson and Nixon attempted to replicate them, they also were not successful.

During World War I and World War II, President Wilson's and President Roosevelt's popularity had soared. In contrast, President Truman's popularity plummeted during the Korean War. President Johnson's and President Nixon's popularity declined during the Vietnam War.

Several situations contributed to the decline in the wartime popularity of later presidents. Journalists, political analysts, and political factions created one of these situations when they provided warnings to the American public about domestic propaganda.

Activity: Anticommunist Rhetoric in the Schools

During the era that followed World War II, government officials believed that communists posed international threats to the United States. They also believed that they posed subversive threats. They warned American citizens to prepare themselves and their children to deal with these threats.

How did groups respond to these adjurations? How did they respond during the early 1950s, an era when the United States was involved in the Korean War? How did they respond during the late 1950s, the era in which the Soviets launched *Sputnik*? How did they respond from the late 1960s through the early 1970s, an era in which the United States was involved in the Vietnam War? To help answer these questions, create a chart.

Along the vertical axis of the chart, place the following groups: parents, teachers, school administrators, members of local school boards, professors of education, liberal politicians, and conservative politicians.

Along the horizontal axis of the chart, arrange several columns. In one column, indicate whether each group primarily supported (+), opposed (-), or

Table 8.3. The Cold War and Its Aftermath

Group	*Early 50s**	*Late 50s**	*Late 60s–Early 70s**	*Rationale*
Parents				
Teachers				
School Administrators				
School Board Members				
Professors of Education				
Liberal Politicians				
Conservative Politicians				

* (+) Supported
(-) Opposed
(+/-) Mixed Commitment

showed a mixed commitment (+/-) to anti-communist rhetoric in the schools during the Korean War. In another column of the chart, indicate each group's attitudes toward anticommunist rhetoric in the schools during the *Sputnik* era. In another column, indicate each group's attitudes toward anticommunist rhetoric in the schools during the Vietnam War.

Your indications about the responses of the groups should be based on assumptions about the vested interests, values, and goals of their members. Although you can use the information in the case study to make some of these assumptions, you may wish to rely on a broader foundation of information.

You can gather additional information from the materials that are listed at the end of this chapter. You may gather it from lectures or discussions.

In a separate column of the chart, or possibly on a separate page, summarize your assumptions about each group.

USING THE PAST TO UNDERSTAND THE PRESENT

Twentieth-century presidents were involved in military conflicts. During the first half of the twentieth century, they sent troops to fight in World War I and World War II. During the second half of the century, they sent troops to Korea and Vietnam. Still later, they sent them to Africa, South America, Asia, and Europe.

Wartime presidents cultivated the support of American citizens. At times, they were elated by that support; at other times, they were disappointed. President Truman had both of these experiences. Immediately after he succeeded Roosevelt, his approval by the public surged. As World War II became more distant, his approval ebbed. His political influence also ebbed.

When he decided to send American troops to Korea, Truman may have hoped to regain the presidential power that he had lost. He was disappointed when an expensive, deadly, and protracted war had the opposite effect. He miscalculated the political temperament of the Chinese communists, the strength of the American military in an Asian campaign, and his own ability to allay homefront dissent.

In all of the military confrontations that followed World War II, American leaders estimated the military and political liabilities associated with the conflicts. However, only afterwards could they verify the accuracy of those assessments. In the early 1960s, President Kennedy was elated by his military decisions.

President George W. Bush was enormously popular during the early years of his administration; he was much less popular at the end of his tenure. He became less popular because he made decisions that had consequences of which constituents disapproved.

Although American wars have affected presidents, they have affected many other persons. They have affected servicepersons and their families; they have affected farmers and industrialists. They also have affected schoolchildren. Some schoolchildren were affected directly when a parent, sibling, or friend engaged in combat. Others were affected indirectly when they learned about war and its threats.

Just as schoolchildren have had opportunities for war to affect them, they had opportunities for domestic wartime propaganda to affect them. They had multiple opportunities to view propaganda during twentieth-century conflicts. Have they had opportunities to view it during recent military conflicts?

To answer the preceding question, identify a twenty-first-century instance of domestic propaganda in the schools. What were the motives of the group that introduced the propaganda? How much political resistance did they encounter? How persuasive was the propaganda? Try to find an instance that occurred in your own state or community.

CHAPTER SUMMARY

During World War I, President Wilson asked a marketing team to cultivate homefront enthusiasm. Most educators responded positively. They distributed domestic propaganda within their schools, communities, and professional associations. They directed young students to sell war bonds, gather recyclable materials, and grow fresh produce. They trained adolescents for wartime jobs and military service.

Two decades after World War I, government leaders duplicated the earlier propaganda campaign. They used it to cultivate national unity during an armed conflict. They also used it to raise awareness about subversive threats. They initially focused on the threats from Japanese Americans; they later shifted their attention to threats from communists.

ADDITIONAL READING

Introductory Passages

Advertising as a weapon of war. (1918). *Printer's Ink, 105* (7), 143–144.

Associated Business Papers. (1942). *Guide to effective wartime advertising.* New York: Author.

Case for advertising. (1940). *Nation's Business, 28* (3), 33–56.

Committee on Public Information. (1918). *Government war advertising: Report of the Division of Advertising.* Washington, DC: Author.

Committee on Public Information. (1972). *The Creel Report: Complete report of the chairman of the Committee on Public Information 1917; 1918; 1919*. New York: Da Capo. (Original work published in 1927.)

Cornebise, A. E. (1984). *War as advertised: The four-minute men and America's crusade, 1917–1918*. Philadelphia: American Philosophical Society.

Fleming, T. (2001). *The New Dealers' war: Franklin D. Roosevelt and the war within World War II*. New York: Basic.

Fox, F. W. (1975). *Madison Avenue goes to war: The strange military career of American advertising, 1941–1945*. Provo, UT: Brigham Young University Press.

Gellerman, W. (1938). *The American Legion as educator*. New York: Teachers College Press.

Goodrum, C., & Dalrymple, H. (1990). *Advertising in America: The first 200 years*. New York: Abrams.

How the 100 best war ads came to be written. (1946, January). *Advertising & Selling*, 85–87.

Jeffries, J. W. (1996). *Wartime America: The World War II home front*. Chicago: Ivan R. Dee.

Nelson, K. L. (1971). *The impact of war on American life: The twentieth-century experience*. New York: Holt, Rinehart, & Winston.

Winkler, A. M. (1986). *Home front USA: America during World War II*. Arlington Heights, IL: Harlan Davidson.

Winter, J., & Baggett, B. (1996). *The Great War and the shaping of the 20th century*. New York: Penguin.

Case Study 8.1: World War I and World War II

Bailey, R. H. (1977). *The home front: U.S.A.* Arlington, VA: Time-Life.

Balfour, M. (1979). *Propaganda in war, 1939–1945: Organizations, policies and publics in Britain and Germany*. London: Routledge & Kegan Paul.

Chambers, J. W., & Culbert, D. (Eds.). (1996). *World War II, film, and history*. Oxford, UK: Oxford University Press.

Combs, J. E., & Combs, S. T. (1994). *Film propaganda and American politics: An analysis and filmography*. New York: Garland.

Culbert, D. H. (Ed.). (1986). *Information control and propaganda: Records of the Office of War Information* (Part II: Office of Policy Coordination. Series A: Propaganda and policy directives for overseas programs, 1942–1945). Frederick, MD: University Press of America.

DeBauche, L. M. (1997). *Reel patriotism: The movies and World War I*. Madison: University of Wisconsin Press.

Dick, B. F. (1985). *The star-spangled screen: The American World War II film*. Lexington: University Press of Kentucky.

Hamlin, C. H. (1973). *Propaganda and myth in time of war: Comprising the war myth in United States History and educators present arms—The use of schools and colleges as agents of war propaganda, 1914–1918*. New York: Vanguard. (Original work published in 1927.)

Hyams, J. (1984). *War movies.* New York: Gallery.
Kane, K. (1982). *Visions of war: Hollywood combat films of World War II.* Ann Arbor: Research Press.
Krugler, D. F. (2000). *The voice of America and the domestic propaganda battles, 1945–1953.* Columbia: University of Missouri Press.
Lasswell, H. D. (1972). *Propaganda technique in the World War.* New York: Garland.
Morella, J., Epstein, E. Z., & Griggs, J. (1973). *The films of World War II.* Secaucus, NJ: Citadel.
Rawls, W. H. (1988). *Wake up, America! World War I and the American poster.* New York: Abbeville.
Renov, M. (1988). *Hollywood's wartime woman: Representation and ideology.* Ann Arbor: Research Press.
Rhodes, A. (1983a). *Propaganda: The art of persuasion: World War II* (Vol. 1). New York: Chelsea House. (Original work published in 1976.)
Rhodes, A. (1983b). *Propaganda: The art of persuasion: World War II* (Vol. 2). New York: Chelsea House. (Original work published in 1976.)
Ross, S. H. (1996). *Propaganda for war: How the United States was conditioned to fight the Great War of 1914–1918.* Jefferson, NC: McFarland.
Rudolph, G. A. (1990). *War posters from 1914 through 1918 in the archives of the University of Nebraska-Lincoln.* Lincoln: University of Nebraska.
Rupp, L. J. (1978). *Mobilizing women for war: German and American propaganda, 1939–1945.* Princeton, NJ: Princeton University Press.
Shale, R. (1982). *Donald Duck joins up: The Walt Disney Studio during World War II.* Ann Arbor: UMI Research Press.
Shindler, C. (1979). *Hollywood goes to war: Films and American society, 1939–1952.* London: Routledge & Kegan Paul.
Short, K. R. M. (1983). *Film & radio propaganda in World War II.* Knoxville: University of Tennessee Press.
Shulman, H. C. (1990). *The Voice of America: Propaganda and democracy, 1941–1945.* Madison: University of Wisconsin Press.
Sorensen, T. C. (1968). *The word war: The story of American propaganda.* New York: Harper & Row.
Steele, R. W. (1999). *Free speech in the good war.* London: Macmillan.
Sweeney, M. S. (2001). *Secrets of victory: The Office of Censorship and the American press and radio in World War II.* Chapel Hill: University of North Carolina Press.
Tuttle, W. M. (1993). America's home front children in World War II. In G. H. Elder, J. Modell, & R. D. Parke. (Eds.), *Children in time and place: Developmental and historical insights* (pp. 27–46). New York: Cambridge University Press.
Woll, A. L. (1983). *The Hollywood musical goes to war.* Chicago: Nelson-Hall.

Case Study 8.2: Japanese Americans

Daniels, R. (1993). *Prisoners without trial: Japanese Americans in World War II.* New York: Hill & Wang.

Daniels, R., Taylor, S. C., & Kitano, H. (Eds.). (1986). *Japanese Americans: From relocation to redress.* Salt Lake City: University of Utah Press.

Davis, D. S. (1982). *Behind barbed wire: The imprisonment of Japanese Americans during World War II.* New York: Dutton.

Gesensway, D., & Roseman, M. (1987). *Beyond words: Images from America's concentration camps.* Ithaca, NY: Cornell University Press.

James, T. (1987). *Exile within: The schooling of Japanese Americans, 1942–1945.* Cambridge, MA: Harvard University Press.

McWilliams, C. (1942). Moving the west-coast Japanese. *Harper's Magazine, 185,* 359–369.

Myer, D. S. (1971). *Uprooted Americans: The Japanese Americans and the war Relocation Authority during World War II.* Tucson: University of Arizona Press.

Nagata, D. K. (1993). *Legacy of injustice: Exploring the cross-generational impact of the Japanese American internment.* New York: Plenum.

Relocating Japanese American students. (1942, September 15). *Education for Victory, 1* (14), 2.

Starr, K. (2003). *Embattled dreams: California in war and peace, 1940–1950.* New York: Oxford University Press.

Taylor, S. C. (1993). *Jewel of the desert: Japanese American internment at Topaz.* Berkeley: University of California Press.

War relocation centers: Education program for evacuees of Japanese ancestry. (1942, November 16). *Education for Victory, 1* (18), 7–9.

Weglyn, M. (1976). *Years of infamy: The untold story of America's concentration camps.* New York: Morrow.

Case Study 8.3: The Cold War and Its Aftermath

Allen, M. L. (1956). *Education or indoctrination.* Caldwell, ID: Caxton.

Bestor, A. E. (1953). *Educational wastelands.* Urbana: University of Illinois Press.

Brameld, T. (1951). *The battle for free schools.* Boston: Beacon.

Counts, G. S. (1951). The need for a great education. *Teachers College Record, 53,* 77–88.

Garber, M., & Walkowitz, R. (Eds.). (1995). *Secret agents: The Rosenberg case, McCarthyism and fifties America.* London: Routledge.

Jones, K., & Olivier, R. (1956). *Progressive education is REDucation.* Boston, MA: Meador.

Kaub, V. P. (1953). *Communist-socialist propaganda in American schools.* Boston, MA: Meador.

Kirk, R. (1954). *A program for conservatives.* Chicago: Regnery.

Kirk, S. A. (1948). Education as national defense. *Progressive Education, 25* (7), 119–120, 144.

Lansner, K. (1958). *Second-rate brains.* New York: Doubleday.

Latimer, J. F. (1958). *What's happened to our high schools?* Washington, DC: Public Affairs Press.

Lynd, A. (1950). *Quackery in the public schools.* Boston, MA: Little, Brown.

McCarthy, J. (1952). *McCarthyism: The fight for America.* New York: Devin-Adair.
Neville, John F. (1995). *Press, the Rosenbergs and the Cold War.* Westport, CT: Greenwood.
Perlstein, R. (2001). *Before the storm: Barry Goldwater and the unmaking of the American consensus.* New York: Hill & Wang.
Perlstein, R. (2008). *Nixonland: The rise of a president and the fracturing of America.* New York: Scribner.
Philipson, I. (1993). *Ethel Rosenberg: Beyond the myths.* Piscataway, NJ: Rutgers University Press.
Radosh, R., & Milton, J. (1997). *The Rosenberg File: A Search for the truth.* New Haven, CT: Yale University Press.
Ravitch, D. (2000). *Left back: A century of school reforms.* New York: Simon & Schuster.
Rickover, H. G. (1957a, December 6). A size-up of what's wrong with American schools. *U.S. News and World Report, 43*, 86–91.
Rickover, H. G. (1957b, March 2). Let's stop wasting our greatest resource. *Saturday Evening Post, 229*, 19, 108–109, 111.
Rickover, H. G. (1959). *Education and freedom.* New York: Dutton.
Rudd, A. J. (1942a). Education for a "new social order." Part One. *National Republic, 30* (1), 5–6, 20, 30.
Rudd, A. J. (1942b). Education for a "new social order." Part Two. *National Republic, 30* (2), 21–22, 32.
Sanford, C. W., Hand, H. C., & Spalding, W. B. (Eds.). (1951). *Schools and national security.* New York: McGraw-Hill.
Smith, M. (1954). *The diminished mind.* Chicago: Regnery.
Smith, M. (1956). *The public schools in crisis: Some critical essays.* Chicago: Regnery.
Tanenhaus, S. (1997). *Whittaker Chambers.* New York: Random House.
Thayer, V. T. (1954). *Public education and its critics.* New York: Macmillan.
Weinstein, A. (1978). *Perjury: The Hiss-Chambers case.* New York: Knopf.
White, G. E. (2005). *Alger Hiss's looking-glass wars: The covert life of a soviet spy.* London: Oxford.

Chapter Nine

Politics: Reacting to Organized Labor

Nineteenth-century social reformers had been concerned about school-age children. They had hoped to educate them and protect them from workplace exploitation. They believed that compulsory schooling was the solution to both problems. Their plan was supported by union members, journalists, religious leaders, and members of the public; it was opposed by some businesspersons and parents. In addition to being concerned about children, the reformers were concerned about teachers. Convinced that teachers had been treated deplorably, they counseled them to form unions.

ORGANIZED LABOR IN TODAY'S SCHOOLS

Many nineteenth- and twentieth-century immigrants to the United States were poor. Their poverty was apparent when they had disembarked from steamships with their possessions in a single trunk, suitcase, basket, or satchel. They frequently lacked the money needed for housing, medical care, clothing, fuel, and food.

Unethical employers, who realized that immigrants were living under dire circumstances, exploited them. They also exploited African Americans, females, and children. They required them to work long hours in dangerous environments for minimal compensation.

Union organizers befriended the workers. They pledged that they would raise their wages and improve their working conditions. They eventually succeeded. They succeeded because of their courage and determination; they also succeeded because of their political savvy. They demonstrated their savvy during the 1930s when they persuaded President Franklin Roosevelt and a coterie of congressional allies to enact helpful legislation.

Members of the public sometimes viewed union leaders positively. They viewed them positively when they learned that they had advanced the interests of oppressed workers. They became skeptical when they learned that they had consorted with gangsters, bullied coworkers, made unrealistic demands of businesses, or led crippling strikes.

After comparing their own wages, benefits, working conditions and job security to those of laborers in other fields, many teachers concluded that they had been treated unfairly. Aware that organized workers had advantages, they resolved that they would form unions.

When teachers made the decision to unionize, they took risks. They risked alienating the groups that traditionally had supported them. Government leaders, school board members, and school administrators feared that unionized teachers might deplete already sparse budgets. Parents feared that unionized teachers would jeopardize their children's education. Members of the public feared that unionized teachers would no longer serve as the altruistic patrons of children.

The National Education Association (NEA), which is the largest teacher union in the United States, is an example of a labor organization that has won support from the public. Members of the NEA won support when they raised the visibility of teachers and the critical contributions that they made to society. They won support when they highlighted educational problems and suggested solutions for them.

At times, members of the NEA lost public support. They lost support when they participated in strikes to raise their salaries. They lost support when they allocated their lobbying budget exclusively to a single political party. They lost support when they opposed test-based accountability, private-school vouchers, teacher merit pay, and incentive pay for teachers with hard-to-locate academic and professional expertise.

The current generation of teachers is affected by the ways in which unions are viewed. In a similar fashion, earlier generations were affected by the complex ways in which unions were viewed. Sometimes they benefited because of these views; at other times they suffered.

CONCERN ABOUT EXPLOITED CHILDREN

When teachers flexed their political muscles on behalf of children, they demonstrated impressive strength, as when they called attention to the many child laborers who were exploited in agriculture, fishing, dining, retailing, mining, manufacturing, industry, and the street trades.

Teachers amassed additional strength through strategic alliances. They worked collaboratively with humanitarians, women's suffrage advocates, journalists, socially progressive authors, the members of religious organizations, and many other persons.

The members of labor organizations agreed with educators about the need to change child labor practices. Although many union members were motivated exclusively by idealistic concerns, some of them had ulterior motives. They hoped that eliminating children from the workforce would improve their own wages and job security.

Beginning in the 1830s, reform-minded legislators in New York, Massachusetts, and several other New England states had passed laws limiting the conditions under which children could labor. Even though the legislators were aware that many young workers were unaffected by these laws, they still were pleased. They were pleased because the new laws helped them publicize their efforts and recruit sympathizers. They hoped that greater support would enable them to enact effective reforms.

TUITION-FREE PUBLIC SCHOOLS

The Massachusetts colonists established public schools during the 1600s. Nonetheless, the families in some of their communities did not have opportunities to send their children to them. Several centuries later, the citizens of Massachusetts resolved that they would solve this problem; they would set up public elementary schools and high schools in all of the major communities of their state.

The citizens of Massachusetts had an educational commitment that extended beyond the elementary schools and high schools. They demonstrated that commitment when they established residential schools for persons with disabilities. They demonstrated it when they began to offer special education in the public schools. They demonstrated it when they established institutions of higher learning. They demonstrated it when they established normal schools.

Not all nineteenth-century families had educational opportunities comparable to those in Massachusetts. The residents of some states had made education a high priority, but others had not. Families that resided in the Northeast and the Midwest generally were pleased with their educational opportunities; families that resided in the South and the West were less pleased.

Those citizens who resided in prosperous regions were able to develop education quickly and robustly. Because the Northeast and Midwest were prosperous regions, the residents of these regions had financial resources. They had abundant resources before the Civil War and they preserved them afterwards. They offered public education uninterruptedly during the war; they continued to support it later. When they decided that racially integrated public schools would meet the needs of both minority and non-minority children, they did not have to cross an economic chasm to implement them.

Southern residents followed a different route than the Northerners. Before the Civil War, they had relied on slavery to maintain an inefficient economy. Even if they had won the war, they would have faced harrowing economic challenges. They would have had to deal with the cost of the war, the physical damage to their property, and the deaths of numerous young males. Having been defeated, they still had to deal with these economic challenges; they also had to deal with the loss of slavery.

As residents of the South set about rebuilding their society, they searched for some way to implement public education. Aware that the era of Reconstruction entailed restrictions, they developed their plans carefully. They resolved that they would create a system of education for non-African American children; they resolved that they would create a separate system for African American children.

Because they had to duplicate services in every school district, Southerners realized that the dual systems of education would be expensive and inefficient. However, they did not realize all of the consequences of their actions.

COMPULSORY SCHOOLING

The reformers who supported tuition-free public education also supported compulsory schooling. They were convinced that both of these developments benefitted children.

Many of the early school administrators agreed with the reformers about the benefits of compulsory schooling; however, they also detected problems. Some of the problems, such as those involving teachers, buildings, equipment, and textbooks, had clear and straightforward solutions. Other problems, such as those involving religious, ethnic, and racial issues, had complicated, difficult-to-discern solutions.

Some school administrators decided that they would address complex problems. Nonetheless, they frequently were confused about how to proceed. Other school administrators decided to simply ignore complex problems.

Dissatisfied and impatient with school administrators, some groups took matters into their own hands. Concerned about religious issues in the public schools, Catholics, Jews, and several other groups established private religious schools. German Americans were concerned about ethnic and cultural issues; they established German-language schools. Southerners who were concerned about racial issues established segregated schools.

Compulsory schooling created practical, religious, ethnic, and racial problems. It also created economic problems. Employers complained that compulsory schooling deprived them of the cheap labor that they needed to make profits. They were able to make this complaint seem more plausible during the Great Depression.

Some poor parents joined the employers who opposed compulsory schooling. Although these parents acknowledged that children were hired because they accepted low wages, succumbed to exploitative managers, and were unprotected by unions, they wished them to remain in the workforce. They explained that they needed their children's wages to live.

UNIONS GROW STRONGER

During the nineteenth and early twentieth centuries, many American citizens were learning about labor unions. They were learning about the influential European labor unions, such as those in Great Britain. They were learning about the influential American unions, such as the Knights of Labor and the American Federation of Labor. They were learning about highly specialized unions, such as the American Railroad Union and the Coal Miners Union.

Many members of the public viewed early workers sympathetically. They viewed them sympathetically after seeing workers struggling in unsafe jobs, earning meager salaries, and coping with abusive supervisors. They viewed them sympathetically after reading novels such as *The Jungle*, which described the early twentieth-century conditions in Chicago's meatpacking industry. They viewed them sympathetically after reading newspaper reports about daring efforts of Eugene Debs and the organizers of the American Railroad Union. Many members of the public were gratified that hundreds of thousands of workers had joined labor unions. They were optimistic that even more would follow.

The union leaders helped workers by arranging shorter workdays, safer workplace conditions, higher wages, and job security. They demanded that employers give their organizers opportunities to recruit new members. They used collective bargaining, threats, and strikes to strengthen these demands.

Many industrialists and businesspersons opposed the union leaders and refused to comply with their demands. They did not hesitate to penalize union members and blacklist organizers. They did not hesitate to take actions that culminated in violence, injury, and death.

Although union leaders had strikes as tools, they also used publicity as a tool. In fact, they had discredited many businesspersons through adverse publicity. Instead of protesting, the businesspersons decided to use this strategy to their own advantage.

The businesspersons used adverse publicity in their conflicts with the labor unions. They circulated information about union leaders who had mismanaged their organizations' finances or collaborated with criminals. They portrayed prominent union spokespersons, such as Upton Sinclair and Eugene Debs, as socialists who were undermining America's economy and government.

During the era that preceded World War I, American businesspersons circulated harmful reports about unions. They warned that the unions imperiled the security of the United States. They reiterated their warnings once combat erupted in Europe.

After communist revolutionaries dismantled Russia's economy and government, American businesspersons sounded their warnings again. They warned Americans to be vigilant about attacks from communist soldiers. They warned them to be vigilant about attacks from the communists' secret agents. The warned them to be vigilant about attacks from those communists' secret agents who had infiltrated the unions.

Case Study 9.1: Child Labor

Well before the Civil War, Northern workers had begun to form labor unions. They had used the unions to lobby for shorter workdays, greater workplace safety, increased job security, and higher wages. They also had used them to lobby for restrictions on child labor.

The members of labor unions believed that they could help children in the workplace. The union members hoped to restrict the wages they could earn, the circumstances under which they could be hired, the number of hours that they could work, and the types of jobs that they could fill.

The employers who hired child workers and the parents who relied on children's wages opposed the reformers. They were upset about the financial difficulties that the reformers would create for them. The employers alleged that the union members had ulterior motives for supporting reforms; they pointed out that they would benefit from reforms that reduced the number of children competing for jobs.

In addition to the financial hardships that they would suffer, employers and parents had other reasons for opposing child labor reforms. They warned that many of the children who lost their jobs would become idle, run free, get into mischief, and turn to lives of crime.

The reformers did not have convincing retorts to the financial objections. They acknowledged that the parents would suffer. They hoped that someday they could prosper without sending their children to work. Although they acknowledged that the employers also would suffer, they felt less sympathy for the employers.

As for the predictions that children would get into trouble and crime, the reformers did have a retort. They responded that the children who were forced out of factories, stores, mines, railroads, bakeries, fishing vessels, newspapers, and other workplaces could go to school. In fact, the reformers wished to make school attendance compulsory.

During the 1840s, the citizens of Massachusetts encouraged all of the children in their state to attend school for at least three months each year. To demonstrate their commitment to this practice, they enacted compulsory school attendance legislation. They combined this legislation with regulations limiting the length of child laborers' workdays. The citizens in several states followed the Massachusetts model; they bundled school-attendance regulations with child labor regulations.

Throughout the 1800s and early 1900s, union members lobbied for legislation to ensure that all children attended school. These legislative acts were largely symbolic; they failed to influence most child laborers. Disappointed by the relatively few children who left the workplace, the union members urged the national Democratic Party to endorse child labor reforms. Although the Democrats agreed to endorse reforms in 1892, they insisted that the reforms affect only children who were fourteen years old or younger. By restricting any new legislation to young children, the Democrats acknowledged the sizeable amount of power that their opponents wielded.

Some state legislators had been able to pass laws prohibiting child labor. Nonetheless, federal legislators had a more difficult time. They faced opponents who insisted that these laws would interfere with the rights of states. They became despondent after the courts agreed with their opponents.

Disappointed by the judicial decisions, the reformers wrote new versions of child labor laws. However, they continued to lose cases in the courts. Therefore, they tried to enact a constitutional amendment that would provide the federal government with the unequivocal right to regulate child labor. They were unable to get the support that they needed for ratification.

Hoping that the prospects for ratification of a child labor amendment had improved during the early 1930s, the reformers once again attempted to attract allies. Even though they were assisted by President Roosevelt, a Democratic congress, labor unions, journalists, religious leaders, educators, and a heterogeneous assemblage of reform-minded allies, they were unsuccessful.

After the reformers were unable to get the support for a constitutional amendment, they decided that they again would try to enact legislation. With the aid of a president who had become enormously powerful, they lobbied for comprehensive workplace reforms. They wanted legislation that would raise workers' wages, protect labor unions, and limit child employment. They judged that the 1938 Fair Labor Standards Act would achieve all of these goals.

Like earlier reformers, the sponsors of the Fair Labor Standards Act wrote their bill in a calculating manner. They argued that the federal government had the right to regulate laborers who handled products that crossed state lines. They explained that the government could restrict child labor not only because of the damage inflicted on children but because of the damage inflicted on interstate commerce.

In the Fair Labor Standards Act, the authors listed specific reasons that child labor should be prohibited. They wrote that it:

1. causes commerce and the channels and instrumentalities of commerce to be used to spread and perpetuate such labor conditions among the workers of the several States;
2. burdens commerce and the free flow of goods in commerce;
3. constitutes an unfair method of competition in commerce;
4. leads to labor disputes burdening and obstructing commerce and the free flow of goods in commerce; and
5. interferes with the orderly and fair marketing of goods in commerce [Fair Labor Standards Act of 1938, p. 1].

On the basis of previous court decisions, opponents anticipated that the Fair Labor Standards Act would be declared unconstitutional. Nonetheless, they feared that Roosevelt was plotting to appoint judges who shared his political philosophy. They became nervous after the president endorsed an initiative to expand the number of justices on the Supreme Court. They listened as the president characterized his initiative as judicial reorganization; they responded that it was an attempt to pack the court with political cronies.

The opponents of child labor reform had accused President Roosevelt of attempting to politically manipulate the Supreme Court. Although they were able to stop him, they still feared that he had enough power to influence the justices.

The Supreme Court justices eventually did agree with the president. They decided that the legislative branch of government, which had the authority to regulate interstate commerce, also had the authority to regulate the child laborers who were involved. Although they responded to legal issues, they may have responded to pressure from the president. They also may have responded to pressure from a public that had become increasingly censorious of child labor.

Activity: Child Labor and the Courts

The questions about which the Supreme Court justices deliberated were connected to legal issues. They also were connected to political and social events. When they deliberated about questions, were the justices influenced by political and social events? To help answer this question, create a chart.

Along the vertical axis of the chart, identify three momentous political or social events that occurred during 1938 or afterwards and that reflect the social and political context for legal questions about which the justices deliberated.

Table 9.1. Child Labor

Political or Social Event	*Significance*	*Influence on the Supreme Court*	*Explanation*

Along the horizontal axis of the chart, arrange several columns. In one of these columns, provide a short explanation about the reason that each event was socially or politically momentous. In still another column, identify one way in which each event might have affected the justices. In a final column, provide a brief explanation for your statements.

Your examples will be based on assumptions about the vested interests, values, and goals of the groups that were involved. Although you can use the information in the case study to make some of these assumptions, you may wish to rely on a broader foundation of information.

You can gather additional information from the materials that are listed at the end of this chapter. You may gather it from lectures or discussions.

Case Study 9.2: Compulsory Education

Educational reformers were troubled when the parents who wished to send children to school could not afford it. Therefore, they campaigned for free public education. However, they were troubled when some poor parents turned down this opportunity; they noted that many poor parents insisted that their children remain in workplaces.

Realizing that their plan still faced formidable opposition, the reformers tried to make school attendance compulsory. To attract supporters, they highlighted their plan's benefits. For example, they provided examples of the multiple ways in which schooling helped children; they noted that it enabled them to stay off the streets, keep away from dangerous workplaces, become literate, and qualify for desirable jobs.

Educational reformers noted that children were only one of the groups that would benefit from compulsory schooling. They pointed out that employers would benefit because the supply of sophisticated workers would increase. They pointed out that the government would benefit because more citizens would be able to communicate in English and meet the qualifications for military service.

They pointed out that organized labor would benefit because the number of persons competing for jobs would decrease.

Even though they expressed confidence in the benefits of compulsory schooling, some persons questioned its cost. Fiscal critics pointed out that the price of education, which already was substantial, would become higher still if all children attended tuition-free schools.

The fiscal critics patiently explained why compulsory schooling would raise the price of education. Those states that instituted compulsory schooling would have to build new schools. They would have to equip the new schools with furniture. They would have to purchase more textbooks. They would have to hire additional teachers, school administrators, clerical staff, and maintenance staff. They would have to hire additional doctors, nurses, social workers, security personnel, and truant officers.

Some state legislators worried about the impact of compulsory schooling on the business community. They feared that they might have to protect the financial interests of business and industry owners who depended on child labor. Some of them worried that they might have to protect the small farm and business owners who depended on child labor.

After they implemented compulsory education, school administrators discovered that numerous problems did accompany this practice. Although they anticipated some of these problems, they did not anticipate others. Furthermore, they were confused about how to react to some of the unanticipated problems; they were confused about how to react to the many nonacademic problems that indigent children created.

School administrators were nonplussed; they did not know how to react to the problems that were associated with poor hygiene, teenage pregnancy, unemployment, substance abuse, disease, malnutrition, emotional disability, and juvenile delinquency. Realizing that they were confronting community-wide problems, they suspected that they should collaborate with knowledgeable personnel in each community. However, they were unclear about how to promote this collaboration.

Like educators in many cities, educators in Chicago were distressed by the problems associated with compulsory schooling. They were especially upset about the problems that sick and unhealthy students created. They were disconcerted when parents complained that once-healthy children had begun to contract debilitating diseases from their classmates.

The educators in Chicago attempted to devise solutions for the problems that poor and sickly children had created. They clothed these children, fed them nutritious meals, and provided them with medical inoculations. They asked specialists to examine their eyes, ears, and teeth; they hired full-time nurses to provide hygienic and medical assistance.

Struck by the greater amount of disease during the winter months, educators in Chicago concluded that the increase was caused by the germ-laden air in the classrooms. Therefore, they bundled children in winter coats and opened the windows of their classrooms. Sometimes they sent them to study on the frigid but supposedly germ-free roofs of their buildings.

Some Chicagoans suspected that old textbooks might be the repositories for germs. In affluent neighborhoods, school administrators replaced old textbooks with new and sanitary volumes; in less affluent neighborhoods, they sprayed the diseased textbooks with disinfectants. In spite of the time, effort, and funds that they expended, they detected few improvements.

Jane Addams was a social reformer who was aware of the diverse problems that the Chicago educators were confronting. She developed an innovative way of responding: She began to combine education with social and health services. During the late 1800s and early 1900s, she provided hybrid services in a community-based facility. Although legions of admirers wished to duplicate her facility and programs, few of them had the necessary resources.

School administrators and teachers were disappointed when they could not solve the complex problems in the schools. Students also were disappointed; they began to drop out of school. Some students dropped out with the approval of their parents; others did not seek it.

Because the early school administrators did not employ uniform reporting procedures, they did not leave records about the precise number of students who dropped out of school. Only during relatively recent decades have school administrators gathered these data. They discovered that thirty percent of students dropped out of school during the 1960s; they discovered that only 10 percent of them dropped out forty years later.

When analysts first began to examine dropout data, they noted that the percentages of male and female high school dropouts were comparable. However, they detected disparate patterns among racial and ethnic groups. They particularly were struck by the high dropout rates among Hispanic Americans.

The analysts noted that the dropout rate among Hispanic American students was a startling thirty-five percent in 1980. They contrasted this with the rates among white and African American students, which were eleven and nineteen percent respectively. Although the Hispanic dropout rate eventually declined to twenty-four percent, it remained higher than those of White and African American students, which respectively fell to seven and eleven percent during that same period.

When early educators worried about students dropping out of school, they turned to remedial educators, counselors, social workers, or truant officers. During recent eras, they have turned to these groups again.

Activity: Campaigning for Compulsory Education

Nineteenth-century reformers took steps so that parents could send their children to free public schools. However, they were upset when parents ignored the schools and sent their children to work in factories, stores, restaurants, and farms. Therefore, they campaigned for compulsory school attendance laws. How

Table 9.2. Compulsory Education

Group	Late 1800*	Early 1900*	Late 1900*	Rationale
Parents—Working Children				
Parents—Non-Working Children				
Hispanic American Parents				
African American Parents				
Members of Labor Unions				
Employers				
Teachers				
School Administrators				
Liberal Politicians				
Conservative Politicians				

* (+) Supported
(-) Opposed
(+/-) Mixed Commitment

did different groups respond to their campaigns? To help answer this question, create a chart.

Along the vertical axis of the chart, arrange the following groups: parents of working children, parents of non working children, Hispanic American parents, African American parents, members of labor unions, employers, teachers, school administrators, liberal politicians, and conservative politicians.

Along the horizontal axis of the chart, arrange several columns. In one column, indicate whether each group primarily supported (+), opposed (-), or showed a mixed commitment (+/-) to regulations promoting compulsory education during the late 1800s. In another column of the chart, indicate the attitudes of each group to regulations promoting compulsory education early in the twentieth century. In still another column of the chart, indicate the attitudes of each group to regulations promoting compulsory education during the late part of the twentieth century.

Your indications about the responses of the groups should be based on assumptions about the vested interests, values, and goals of their members. Although you can use the information in the case study to make some of these assumptions, you may wish to rely on a broader foundation of information.

You can gather additional information from the materials that are listed at the end of this chapter. You may gather it from lectures or discussions.

In a separate column, or possibly on a separate page, summarize your assumptions about each group.

Case Study 9.3: Teachers Join Organized Labor

Workers had different reasons for joining unions. Some of them joined because they were paid low wages; others joined because they lacked job security, toiled for extended periods, or faced hazards. Some workers, such as those in the steel, railroad, textile, meatpacking, and mining industries, joined because they had to deal with all of these adverse conditions.

Even though the conditions under which early teachers had labored were not utterly bleak, they were far from ideal. For example, teachers could be discharged peremptorily. They might be fired if their supervisors judged them to be immoral; they might be fired if they judged them to be indecorous. They might be fired if their supervisors judged them to be associated with a rival political faction.

Teachers were worried about the precarious conditions under which they were hired and retained. They eventually asked professional organizations to protect them. However, these organizations were not labor unions. Even the founders of those organizations had not viewed them as labor unions.

When educators decided to establish a national organization in 1857, they set relatively modest goals. They had hoped that their organization, the National Teaching Association, would "promote the general welfare of [their] country," concentrate "the wisdom and power of numerous minds," and "advance the dignity, respectability and usefulness of their calling" (Valentine, 1857, p. 1).

The National Teaching Association grew rapidly. It grew by attracting new members. It also grew by merging with other organizations, such as those that had represented male college professors, male normal-school faculty members, and male school administrators. Because mergers had expanded the types of school personnel within the National Teaching Association, the officers decided to change the organization's name. They renamed it the National Education Association (NEA).

The members of the NEA had taken a daring step when they started their organization; they took another daring step when they allowed females to join it. This decision could have been anticipated because so many new teachers were females. However, the decision also was predictable because of the members' liberal political attitudes. During the late 1800s and early 1900s, they displayed those attitudes by inviting African American educators to address them, endorsing women's suffrage, and eventually electing a female as president.

In the early 1900s, the leaders of the NEA decided to make another important organizational change; they decided to convert their association into a labor union. They then analyzed data about teacher salaries and demonstrated that females earned less than males. They urged school administrators and community leaders to redress these salary inequities. They also urged them to provide job security and retirement pensions to both female and male teachers.

In order to effectively promote their lobbying agenda, the officers of the NEA relocated their headquarters from Minnesota to Washington, D.C. From this location, they were able to lobby federal lawmakers. In 1972, they amplified their lobbying efforts by disbursing funds to responsive lawmakers.

Activity: Teachers Join the Labor Movement

Educational reformers were concerned that some students and teachers were not treated fairly. They decided that educational unions could provide platforms from which to address both issues. They encouraged teachers to join them.

During distinct eras, how did different groups respond to teachers in unions? To help answer this question, create a chart.

Along the vertical axis of the chart, arrange the following groups: parents, employers, members of non-educational labor unions, school administrators, members of local school boards, liberal politicians, and conservative politicians.

Along the horizontal axis of the chart, arrange several columns. In one column, indicate whether each group primarily supported (+), opposed (-), or showed a mixed commitment (+/-) to unionized teachers during the early 1900s.

In another column of the chart, indicate each group's attitudes toward unionized teachers during the late 1900s. In still another column, indicate each group's recent attitudes toward unionized teachers.

Your indications about the responses of the groups during different eras should be based on assumptions about the vested interests, values, and goals of their members. Although you can use the information in the case study to make some of these assumptions, you may wish to rely on a broader foundation of information.

You can gather additional information from the materials that are listed at the end of this chapter. You may gather it from lectures or discussions.

Table 9.3. Teachers Join Organized Labor

Group	*Early 1900**	*Late 1900**	*Post-2000**	*Rationale*
Parents				
Employers				
Members of Non-Education Labor Unions				
School Administrators				
School Board Members				
Liberal Politicians				
Conservative Politicians				

* (+) Supported
(-) Opposed
(+/-) Mixed Commitment

In a separate column of the chart, or possibly on a separate page, summarize your assumptions about each group.

USING THE PAST TO UNDERSTAND THE PRESENT

During the nineteenth century, government and community leaders wished to dispense services to the children who were facing severe economic and social hardships. However, they had to identify institutions that would deliver those services. They searched for institutions that were ubiquitous and that had staffs trained to handle children. Realizing that local schools had these characteristics, they proposed that the schools enroll more children; they proposed that the schools enroll many more children from impoverished families.

When educators were asked to enroll more students, they agreed. However, they were unprepared for the numbers of children that came to them. They struggled because they did not have enough classrooms or teachers. They also struggled because they did not have enough textbooks and other learning materials.

Educators realized that the shortages of facilities, personnel, and equipment were problems that had clear and straightforward solutions. However, they were more worried about problems for which the solutions were murky and complex.

For example, educators were unsure about ways to help the many children with limited proficiency in English. They were unsure about ways to help children with part-time jobs. They were unsure about ways to help children who lacked appropriate clothing, nourishment, inoculations, and medical care. They were unsure about ways to help children who confronted crime, alcoholism, and drug abuse in their homes and neighborhoods.

Although teachers displayed sensitivity to their new students, they still asked practical questions about the best ways to help them. They also asked practical questions about themselves. They asked how they could protect themselves from personal and professional exploitation. Some teachers believed that teacher unionization contained the answers to both questions.

The early teachers were conflicted when they simultaneously attempted to help children and protect themselves. Do current teachers experience similar conflicts? To answer this question, identify a recent incident that reveals conflicting issues about which teachers were concerned. Identify an incident that has been reported by the media. How were the teachers' concerns about children's interests portrayed by the media? How were their concerns about their own professional interests portrayed? Ideally, locate an incident that transpired in your own state or community.

CHAPTER SUMMARY

Nineteenth-century reformers were convinced that all children should attend school. However, they were opposed by those employers who depended on children's labor. They also were opposed by those parents who depended on their children's income.

Distressed by the resistance that they had encountered, the reformers wished to make schooling mandatory. They pointed out the multiple ways in which mandatory schooling would help children. Children would benefit from academic learning; they also would benefit from the nutritious meals, medical checkups, inoculations, health care, and social services that the schools could provide.

The reformers pointed to ways in which mandatory schooling would help society. The military and the government would benefit from a better-educated citizenry. Employers would benefit from a better educated workforce.

Although they were concerned about students, the reformers also were concerned about teachers. They noted that teachers had been paid low wages, treated poorly, and deprived of job security. They counseled them to form labor unions.

ADDITIONAL READING

Introductory Passages

Hindman, H. D. (2002). *Child labor: An American history* (rev. ed.). Armonk, NY: Sharpe.

Lavalette, M. (Ed.). (1999). *A thing of the past: Child labour in Britain in the nineteenth and twentieth centuries.* New York: Palgrave Macmillan.

Sallee, S. (2004). *The whiteness of child labor reform in the New South.* Athens: University of Georgia Press.

Sinclair, U. (2003). *The Jungle: The uncensored original edition.* Tucson, AZ: See Sharp Press. (Original work published in 1906.)

Weston, B. H. (Ed.). (2005). *Child labor and human rights: Making children matter.* Boulder, CO: Rienner.

Whittaker, W. G. (2003). *Child labor in America: History, policy and legislative issues.* New York: Novinka.

Case Study 9.1: Child Labor

Finkelman, P., & Urofsky, M. I. (2007). *Landmark decisions of the United States Supreme Court* (2nd ed.). Washington, DC: CQ Press.

Greenburg, J. C. (2007). *Supreme conflict: The inside story of the struggle for control of the United States Supreme Court.* New York: Penguin.

Hartman, G. R., Mersky, R. M., & Tate, C. L. (2006). *Landmark Supreme Court cases: The most influential decisions of the Supreme Court of the United States.* New York: Checkmark.

Rosen, J. (2007). *The Supreme Court: The personalities and rivalries that defined America.* New York: Times.

Schwartz, B. (1994). *A History of the Supreme Court.* New York: Oxford University Press.

Case Study 9.2: Compulsory Education

Cremin, L. A. (1970). *American education: The colonial experience, 1607–1783.* New York: Harper & Row.

Cremin, L. A. (1980). *American education: The national experience, 1783–1876.* New York: HarperCollins.

Cremin, L. A. (1990). *American education: The metropolitan experience, 1876–1980.* New York: HarperCollins.

Dorn, S. (1996). *Creating the dropout: An institutional and social history of school failure.* New York: Praeger.

Fry, R. (2003). *Hispanic youth dropping out of U.S. schools: Measuring the challenge.* Pew Hispanic Center. (Retrieved on 6 November 2008 from: http://pewhispanic.org/reports/report.php?ReportID=19.)

National Institute on the Education of At-Risk Students. (1996). *High school dropout rates.* Washington, DC: U.S. Department of Education. (Retrieved on 6 November 2008 from: http://www.ed.gov/pubs/OR/ConsumerGuides/dropout.html.)

Parkerson, D. H., & Parkerson, J. (1998). *The emergence of the common school in the U.S. countryside.* Lewiston, NY: Mellen.

Ravitch, D. (2000). *Left back: A century of failed school reforms.* New York: Simon & Schuster.

Reese, W. J. (1995). *The origins of the American high school.* New Haven, CT: Yale University Press.

U.S. Census Bureau. (2002). *School enrollment: Social and economic characteristics of students, October 2002.* Washington, DC: Author. (Retrieved on 6 November 2008 from: http://www.census.gov/population/www/socdemo/school/cps2002.html.)

U.S. Census Bureau. (2003). *School enrollment: Social and economic characteristics of students, October 2003.* Washington, DC: Author. (Retrieved on 6 November 2008 from: http://www.census.gov/population/www/socdemo/school/cps2003.html.)

U.S. Census Bureau. (2004). *School enrollment: Social and economic characteristics of students, October 2004.* Washington, DC: Author. (Retrieved on 6 November 2008 from: http://www.census.gov/population/www/socdemo/school/cps2004.html.)

U.S. Department of Education. (2001). *Dropout rates in the United States: 2000.* Washington, DC: Author. (Retrieved on 6 November 2008 from: http://nces.ed.gov/pubs2002/droppub_2001.)

U.S. Department of Education. (2004). *Issue brief: Educational attainment of high school drop outs eight years later.* Washington, DC: Author. (Retrieved on 6 November 2008 from: http://nces.ed.gov/pubs2005/2005026.pdf.)

Case Study 9.3: Teachers Join Organized Labor

Blewett, M. H. (1990). *Men, women, and work: Class, gender, and protest in the New England shoe industry, 1780–1910.* Champagne: University of Illinois Press.

Cobble, D. S. (2003). *The other women's movement: Workplace justice and social rights in modern America.* Princeton, NJ: Princeton University Press.

Devault, I. A. (1995). *Sons and daughters of labor: Class and clerical work in turn-of-the-century Pittsburgh.* Cornell, NY: Cornell University Press. (Original work published in 1990.)

Dubofsky, M., & Dulles, F. R. (2004). *Labor in America: A history* (7th ed.). Wheeling, IL: Harlan Davidson.

Jacobs, J. (2007). *Mobsters, unions, and feds: The Mafia and the American labor movement.* New York: New York University Press.

Kessler-Harris, A. (2006). *Gendering labor history.* Champagne: University of Illinois Press.

Lichtenstein, N. (2003). *State of the union: A century of American labor.* Princeton, NJ: Princeton University Press.

O'Farrell, B., & Kornbluh, J. L. (Eds.). (1996). *Rocking the boat: Union women's voices, 1915–1975.* New Brunswick, NJ: Rutgers University Press.

Chapter Ten

Curriculum: Promoting Quality with Tests

To determine whether students were learning, early educators made them recite key pieces of information. However, the teachers were faulted for inefficiency and bias. Therefore, they searched for an alternative assessment procedure. They hoped to find a procedure that was reliable, objective, easy to administer, and simple to score. Although some of them judged that standardized testing had these characteristics, they had difficulty responding to questions from skeptics.

TESTING TODAY

People wanted evidence about the schools. Parents wanted evidence that children were learning. Employers wanted evidence that workers were prepared for jobs. Military leaders wanted evidence that young men were ready for the armed services. Taxpayers wanted evidence that the schools were operating efficiently.

In response to these demands, standardized tests were introduced into schools in the early twentieth century. However, many teachers resisted them. Some of them resisted because they did not understand the hermetic concepts on which the new tests were based. Some resisted because they had difficulty reconciling the new tests with their humanistic philosophies. Some resisted because they feared that the new tests would be used to challenge their effectiveness as instructors.

Just as early educators had focused their attention on standardized tests, so did later generations. In fact, they became especially concerned about tests during the era of high-stakes assessment. The members of disputing factions used the phrase *high-stakes* for distinct rhetorical purposes. Proponents of testing used it to promote accountability; opponents used it to illustrate the excessive politicizing of education.

When the proponents and opponents of high-stakes testing had disputes, the proponents usually prevailed. They prevailed because they were able to attract political allies. For example, they attracted those parents who agreed with the philosophical assumptions on which standardized testing was based.

The proponents of high-stakes testing attracted even those parents who were skeptical about the philosophical assumptions of standardized testing. The skeptical parents sided with the proponents of tests because they were pragmatists; they recognized that tests influenced the academic, vocational, and social opportunities that were available to their children. They concluded that their children had no alternative other than to prepare for a world in which performances on tests mattered.

EARLY ACADEMIC TESTS

Most nineteenth-century teachers had relied on oral recitations to evaluate their students; some had supplemented with written exams that they had created. The early teachers had a hard time implementing these informal assessment procedures; they also had a hard time demonstrating that the procedures were objective and reliable.

Early twentieth-century educators began to look for a new approach to assessment. They were impressed with the standardized tests that psychologists had developed. They hoped that they could use some of their psychological tests in the schools; they hoped that they could develop academic tests that had similar characteristics. They hoped that the new assessment instruments could be administered rapidly and scored objectively.

Critics of the schools were concerned about assessment in the schools. They were concerned about assessments being done by the many teachers who had defined their own curricula; they especially were concerned when these assessments were performed by poorly trained teachers. To protect children from incompetent instructors, the critics insisted that teachers rely on textbooks (Giordano, 2003). They viewed standardized testing as a way of strengthening that protection.

Educational critics who were philosophically and politically entwined with the standards and efficiency movement valued testing. They were not the only group. Many scholars valued testing. The scholars believed that testing could be the basis for scientific educational progress. These scholars called attention to the innovative research studies that J. M. Rice had conducted.

Rice was a medical doctor who was concerned about the many teachers who relied excessively on spelling. In two key reports (Rice 1897a; 1897b), he analyzed the relationship between the amount of classroom time that students spent on spelling activities and the scores they earned on spelling tests. He concluded that scores on tests had not necessarily increased after students had increased the amount of time that they spent on spelling.

Educators who emphasized spelling were upset by Rice. Some of them may have been annoyed because he was a physician rather than a professional educator. Others were annoyed by the philosophical chasm that separated Rice's ideas from their own ideas. They berated Rice for failing to realize that the objective of classroom spelling exercises was to nurture the intellect. They were ready to substantiate this contention through observations made in their classrooms.

The early proponents of standardized assessment were able to design tests to measure whether students had mastered the content in academic subjects. They readily developed tests for mathematics and spelling. Although they faced challenges, they developed tests for reading, history, handwriting, foreign languages, and the sciences. They also developed assessment instruments for specialized subjects, such as art appreciation, bookkeeping, dictionary use, and political science. They even created diagnostic tests to detect the reasons that students were not progressing.

OPPOSITION TO STANDARDIZED TESTS

Early twentieth-century critics of standardized tests believed that the new assessment instruments were invalid. They warned that they could be used to foster racial and ethnic discrimination.

Although later critics remained concerned about the link between testing and discrimination, they fretted about new issues. They alleged that the large and powerful test publishers had abused their responsibilities. They gave examples of these abuses; they claimed that the publishers had exhibited conflicts of interests, demonstrated meager respect for consumers, and made excessive profits. They were extremely critical of the Educational Testing Service.

The directors of three nonprofit organizations had established the Educational Testing Service in 1947. Anticipating that the organization someday would be attacked, they designed it to withstand even the most intense assaults.

Thirty-three years after the Educational Testing Service was founded, Ralph Nader and a group of political activists made an intense assault on this organization. Nader accused the Educational Testing Service of employing invalid tests; he also accused it of ruthlessness and greed. Although he did not have evidence with which to prove these charges, Nader claimed that the organization's clandestine methods of operation constituted circumstantial indications of guilt.

TESTING EXPANDS

The testing industry initially began to expand after World War I. Postwar businesspersons who already had realized that textbooks were profitable suspected that educational testing could be equally profitable. Some of them wondered whether it might be even more profitable.

Publishers devised tests for the new markets that were emerging; they devised them for elementary schools, high schools, vocational schools, institutions of higher learning, the government, the military, commerce, and industry. Observers were struck by the speed with which these testing markets expanded. By the early 1930s, over 3,500 assessment instruments were available (Hildreth, 1933).

As the number of tests that were on the market increased, the number of tests that were purchased increased. In the early twentieth century, most school districts spent only modest amounts of money on tests. In fact, one alarmed critic had written that New York City had been spending "hardly a dollar" on assessment (unidentified editorialist, quoted by Taylor, 1912, p. 348). Although the annual assessment budget for the New York City schools may have been modest in the early 1900s, it grew noticeably. By 1924, it had mushroomed to $100,000 (Cardozo, 1924).

By the 1920s, many school districts had established assessment budgets. However, they did not place uniform amounts of money in them. The assessment budgets in California's rural school districts ranged from $35 to $2,000 during the early 1920s (Russell, 1925). These budgets contained only the money that the districts used to purchase tests; they did not contain the funds spent on labor, facilities, and equipment needed to administer tests. As a result, the genuine expenditures on standardized assessment were greater than budgetary ledgers revealed.

Case Study 10.1: High-Stakes Tests Emerge

At the beginning of the twentieth century, most persons were unaware of the mental tests that psychologists already had developed. However, they learned about them after the United States entered World War I.

Military leaders had been assessing the physical aptitudes of new soldiers; they wondered whether they should assess their mental aptitudes as well. They hired Robert Yerkes, an expert in psychological assessment, to help them. They gave him $2,500 to experimentally classify four thousand soldiers. They asked him to classify those soldiers who were fit for service, those who were unfit for service, and those who were extremely talented.

Yerkes used his budget to print materials, equip examination rooms, and pay for test administrators. He then conducted his experiment, analyzed the results, and wrote a report. His report convinced the military leaders that testing was invaluable.

The military leaders established a school for training specialized test administrators. Persons were taught to administer and score the alpha test. Yerkes had designed this test for the large group of hundreds of thousands of soldiers who could speak, read, and write in English.

The persons who attended the testing school also learned to administer the beta test. Although they gave this test to persons with mental disabilities, they gave it primarily to soldiers who had normal intelligence but who could not speak, read, or write in English. When they administered this test, they gave it to small groups, explained the requirements through gestures, and supplemented with pictorial instructions.

Yerkes had the background to assess soldiers' intelligence and their emotional stability. However, he had other useful experiences. He had collaborated with prewar industrialists to test workers' career aptitudes, vocational achievements, and technical proficiencies. Army leaders asked Yerkes to develop tests of this sort for armed forces personnel. They also asked him to develop special tests to assess aptitudes for some of the military's distinctive vocations, such as piloting combat planes and calling in artillery strikes.

Members of the public became interested in military testing for several reasons. They were interested in it because of its large scale; they were impressed that hundreds of thousands of recruits were being evaluated. They were interested in it because of its novelty; they were amazed that soldiers could be assessed and classified in only several hours. They were interested in it because of its practicality; they hoped that testing represented a solution to a critical wartime problem.

Although the military's testing program generated curiosity, it also generated apprehension. Some people were apprehensive when they learned about the low scores that servicemen were earning. They became even more apprehensive after they read alarmist editorials about those scores.

Robert Yerkes disagreed with the journalists who wrote sensational reports in the newspapers. Nonetheless, he acknowledged the damage that they were causing. Yerkes quoted a passage that had been written by one of these critics.

> The army mental tests have shown that there are, roughly, forty-five million people in this country who have no sense. Their mental powers will never be greater than those of twelve-year-old children. The vast majority of these will never attain even this meager intelligence [Unidentified wartime editorialist, quoted by Yerkes, 1923, p. 358].

Political conservatives had believed that testing in the armed services promoted efficiency. Political conservatives also were enthusiastic about testing in the schools, where they believed that it could promote fiscal accountability (Giordano, 2004). Comparing education to business, they urged school administrators to adopt the principles that managers were implementing in industry, retail, and service enterprises.

During World War I, conservatives detected another reason for administering standardized tests in the schools. Startled by the scores that servicemen were earning on the military tests, they alleged that their low scores were symptoms of national weaknesses. They blamed the schools for these weaknesses.

Alarmed by the educational conditions that testing had revealed, conservative critics were convinced that national security was threatened. They demanded that school administrators take protective steps. One of these steps was continued testing. Some of them urged continued testing in order to monitor students; others urged it to monitor teachers.

The conservative critics had another protective measure that they wanted the school administrators to implement. They urged them to maintain the special programs that they had started during the war. In fact, they urged them to expand these programs.

Political liberals were not impressed by the educational problems to which the conservatives had pointed; they did not share their confidence in standardized testing. They also were not impressed with the protective measures that the conservatives had recommended. They disapproved of their proposals to assess students and teachers through standardized tests; they disapproved of their proposal to retain the wartime school initiatives.

When the United States was engaged in World War I, military leaders had relied on testing. However, they halted the testing program at the end of the war. They may have made this decision because they no longer had to deal with millions of conscripts. They also may have succumbed to pressure from those military authorities who were questioning the value of the testing program (Giordano, 2004).

Once the military leaders had terminated their testing program, they discharged the psychologists that they had trained. The director of the United States Bureau of Education encouraged school administrators to hire the discharged psychologists immediately. He explained that they could rely on the psychologists to measure the results of teaching, classify children with disabilities, identify students who were gifted, determine criteria for promotion, make suggestions about organizing classrooms, and give advice about operating special schools (Claxton, 1919).

Activity: Early High-Stakes Testing in the Schools

Early twentieth-century educators were criticized for the cumbersome and subjective ways in which they had assessed students. They looked for an alternative

Table 10.1. Tests Emerge

Group	*Support**	*Explanation*
Parents		
Teachers		
School Psychologists		
School Administrators		
School Board Members		
Employers		
Liberal Politicians		
Conservative Politicians		
Commercial Publishers		

* (+) Supported
(-) Opposed
(+/-) Mixed Commitment

assessment technique. Hoping that standardized testing would satisfy their critics, they introduced it into the schools.

How do you think groups responded to the introduction of standardized educational testing? To help answer this question, create a chart.

Along the vertical axis of the chart, arrange the following groups: parents, teachers, school psychologists, school administrators, members of local school boards, employers, liberal politicians, conservative politicians, and commercial publishers.

Along the horizontal axis of the chart, arrange several columns. In one column, indicate whether each group primarily supported (+), opposed (-), or showed a mixed commitment (+/-) to standardized educational testing.

Your indications about the responses of the groups should be based on assumptions about the vested interests, values, and goals of their members.

Although you can use the information in the case study to make some of these assumptions, you may wish to rely on a broader foundation of information.

You can gather additional information from the materials that are listed at the end of this chapter. You may gather it from lectures or discussions.

In a separate column of the chart, or possibly on a separate page, summarize your assumptions about each group.

Case Study 10.2: Opposition to Tests

Supporters of standardized educational tests were able to articulate reasons for using them. However, the opponents were equally articulate. The opponents were skeptical of tests for practical reasons. They claimed that they were priced too high, required too much time to administer, comprised hermitic concepts, contained poorly worded questions, and robbed students of instructional time.

Some of the opponents of standardized tests were disturbed for additional reasons. They were disturbed by the philosophical implications of the new assessment instruments. They alleged that standardized tests were based on research by animal psychologists; they questioned whether this research could be generalized to humans.

Some critics attacked tests for promoting social and political injustice. They were outraged after the advocates of eugenics cited test scores to justify racist policies. Critics such as Walter Lipmann (1922) confronted the eugenicists; he contended that low test scores by minority groups were the result of cultural biases within the tests. He fumed at his opponents for attempting to replace egalitarian education with an "intellectual caste system."

Forty years after Lippmann had fired his broadsides against standardized testing, critics continued to blame it for advancing elitism. A group of scholars within the American Psychological Association claimed that it advanced racism. They counseled professionals "to use educational and psychological tests with minority group children in ways that will enable these children to attain the full promise that America holds out to all of its children" (Fishman, Deutsch, Kogan, North, and Whiteman, 1963, p. 1).

One group of mental health professionals worried that African American children would be placed at a disadvantage if they were examined by non-African American psychologists. Therefore, they recommended that African Americans oppose all assessments that were not administered by minority psychologists.

The members of the New York City Board of Education were extremely concerned about the ways in which tests might influence students from minority groups. Therefore, they banned all group-administered intelligence testing in their schools (Loretan, 1965).

In the late 1960s, the members of the National Association of Black Psychologists encouraged parents to block the administration of standardized tests to African American children. However, they made this advice even more restrictive during the early 1970s. They encouraged the parents to examine their children's scholastic records and then remove "all quantitative and qualitative data obtained from performance on past and presently used standard psychometric, educational achievement, employment, general aptitude and mental ability tests" (Resolution from the Association of Black Psychologists, 1972, quoted by Rivers, Mitchell, and Williams, 1975, p. 63).

During the late 1970s, members of the public were confused by the debates about the benefits and liabilities of standardized testing. The members of local school boards demonstrated their confusion when they responded to a survey about testing programs. More than a third of the respondents indicated that the assessment programs in their districts were not worth the time and money that they were investing in them (National School Boards Association, 1977).

Activity: Debates About Testing during the 1960s and 1970s

Early twentieth-century critics had doubts about standardized educational tests. They had questioned their cost, practicality, validity, and the philosophy on

Table 10.2. Opposition to Tests

Group	*Support**	*Explanation*
Minority Parents		
Non–Minority Parents		
Teachers		
School Administrators		
School Board Members		
Liberal Politicians		
Conservative Politicians		

* (+) Supported
(-) Opposed
(+/-) Mixed Commitment

which they were based. They had worried that they could reinforce social injustices.

During the 1960s and the 1970s, critics continued to question standardized tests. They continued to debate with the advocates of tests. They continued to influence the ways in which teachers, professionals, and the general public viewed tests.

How did groups view standardized educational tests during the 1960s and the 1970s? To help answer this question, create a chart.

Along the vertical axis of the chart, arrange the following groups: parents from minority groups, nonminority parents, teachers, school administrators, members of local school boards, liberal politicians, and conservative politicians.

Along the horizontal axis of the chart, arrange several columns. In one column, indicate whether each group primarily supported (+), opposed (-), or showed a mixed commitment (+/-) to standardized educational tests during the 1960s and the 1970s.

Your indications about the responses of the groups should be based on assumptions about the vested interests, values, and goals of their members. Although you can use the information in the case study to make some of these assumptions, you may wish to rely on a broader foundation of information.

You can gather additional information from the materials that are listed at the end of this chapter. You may gather it from lectures or discussions.

In a separate column of the chart, or possibly on a separate page, summarize your assumptions about each group.

Case Study 10.3: Standardized Tests Reemerge in California

During the 1980s, Californians had watched their population expand rapidly. As their schools attracted many new students, they had to address numerous questions. They had to address questions about educational facilities, teachers, learning materials, and curricula.

Californians also had to address questions about instruction. In fact, two highly opinionated factions had emerged. The members of one faction had recommended that students master uniform academic skills. They were advocates of skills-based instruction and textbooks.

The members of the other California faction had supported holistic instruction. They had recommended that individual students learn only those academic skills for which they were developmentally ready. They were sympathetic to the pedagogical philosophy on which progressive educators once had relied.

The Californians argued about instruction in the various subjects of the curriculum. Nonetheless, they had a special interest in reading. The advocates of skills-based instruction insisted that teachers identify precise literacy skills, sequence them, and reinforce them with structured learning materials.

The advocates of whole language disagreed. They believed that reading was a natural process; they recommend that teachers synchronize literacy skills to oral language skills. They discouraged the use of textbooks and promoted the use of children's literature.

Californians were concerned about the millions of minority students with limited proficiency in English. One faction stipulated that the skills-based approach was ideal for these learners; they argued that the children would benefit as they simultaneously learned to read and speak in English.

The opponents of skills-based instruction had a different opinion. They argued that the pronunciation of words in English needlessly complicated reading. Pointing to the historically high rate at which minority students had failed in phonics-centered literacy programs, they claimed that many of these students would have been successful had their teachers used whole language.

The opponents of skills-based instruction recommended a holistic approach. They reasoned that a holistic approach would enable bilingual learners to rely on English, Spanish, or both languages while they were attempting to decipher the meanings of written passages.

The California dispute attracted the attention of a national audience. Literacy experts, the members of professional educational associations, and representatives of teachers unions became involved. Politicians also became involved.

Conservative California politicians tended to endorse the skills-based programs. However, the conservatives had lost credibility with some of their constituents. They alienated Hispanic residents when they attempted to reduce the number of illegal immigrants in their state, bar children of illegal immigrants from school services, reduce the funding for bilingual education, and promote the exclusive use of the English language in government transactions. When they endorsed skills-based instruction, they were censured for promoting their political interests.

Liberal California politicians tended to endorse whole language. They had won the confidence of many Hispanic residents through the political initiatives that they endorsed. However, they had alienated some other influential groups. When they endorsed whole language, the groups they had antagonized censured them for promoting their political interests.

Californians needed research to help them sort through their complex educational problems. They needed research about students who had learned with skills-based and holistic programs. Although they agreed about the research questions that they wanted to resolve, they did not agree about the type of test they would employ to answer those questions.

Most supporters of skills-based instruction believed that phonics skills were invaluable; therefore, they recommended that students complete tests that incorporated phonics. The supporters of whole language disagreed. They viewed reading as an individualized process that could be measured best by classroom observations. They thought that teachers should observe the amount of time that children spent reading, the number of books that they read, and the types of books that they read.

Traditionally, authorities at the California Department of Education had allowed teachers to employ both skills-based and holistic approaches. Beginning in 1988, they required them to employ whole language exclusively. They then directed them to measure the results with holistic procedures.

Because of state-mandated restrictions, California residents had difficulty gauging their children's performance on standardized tests. Nonetheless, they still had access to some data from standardized tests; they had access to the National Assessment of Educational Progress. The National Assessment of Educational Progress was a federally managed initiative that compared the academic achievements of students, including those in California; it relied on standardized tests.

Traditionally, students in California had scored in the upper percentiles on standardized academic achievement tests. However, their literacy scores plummeted during the 1990s. California's teachers, school administrators, parents, employers, community leaders, politicians, and journalists noticed the falling scores. A national audience also noticed.

Once the declining test scores had been brought to their attention, many Californians were upset. However, the proponents of whole language pointed out that the number of academically unprepared students in the schools had been increasing. They hypothesized that many of the low scores had been earned by students who had arrived recently in the United States, who spoke limited English, and who would have received low scores on any standardized English-language test.

The proponents of whole language criticized the National Assessment of Educational Progress. They alleged that this initiative had underestimated the number of students who were making genuine progress. They directed their critics to examine informal assessment measures in order to discern that progress.

California's legislators were not impressed with the recommendations from the proponents of whole language. Instead of following their advice, the legislators enacted laws to restrict the instruction and assessment of reading in their state.

Activity: Standardized Tests Reemerge in the California Schools

Californians had searched for the optimal way to nurture and assess reading. Some of them supported skills-based approaches; others supported whole language.

In the late 1980s, holistic instruction and assessment became mandatory in California. However, students' scores on standardized reading tests soon declined. Eventually, skills-based instruction reemerged, and so did standardized testing.

How did groups react to the reemergence of standardized testing in California? To help answer this question, create a chart.

Along the vertical axis of the chart, arrange the following groups: parents, school administrators, members of local school boards, employers, liberal poli-

Table 10.3. Standardized Tests Reemerge in California

Group	*Support**	*Explanation*
Parents		
School Administrators		
School Board Members		
Employers		
Liberal Politicians		
Conservative Politicians		
Scholastic Publishers		

* (+) Supported
(-) Opposed
(+/-) Mixed Commitment

ticians, conservative politicians, and scholastic publishers. Along the horizontal axis of the chart, arrange several columns. In one column, indicate whether each group primarily supported (+), opposed (-), or showed a mixed commitment (+/-) to the expansion of high-stakes testing.

Your indications about the responses of the groups should be based on assumptions about the vested interests, values, and goals of their members. Although you can use the information in the case study to make some of these assumptions, you may wish to rely on a broader foundation of information.

You can gather additional information from the materials that are listed at the end of this chapter. You may gather it from lectures or discussions.

In a separate column of the chart, or possibly on a separate page, summarize your assumptions about each group.

USING THE PAST TO UNDERSTAND THE PRESENT

Critics worried that American students might be taking an excessive number of standardized tests. One critic estimated that they were completing more than 100,000,000 tests annually during the 1980s (Fiske, 1988). Another critic speculated that this number rose to 400,000,000 during the 1990s (Sacks, 1999).

Critics objected to excessive testing; they also objected to the cost of that testing. A 1980s critic reported that elementary and high school tests enabled publishers to earn annual profits that were greater than $100,000,000 (Bencivenga, 1985). Another critic alleged that the citizens of Texas had spent nearly this amount on a test that they had adopted during the 1990s. This critic opined that the scholastic publishers had been the clear beneficiaries of the Texas testing initiative (Sacks, 1999).

The critics and the advocates of standardized assessment disagreed about the number of tests that were administered, the reasons that they were administered, their costs, and their benefits. However, they agreed that scholastic testing had been growing. They also agreed that this growth would not have transpired without the cooperation of businesspersons, politicians, and educators.

To what extent has cooperation among businesspersons, politicians, and educators contributed to the expansion of educational testing? To answer this question, identify a recent incident in which these groups have collaborated. Describe the ways in which they collaborated. Attempt to find an incident that transpired in your state or community.

CHAPTER SUMMARY

Critics were disappointed with the ways in which the early educators had assessed their students. They urged them to find a technique that was reliable, valid, easy to administer, and simple to score. Many educators believed that standardized testing had these features.

Although some educators admired standardized tests, others opposed them. They opposed them for several reasons. They questioned the philosophical base for standardized tests. They worried that standardized tests might perpetuate social injustice. They feared that student performance on standardized tests would be used to evaluate teachers.

ADDITIONAL READING

Introductory Passages

Bracey, G. W. (2003). *What you should know about the war against America's public schools.* Boston, MA: Allyn & Bacon.

Committee for Economic Development. (2001). *Measuring what matters: Using assessment and accountability to improve student learning.* (Retrieved on 25 July 2007 from: http://www.ced.org/docs/report/report_education.pdf.)

Cross, C. T. (2004). *Political education: National policy comes of age.* New York: Teachers College Press.

Finn, C. E., Jr., & Ravitch, D. (1987). Survey results: U.S. 17-year-olds know shockingly little about history and literature. *American School Board Journal, 174* (10), 31–33.

Giordano, G. (2005). *How testing came to dominate American schools: The history of educational assessment.* New York: Peter Lang.

Case Study 10.1: Tests Emerge

Gilliland, A. R., & Jordan, R. H. (1924). *Educational measurements and the classroom teacher.* New York: Century.

Goodenough, F. L. (1949). *Mental testing: Its history, principles, and applications.* New York: Rinehart.

Hawkes, H. E., Lindquist, E. F., & Mann, C. R. (Eds.). (1936). *The construction and use of achievement examinations.* Boston, MA: Houghton Mifflin.

Hull, C. L. (1928). *Aptitude testing.* New York: World.

Kepner, P. T. (1923). A survey of the test movement in history. *Journal of Educational Research, 7,* 309–325.

McGiverin, R. H. (1990). *Educational and psychological tests in the academic library.* New York: Haworth.

Monroe, W. S., DeVoss, J. C., & Kelly, F. J. (1917). *Educational tests and measurements.* Boston, MA: Houghton Mifflin.

Yoakum, C. S., & Yerkes, R. M. (Eds.). (1920). *Army mental tests.* New York: Holt.

Young, K. (1923). The history of mental testing. *Pedagogical Seminary, 31,* 1–48.

Case Study 10.2: Opposition to Tests

Gifford, B. (Ed.). (1989). *Test policy and test performance: Education, language, and culture.* Boston, MA: Kluwer.

Goodman, K. S. (1965). Dialect barriers to reading comprehension. *Elementary English, 42,* 853–860.

Graham, H. D. (1990). *The civil rights era: Origins and development of national policy, 1960–1972.* New York: Oxford University Press.

Gross, M. L. (1962). *The brain watchers.* New York: Random House.

Hartshorne, H., & May, M. A. (1928). *Studies in deceit: Book one—General methods and results.* New York: Macmillan.

Houts, P. L. (Ed.). (1977). *The myth of measurability.* New York: Hart.

Lemann, N. (1999). *The big test: The secret history of the American meritocracy.* New York: Farrar, Straus & Giroux.

Case Study 10.3: High-Stakes Tests

Carlos, L., & Kirst, M. (1997). California curriculum policy in the 1990s: "We don't have to be in front to lead." (*Research Reports and Case Studies.*) San Francisco, CA: WestEd. (Retrieved on 11 October 2007 from: http://www.wested.org/policy/pubs/full_text/pb_ft_cacuric.htm.)

Flesch, R. (1986). *Why Johnny can't read: And what you can do about it.* New York: Harper & Row. (Original work published in 1955.)

Gutloff, K. (1999). High-stakes tests: Rethinking curriculum. *NEA Today, 17* (6), 4–5.

Haney, W., Madaus, G. F., & Lyons, R. (1993). *The fractured marketplace for standardized testing.* Boston, MA: Kluwer Academic.

Hillocks, G., Jr. (2002). *The testing trap: How state writing assessments control learning.* New York: Teachers College Press.

Jennings, J. F. (1998). *Why national standards and tests: Politics and the quest for better schools.* Thousand Oaks, CA: Sage.

Jones, M. G., Jones, B. D., & Hargrove, T. Y. (2003). *The unintended consequences of high-stakes testing.* Lanham, MD: Rowman & Littlefield.

Kohn, A. (2000). *The case against standardized testing: Raising the scores, ruining the schools.* Portsmouth, NH: Heinemann.

Neill, M. (1999). Is high-stakes testing fair? *NEA Today, 17* (6), 6.

Nichols, S. L., & Berliner, D. C. (2007). *Collateral damage: How high-stakes testing corrupts America's schools.* Cambridge, MA: Harvard University Press.

Owen, D. (1999). *None of the above: The truth behind the SATs, revised and updated.* Lanham, MD: Rowman & Littlefield.

Popham, W. J. (2000). *Testing! Testing! What every parent should know about school tests.* Boston, MA: Allyn & Bacon.

Chapter Eleven

Learners: Helping Students with Disabilities

Many nineteenth-century Americans wished to send children with disabilities to asylums. The parents and relatives of children with disabilities objected to the inhumane treatments at the asylums. Frugal taxpayers objected to their high costs. Pressured by both groups, civic leaders searched for an alternative system of care. They asked school administrators to help by enrolling children with disabilities in the public schools. Even though school administrators agreed to accept the new students, they had to deal with numerous practical problems. They had to recruit specially trained teachers. They also had to devise special curricula, instructional strategies, and learning materials for them.

STUDENTS WITH DISABILITIES TODAY

Throughout the course of American history, minority groups have searched for ways to make social changes. Some of them created political friction in order to make changes. Persons with disabilities employed this strategy. They and their advocates created political friction to reduce bias and promote equity.

The parents of children with disabilities were visible advocates for their children; they advocated unrelentingly for educational reform. At the beginning of the twentieth century, most of them could obtain public care only at asylums or residential hospitals. However, they had a difficult time locating residential facilities that were not overcrowded. They also had a difficult time locating facilities that were not poorly maintained and inadequately staffed.

Parents of children with disabilities were excited about school-based care. They hoped that teachers would treat their children in a sensitive and caring manner; they hoped that they might educate them.

School administrators anticipated that parents of children with disabilities would support school-based care. However, they underestimated the resistance from other groups. Some persons opposed the plan because they feared that it would take a disproportionate amount of the teachers' time and energy. Some opposed it because they feared that it would gobble up educational budgets. Some opposed it because they feared that learners with disabilities would be destructive or violent.

Nineteenth-century American citizens frequently displayed fear toward persons with disabilities. Although twentieth-century citizens expressed those fears less often, they continued to harbor them. They feared that persons with disabilities would reduce public safety, public morality, and government budgets; they even feared that they would reduce the quality of the nation's genetic stock.

In spite of the pervasive prejudice, reformers attempted to make changes. They implored legislators to ensure that children with disabilities had access to the schools. They also implored them to enact laws ensuring access to public facilities and events.

The reformers were concerned that physical and architectural impediments could restrict mobility. They also were concerned that cultural and societal stereotypes could restrict independence, employment, health, civil rights, and human dignity.

Persons with disabilities campaigned for opportunities similar to those of other citizens. However, they faced obstacles. They realized that entrenched social attitudes comprised a major obstacle. They were struck by the number of adults who had biased attitudes but who did not have opportunities to interact with persons with disabilities. They worried that their limited opportunities for interaction had contributed to their biased attitudes.

Persons with disabilities realized that children were in different situations than adults. They noted that children in the schools had daily opportunities to interact and communicate with peers who had disabilities. They hoped that this situation would foster unbiased attitudes. They hoped that it would provide the basis for pervasive and genuine social change.

ASYLUMS

Early Americans had cared for family members with disabilities. Both wealthy and poor families historically had assumed this responsibility. Wealthy families were in better situations than impoverished families; they were able to hire knowledgeable, kind, and respectful caretakers.

Impoverished families lacked the financial means to hire professional help for relatives with disabilities. They lacked the training to provide this help themselves. When the parents as well as the siblings in these families were employed, the families even lacked the time to provide care.

Children with disabilities attracted attention in their communities. Some of them attracted attention because they were crippled, blind, deaf, or unable to speak. Some of them attracted attention because they were asocial or violent. Some of them attracted attention because they were neglected or abandoned.

During the nineteenth century, some Americans believed that persons with disabilities were genetically inferior and sexually promiscuous. They claimed that these traits assured that they would have children with the identical characteristics. They demanded that government officials prevent persons with disabilities from procreating; they demanded that they send them to asylums. When they discovered that the asylums were too crowded to accept new inmates, they urged the government to build more institutions.

Although some members of the community were upset with the asylums because they could not accommodate new patients, others were upset for different reasons. They were angry about the squalid conditions and inhumane practices at them. They urged the government to build clean and comfortable asylums.

Fiscally conservative critics formed another disgruntled group. Although they believed that persons with disabilities were a threat to society, they opposed asylums. They opposed them because they were expensive to build, maintain, and staff. They preferred to send persons with disabilities to relatively inexpensive facilities, such as jails, workhouses, poorhouses, or reformatories. They were distressed when they learned that these facilities were too crowded to accommodate additional inmates.

PUBLIC SCHOOLS

Parents had difficulty locating institutions to care for children with disabilities. Even parents who were able to make arrangements had grave reservations about them. The parents were dismayed that they would have limited opportunities to visit their children after the children became residential patients. They also were upset about the deplorable conditions to which their children would be subjected.

Civic leaders attempted to find some way to deal with the children with disabilities that were in their communities. They wished to find a way that would appease constituents who were frightened by these children, those who were concerned about the mistreatments in asylums, and those who thought that asylums were too expensive. They looked for new places to which they could send children with disabilities.

At the end of the nineteenth century, civic leaders believed that they had found the ideal places for children with disabilities; they would send them to the public schools. Because schools were situated in every neighborhood, they were accessible. Because schools were staffed by persons who were used to caring for children, they could provide humane care.

The civic leaders reasoned that parents would be happy to send their children to local schools rather than distant asylums. They assumed that they would be happy to assign them to loving teachers rather than uncaring staffs. They assumed that they would be even happier if their children were able to develop useful skills at the schools.

The civic leaders predicted that frugal taxpayers also would be pleased with their solution to the problem. After all, the schools would provide supervision at an extremely reasonable price. They hoped that even those persons who had insisted on restrictive supervision would be pleased; they hoped that these people would view the plan as an expedient way to increase the number of children with disabilities who were being supervised.

When school administrators in Boston, New York, Philadelphia, and several other large cities hired the first special educators, they asked them only to provide day care. However, the teachers were ambitious. They decided that they could not only care for the children but instruct them.

The special educators taught academic skills to children with moderate disabilities. They taught functional living skills to children with severe disabilities. They hoped that some of these students would progress to levels that would enable them to join regular education classrooms.

In addition to academic and living skills, special educators nurtured vocational skills. They hoped that vocational learning would keep students occupied during the course of the school day. They hoped that it would enable them to help with janitorial, culinary, and clerical tasks around the schools. They hoped that it would enable them to earn money. They hoped that it would enable some of them to live independently.

TEACHERS

School administrators who implemented special education programs faced practical problems. They needed space, instructional materials, and equipment. They desperately needed teachers. Although they initially reassigned primary-grade teachers to special education classrooms, they soon realized that the new teachers required a distinctive type of training.

The school administrators in large school districts such as New York and Boston attempted to prepare special education teachers through apprenticeships. However, they could not keep up with the demand for teachers. Therefore, they asked the colleges that had been training teachers for regular education to train them for special education as well. Many of the colleges complied.

Once they were appointed, the special education teachers were challenged by practical problems. One of their problems involved terminology. Although they relied on phrases such as "feeble-minded" or "backward" to describe students, some of them considered these terms to be demeaning. Furthermore, they could not agree about the meaning of these terms.

Because of disputes about terminology, the early special educators had difficulty making decisions about the students that they would admit into their programs. They also had difficulty communicating with the public and with their colleagues in regular education. They even had difficulty communicating with each other.

REVOLUTION

Persons with disabilities faced daunting challenges in the schools. They noted that African Americans also had faced overwhelming challenges. Impressed by the ways in which African American citizens had responded to their challenges, the persons decided to incorporate some of their strategies into their own educational crusade.

African Americans had achieved a legal milestone in 1954 when in the case of *Brown v. Board of Education of Topeka* the Supreme Court ruled that segregated schools were unconstitutional. However, those African Americans who had assumed that nationwide educational reforms would follow became disheartened when many communities refused to desegregate their schools.

African Americans continued to press for reforms. Through legislation, federal intervention, public protests, and litigation, they raised national awareness about the plight of minority children in the schools. They eventually forced communities to comply with the Supreme Court's directive. With their political allies, they created a social and educational revolution.

Other minority groups hoped to replicate the educational and political achievements of African Americans. Hispanic Americans lobbied for bilingual education. Females lobbied for education that was free of gender bias.

Persons with disabilities lobbied for education that was accessible to all children, including those with disabilities.

Persons with disabilities waged a complex political campaign. They attracted a broad alliance that included persons with disabilities, their relatives, community leaders, teachers, health care professionals, lawyers, judges, lawmakers, businesspersons, journalists, and social activists. Simultaneously pursuing redress in the courts, the legislature, and the media, they called attention to the many ways in which children with disabilities were suffering. They demanded revolutionary changes throughout society, including in the schools.

Case Study 11.1: Vacating Asylums

Even though nineteenth-century citizens worried about all adults with disabilities, they worried especially about women. One scholar warned that women were susceptible to disabilities because they "possess a more delicate organization, more refined sensibilities, more exquisite perceptions, and are, moreover, the subjects of repeated constitutional changes and developments of a magnitude and importance unknown to the other sex" (Churchill, 1851, p. 260).

Censorious citizens focused their attention on pregnant women. They claimed that pregnant women who did not display a motherly demeanor had disabilities; they warned that these women also tended to conceive children with disabilities. They cautioned that this tendency was even stronger when the women behaved immorally.

Some critics assumed that all women with disabilities were innately immoral. Relying on faulty logic, they inferred that all women who behaved immorally had disabilities. They advised authorities to round up and confine women with disabilities and women who were behaving immorally. Authorities in New York acted on this advice. During the late 1800s, they built detention facilities for women that were quickly filled with inmates.

Some critics were alarmed about the children of women with disabilities. They were convinced that heredity predestined these young persons to disreputable lives. They predicted that they eventually would engage in criminal acts, use illegal drugs, behave promiscuously, seduce persons, parent children with disabilities, and create a plague of inherited diseases. They demanded lifelong institutionalization of all children with disabilities; some of them demanded sterilization as well.

Scholars, educators, medical personnel, lawmakers, law enforcement personnel, social workers, and members of the public listened to alarmist warnings about the connection between disabilities, immorality, and crime. However, some of them were skeptical. They could identify numerous delinquent youths who did not have disabilities; they also could identify many well behaved youths who did have disabilities.

The skeptics questioned the warnings that the alarmists had provided; they also questioned the treatments that they had recommended. They wondered whether juvenile delinquents and youths with disabilities could be transformed into productive citizens. They began to side with the social reformers, who believed that juvenile delinquents and youths with disabilities could develop social, academic, and vocational skills and use these to lead productive lives.

The social reformers wanted to help delinquent youths; they also wanted to help those youths who had not yet become delinquents. They identified the public schools as the ideal places at which to establish inexpensive yet effective programs. They hoped that these programs could solve some of the social and economic problems that contributed to juvenile delinquency. They implored educators to assist them.

Reform-minded school administrators in Boston, New York, Detroit, and other large cities began to establish special education programs in the schools. They designed these programs for miscreant children as well as children with disabilities. They believed that their programs would reduce current incidents of misbehaviors; they hoped that they would reduce future incidents as well.

A school administrator in Detroit agreed with the reformers. He articulated the philosophy that guided the programs that he and his colleagues had established. He wrote that "while it may be true that the mentally retarded child is a potential sinner, it is equally true that he is also a potential saint, and whether he becomes a saint or a sinner will depend in large measure upon the type of training he receives" (Berry, 1923, p. 766).

Activity: Special Education

Nineteenth-century citizens were fearful of persons with disabilities; they wished to imprison them in asylums, reformatories, or restrictive facilities. Parents of children with disabilities objected because institutionalization was cruel. Frugal taxpayers objected because it was expensive. Pressured by constituents, civic leaders searched for an alternative to institutionalization. They eventually established day care programs in the schools.

How do you think groups responded when children with disabilities initially were placed in the public schools? To help answer this question, create a chart.

Along the vertical axis of the chart, arrange the following groups: parents of children with disabilities, parents of children without disabilities, teachers, school administrators, directors of asylums, wardens, religious leaders, liberal politicians, and conservative politicians.

Along the horizontal axis of the chart, arrange several columns. In one column, indicate whether each group primarily supported (+), opposed (-), or showed a mixed commitment (+/-) to the introduction of special education in the public schools.

Your indications about the responses of the groups should be based on assumptions about the vested interests, values, and goals of their members.

Table 11.1. Vacating Asylums

Group	*Support**	*Explanation*
Parents—Children with Disabilities		
Parents—Children without Disabilities		
Teachers		
School Administrators		
Asylum Directors		
Wardens		
Religious Leaders		
Liberal Politicians		
Conservative Politicians		

* (+) Supported
(-) Opposed
(+/-) Mixed Commitment

Although you can use the information in the case study to make some of these assumptions, you may wish to rely on a broader foundation of information.

You can gather additional information from the materials that are listed at the end of this chapter. You may gather it from lectures or discussions.

In a separate column of the chart, or possibly on a separate page, summarize your assumptions about each group.

Case Study 11.2: Practical Problems

Nineteenth-century American social reformers had pledged to help persons with disabilities. After several decades, they had made little progress. They were unsure about how they should proceed; they were unsure about how they should solve the many practical problems that they faced.

The Americans noticed that European educators had established impressive programs at asylums and then moved them into the public schools. Hopeful that the Europeans could give them advice, they invited them for a visit.

When the European consultants arrived, they were disappointed with the Americans. They were disappointed because the Americans had set their goals so low. They reported that the American guards and caregivers at asylums felt contempt for the persons that they were supervising; the Europeans added that they did not even try to conceal that contempt.

In spite of the many challenges that they faced, the Americans were optimistic that they could reform the care and education of persons with disabilities. They were gratified that many politically progressive members of the public agreed with them. They considered these persons to be allies; they hoped that additional allies would join them.

The American reformers recognized that they had to deal with pressing practical problems. Even though they were able to provide education in a few asylums, they were unable to introduce it into the public schools. They concluded that they would not be successful with their plan unless school administrators became their allies.

Those school administrators who questioned special education were formidable adversaries. Some of them questioned it because they were confused about disabilities and their origins. Their confusion was evident during their early attempts to help children with disabilities.

Prior to the introduction of special education, superintendents and principals in New York City persuaded physicians to help children with disabilities (Farrell, 1914). They originally invited the physicians into the schools to promote hygiene and health. Some of them asked the physicians to identify children with physical ailments. Some of them asked the physicians to treat them.

The school administrators believed that the diagnosis and treatment of physical ailments would reduce physical disabilities; they hoped that it also would reduce mental disabilities. In fact, some of them hoped that these efforts would eliminate mental disabilities in the schools.

The school administrators realized that the physicians were having little impact on hygiene, health, and physical disabilities. They eventually realized that they were having no impact on mental disabilities. They became discouraged.

In 1896, school administrators in Providence, Rhode Island, tried a novel strategy; they established a classroom for children with disabilities. Colleagues in New York, Philadelphia, Boston, and several other cities followed their example. However, the school administrators must have been disconsolate after critics referred to the new sessions as "fool classes." They realized that these critics were trying to disparage not only their new students but also the educators who had invited them into the schools. In spite of the criticism, they continued to enroll children with disabilities.

Parents requested that teachers make special adaptations for children with disabilities. Some school administrators ignored these requests. Others became angry; they retorted that teachers lacked the time and the training to make instructional adaptations for individual students. However, some school administrators sympathized with the parents; they agreed that the teachers should be sensitive to the individual needs of students.

American school administrators looked to Great Britain for strategies with which to individualize special education. They noted that the British educators grouped students to make it easier for them to prepare lessons and learning materials. For example, they instructed children who had physical disabilities separately from those who had mental disabilities. They even differentiated between children with certain types of physical disabilities, such as those that affected speech, hearing, vision, or mobility.

Although American educators saw the benefits of the British strategy, they had doubts about their ability to employ it. Some of them lacked the requisite financial resources. Even those educators who had funding could not proceed because of their feuding. They continually feuded about numerous topics, including the terminology with which to identify disabilities.

Unable to agree on terminology, American educators relied on their intuitions when they had to make critical decisions. For example, they relied on their intuitions when they admitted students to special education programs. As a result, some of them admitted students only because the students were odd or unable to speak in English.

By relying on informal admission procedures, educators filled classes with heterogeneous learners. They increased the confusion by randomly grouping learners with disabilities in a single room. Some of them grouped learners with mental, behavioral, visual, hearing, speech, and physical disabilities in the same classroom.

American special educators eventually realized that their students required distinctive types of instruction. To help them individualize instruction, some of them began to examine students' backgrounds. They used informal inventories to compile histories of familial illnesses and ancestral disabilities. They also collected information about nutritional habits, physical growth, and intellectual development. They even tried to compile records about immoral activities in which children might have engaged.

The special education teachers in New York City used information about students' backgrounds to design ingenious and unconventional instructional activities. They then shared their lessons with colleagues throughout the city, state, and region.

Educators sometimes developed eccentric lessons for children with disabilities. For example, they filled a room with items that appealed to a single sense. They hoped that students' experiences in this room would enable them to rely on that sense when they were learning. They reasoned that students with impaired vision would benefit from learning activities that required them to use nasal, tactile, auditory, or gustatory cues.

Although some special education teachers employed eccentric instructional methods and learning materials, most of them used methods and materials similar to those of the teachers in regular education classrooms. However, they implemented instruction in ways that were sensitive to individual learners.

The parents of children with disabilities praised the special education teachers for motivating their children and raising their academic achievement. The parents of children in regular education classrooms also took notice of the new teachers; they wondered whether their innovative instructional approaches could be transferred to their children's classrooms.

School administrators began to see the advantages of educating students with disabilities. They also began to see the advantages of educating them with distinctive instructional strategies and materials. Nonetheless, they realized that cost made these innovations difficult to implement. They realized that the cost increased when the innovations were augmented by novel technologies, assessment procedures, psychological services, and medical care.

In order to effectively implement special education programs, school administrators had to procure facilities, equipment, and supplies; they also had to find the funding with which to hire trained teachers and auxiliary staff. In many cases, they solved these problems by transferring money from other programs. However, they quickly realized that each of the programs from which they diverted funds had ardent proponents.

Activity: Solving Practical Problems

After school administrators began to admit children with disabilities to the public schools, they had to solve practical problems. They had to devise admission criteria, find facilities, gather learning materials, designate methods of instruction, and hire teachers.

How do you think groups responded to the practical problems that were associated with the early special education programs? To help answer this question, create a chart.

Along the vertical axis of the chart, arrange the following groups: school administrators, regular education teachers, health care professionals in the schools, school psychologists, and local school board members.

Along the horizontal axis of the chart, arrange several columns. In one column, indicate the importance that each group assigned to solving the practical problems associated with early special education programs. Select the value *1* if they viewed this as a matter of low importance, *2* if they viewed this as a matter of moderate importance, and *3* if they viewed this as a matter of great importance.

Your indications about the responses of the groups should be based on assumptions about the vested interests, values, and goals of their members. Although you can use the information in the case study to make some of these assumptions, you may wish to rely on a broader foundation of information.

You can gather additional information from the materials that are listed at the end of this chapter. You may gather it from lectures or discussions.

Table 11.2. Practical Problems

Group	*Practical Problems Associated with Special Education**	*Explanation*
School Administrators		
Regular Education Teachers		
Health Care Professionals		
School Psychologists		
School Board Members		

* 1: Low Importance
2: Moderate Importance
3: Great Importance

In a separate column of the chart, or possibly on a separate page, summarize your assumptions about each group.

Case Study 11.3: Politicians

During the nineteenth century, citizens in different states assigned distinct priorities to education. Residents in the Northeast were committed to education; in particular, residents in Massachusetts were strongly committed to it.

Citizens in many states were impressed by the way in which Massachusetts residents had educated their youths. They also had been impressed by the manner in which they cared for persons with disabilities.

In 1846, the Massachusetts residents appointed a commission to determine an appropriate way to provide care for persons with disabilities. On the basis of that commission's recommendations, they established a residential institution. They soon began to offer education to the inmates at that institution; they followed with other innovative programs for the inmates. They were one of the initial groups to invite children with disabilities into the schools.

Although many states implemented educational programs for adults and children with disabilities, they did not follow the schedule that Massachusetts had set. Many of them delayed their programs for decades. At the end of the nineteenth century, some states did not offer educational services to children with disabilities.

In most late nineteenth-century American communities, parents of children with disabilities had two opportunities to educate their children. They could keep them at home or they could send them to asylums. Those parents who kept their children at home faced problems; they lacked the prerequisite skills, time, and resources.

Those parents who wished to send their children to asylums also faced problems. Many of them could not locate an asylum that was not overcrowded. They noted that some institutions were so crowded that their staffs would admit additional patients only when ordered by the courts. Even when parents were able to find institutions that would accept their children, they were depressed by the dismal conditions and abusive staffs at them.

Educational reformers wanted to create new opportunities for children with disabilities. They insisted that they be assigned to local day care programs. They insisted that the children be treated humanely. They insisted that the children be given opportunities to learn skills and improve the quality of their lives.

The educational reformers were adamant about helping children with disabilities. The persons who opposed them were equally adamant. The opponents demanded programs that would protect society from children with disabilities. In fact, many of them believed that these children should be sexually sterilized and permanently imprisoned. Some of them wished to exterminate children with disabilities.

In spite of an anxious social mood, the reformers made progress. They made progress because they were able to attract political supporters. They attracted supporters from religious and charitable groups. They attracted supporters who wished to help children who were crippled, blind, or deaf. Although they had a more difficult time attracting persons to help children with behavioral and mental problems, they eventually did recruit them.

The reformers recommended that state governments assume the responsibility for helping children with disabilities. They were supported by physicians and psychologists and even law enforcement personnel. Accompanied by this powerful assembly, the reformers asked state legislators to designate public institutions that would provide care for children with disabilities. This political process was illustrated in Michigan.

Prior to 1871, Michigan's residents did not have access to state-managed programs for children with disabilities. Instead of sending children to state facilities, they sent them to county-funded poorhouses or church-funded asylums. The Michigan legislators then reimbursed the local governments or churches for these services.

Reformers in Michigan had questioned the quality of the care at the county-funded poorhouses and church-funded asylums. Furthermore, they had documented flagrant conflicts of interests. They were able to persuade their legislators to redirect the funding from the private and county programs to state-managed institutions.

Soon after the legislators in Michigan acted, New York's lawmakers passed similar legislation. Like the Michigan officials, the New Yorkers had been sending children with disabilities to local poorhouses and to church-based asylums. As had been the case in Michigan, they had changed their system after reformers had documented financial mismanagement, conflicts of interest, and poor care.

During the era when states began to create public institutions for children with disabilities, many legislators were concerned about the expense of the new programs (Best, 1930). Critics predicted that the special programs would affect regular education programs. When the public schools became the sites for special programs, the competition for limited funds was highlighted.

The reformers retorted that the education of persons with disabilities was not as expensive as the critics had portrayed it. They claimed that it was in some ways economical. They claimed that it was economical because it enabled participants to become independent.

The advocates of special education claimed that it was economical because it benefitted all children. They explained that it relieved regular education classrooms of those learners who required extraordinary amounts of attention. They identified an additional way in which special education helped all of the students in every school district. They claimed that the instructional techniques that were devised in special education classrooms could be adapted for use in regular education classrooms.

Nineteenth-century teachers had changed their attitudes toward learners with disabilities; twentieth-century teachers also changed their attitudes. They revealed those changes in the actions they took within their professional education organizations. For example, the members of the National Education Association formally recognized special education at their 1902 convention. One observer noted that these educators had taken this action because they had realized "that the line between a defective and a normal child cannot be drawn hard and fast" (Allen, 1904, p. 773).

The advocates of special education detected a favorable political situation during World War I. They realized that government leaders had been supporting vocational programs and trade schools because they were convinced that these programs increased the supply of trained homefront workers. They convinced government leaders that special vocational programs would have the same effect.

The advocates of special education continued to benefit from the political situation after World War I. This was an era when the federal government had established rehabilitation programs for physically and emotionally impaired veterans. The advocates of special education pointed to ways in which the government-funded rehabilitation programs resembled their own programs. In fact, they noticed that many rehabilitating veterans behaved like adults with developmental disabilities.

During World War II and the postwar years, the public again felt great sympathy for wounded veterans. As they had done during the earlier war, the advocates of special education took advantage of this situation to emphasize the benefits of their programs.

During the 1950s and 1960s, proponents of special education acknowledged that remarkable progress had transpired. Nonetheless, they were disturbed that many children with disabilities did not attend the public schools; they also were disturbed because some of those who were attending did not receive appropriate instruction.

The proponents of special education wanted educational reforms. They organized a political movement to create these reforms. Parents of children with disabilities assumed central roles in this movement. Displeased by the varying laws and regulations that affected special education in different states, they called for a nationwide template. They also wanted the funding to implement the new template.

In response to pressure from the reformers, Congress passed Public Law 94-142 (Education for All Handicapped Children Act, 1975). The authors of this bill acknowledged that many children with disabilities had been barred from the schools; in fact, they estimated that as many as 1,000,000 children had been excluded.

The authors of Public Law 94-142 defined the educational rights of children with disabilities. They also developed a national template to guide the provision of services to these children. Recognizing that funding was critical to solving this problem, they provided money to improve and expand special education.

A heterogeneous group of reformers had lobbied for Public Law 94-142; the group comprised adults with disabilities, the parents of children with disabilities, and professionals from health care, social services, and education. Although the reformers were pleased with the new law, they continued to call for the educational and social changes to which persons with disabilities were entitled.

Activity: Impact of Legislation on Special Education

Twentieth-century reformers assembled an alliance to change the ways that persons with disabilities were viewed. They attracted persons with disabilities, members of their families, and numerous professionals to this alliance.

As the reformers detected social changes, they insisted that school administrators be responsive. They asked them to implement comprehensive reforms. However, they were disappointed by the limited reactions of the school administrators. The reformers eventually asked federal legislators to mandate comprehensive school reforms. During the 1970s, the legislators acted.

Which groups do you think had substantive impacts on the legislators? To help answer this question, create a chart.

Along the vertical axis of the chart, arrange the following groups: adults with disabilities, parents of children with disabilities, educators, medical practitioners, and journalists.

Along the horizontal axis of the chart, arrange several columns. In one column, indicate the impact that each group had on federal legislators. Select the

Table 11.3. Politicians

Group	*Impact on Legislators**	*Explanation*
Adults with Disabilities		
Parents of Children with Disabilities		
Educators		
Medical Practitioners		
Journalists		

* (1) Minor
(2) Moderate
(3) Major

value *1* if they had a minor impact, *2* if they had a moderate impact, and *3* if they had a great impact.

Your indications about the impact of the groups should be based on assumptions about the vested interests, values, and goals of their members; it should also be based on assumptions about the vested interests, values, and goals of the legislators. Although you can use the information in the case study to make some of these assumptions, you may wish to rely on a broader foundation of information.

You can gather additional information from the materials that are listed at the end of this chapter. You may gather it from lectures or discussions.

In a separate column, or possibly on a separate page, summarize your assumptions about the ways that the legislators reacted to each group.

USING THE PAST TO UNDERSTAND THE PRESENT

During the 1970s, Congress enacted legislation to define, protect, and fund education for learners with disabilities. Political liberals and conservatives supported this legislation. After signing the legislation, President Ford directed the U.S. Department of Education to monitor and administer the provisions within it. President Carter continued to implement and fund this congressional initiative.

Presidents Ford and Carter had funded the expansion of special education services. After President Reagan took office, he signaled new priorities for federal spending in a widely publicized report, *A Nation at Risk* (National Commission on Excellence in Education, 1983).

The authors of *A Nation at Risk* claimed that a dysfunctional educational system imperiled the country. They recommended that the U.S. Department of Education use its resources to monitor academic achievement. They recommended that it rely on rigorous and comprehensive testing.

During the 1980s, advocates for special education realized that most members of the public agreed with the new educational priorities. Although they were disappointed that the national agenda had shifted, they resolved that they would continue to press for changes. They resolved that they would show the same type of determination that earlier reformers had exhibited when they were facing challenges.

Do current advocates for special education confront problems that are similar to those that earlier reformers confronted? To help answer this question, identify a recent incident in which at least two parties have disagreed about the education of children with disabilities. Identify the parties that were involved and the basis for their disagreement. Did any of the disputants display stereotypes about students with disabilities? Did they reveal concerns about limited school budgets? Attempt to find an incident that transpired in your own state or community.

CHAPTER SUMMARY

Nineteenth-century citizens became increasingly concerned about persons with disabilities. Some of them wished to confine them in asylums, reformatories, and restrictive facilities. The families of persons with disabilities objected that this treatment was too cruel; frugal taxpayers objected that it was too expensive. They asked community leaders to find some other solution for this problem.

Community leaders turned to the public schools. They urged educators to establish day care programs for children with disabilities. The educators agreed to provide care; they also agreed to provide instruction. However, they faced practical problems. They had to develop special assessment procedures, learning materials, adaptive equipment, instructional techniques, and curricula. They also had to recruit qualified personnel. Federal legislators eventually codified the procedures that they were to follow when addressing these problems.

ADDITIONAL READING

Introductory Passages

Barkan, E. (1992). *The retreat of scientific racism: Changing concepts of race in Britain and the United States between the world wars.* New York: Cambridge University Press.

Giordano, G. (2007). *American special education: A history of early political advocacy.* New York: Peter Lang.

Gould, S. J. (1996). *The mismeasure of man* (revised ed.). New York: Norton.

Gross, P. R. & Levitt, N. (1994). *Higher superstition: The academic left and its quarrels with science.* Baltimore: The Johns Hopkins University Press.

Hockenberry, J. (1995). *Moving violations: War zones, wheelchairs, and declarations of independence.* New York: Hyperion.

Kevles, D. (1985). *In the name of eugenics: Genetics and the uses of human heredity.* New York: Knopf.

Kühl, S. (1994). *The Nazi connection: Eugenics, American racism, and German national socialism.* New York: Oxford University Press.

Lifchez, R. (1987). *Rethinking architecture: Design students and physically disabled people.* Berkeley: University of California Press.

Ogletree, C. J. (2004). *All deliberate speed: Reflections on the first half century of Brown v. Board of Education.* New York: Norton.

Patterson, J. T. (2001). *Brown v. Board of Education: A civil rights milestone and its troubled legacy.* New York: Oxford University Press.

Paul, D. B. (1995). *Controlling human heredity, 1865 to the present.* Atlantic Highlands, NJ: Humanities Press.

Selden, S. (1999). *Inheriting shame: The story of eugenics and racism in America.* New York: Teachers College Press.

Sokol, J. (2006). *There goes my everything: White southerners in the age of civil rights, 1945–1975.* New York: Knopf.

Case Study 11.1: Vacating Asylums

Hoffman, E. (1975). The American public school and the deviant child: The origins of their involvement. *Journal of Special Education, 9* (4), 416–423.

Noll, S. (1995). *Feeble-minded in our midst: Institutions for the mentally retarded in the South, 1900–1940.* Chapel Hill: University of North Carolina Press.

Osgood, R. L. (2000). *For "children who vary from the normal type": Special education in Boston, 1838–1930.* Washington, DC: Gallaudet University Press.

Safford, P. L., & Safford, E. J. (1996). *A history of childhood and disability.* New York: Teachers College Press.

Scheerenberger, R. C. (1987). *A history of mental retardation: A quarter century of promise.* Baltimore: Brookes.

Case Study 11.2: Practical Problems

Anderson, M. L. (1917). *Education of defectives in the public schools.* New York: World.

Anderson, V. V. (1921). Education of mental defectives in state and private institutions and in special classes in public schools in the United States. *Mental Hygiene, 5,* 85–122.

Barnes, E. (1908). The public school and the special child. *National Education Association Journal of Proceedings and Addresses of the Forty-sixth Annual Meeting,* 1118–1123.

Barr, M. W. (1899–1900). The how, the why, and the wherefore of the training of feeble-minded children. *Journal of Psycho-Asthenics, 4,* 204–212.

Best, H. (1930). A comparison of the educational treatment of the deaf, the blind, and the feeble-minded. *American Journal of Sociology, 35,* 631–639.

Bolton, F. E. (1912). Public education of exceptional children. *Educational Review, 44,* 62–69.

Giordano, G. (2005). *How testing came to dominate American schools: The history of educational assessment.* New York: Peter Lang.

Goddard, H. H. (1923). *School training of defective children* (4th ed.). New York: World.

Groszmann, M. P. E. (1917). *The exceptional child.* New York: Scribner's Sons.

Hollingworth, L. S. (1923). *Special talents and defects: Their significance for education.* New York: Macmillan.

Holmes, A. (1915). *Backward children.* Indianapolis, IN: Bobbs-Merrill.

Inskeep, A. D. (1926). *Teaching dull and retarded children.* New York: Macmillan.

Maennel, B. (1909). *Auxiliary education: The training of backward children* (E. Sylvester, Trans.). New York: Doubleday, Page.

Mateer, F. (1924). *The unstable child.* New York: Appleton.

Sherlock, E. B. (1911). *The feeble-minded: A guide to study and practice.* London: Macmillan.

Young, M. (1916). *The mentally defective child.* London: Lewis.

Case Study 11.3: Politicians

Arnold, J. (1936). A sterilization law for Kentucky: Its constitutionality. *Kentucky Law Review, 24,* 220–229.

Blatt, B. (1973). *Souls in extremis: An anthology on victims and victimizers.* Boston, MA: Allyn & Bacon.

Blatt, B. (1981). *In and out of mental retardation.* Baltimore: University Park Press.

Blatt, B., & Kaplan, F. (1966). *Christmas in purgatory: A photographic essay on mental retardation.* Boston, MA: Allyn & Bacon.

Braddock, D. (1987). *Federal policy toward mental retardation and developmental disabilities.* Baltimore: Brookes.

Cross, C. T. (2004). *Political education: National policy comes of age.* New York: Teachers College Press.

Hill, A. S. (1957). *The forward look: The severely retarded child goes to school.* Washington, DC: United Sates Government Printing Office. (Original work published in 1952.)

Kirp, D., Buss, W., & Kuriloff, P. (1974). Legal reform and special education: Empirical studies and procedural proposals. *California Law Review, 62* (1), 40–155.

Mesibov, G. B. (1976). Mentally retarded people: 200 years in America. *Journal of Clinical Child Psychology, 5* (3), 25–29.

Sage, D., & Burrello, L. C. (1986). *Policy and management in special education.* Englewood Cliffs, NJ: Prentice-Hall.

Sales, B. D., Powell, D. M., & Duizend, R. V. (1982). *Disabled persons and the law: State legislative issues.* New York: Plenum.

Zedler, E. Y. (1953). Public opinion and public education for the exceptional child–court decisions, 1873–1950. *Exceptional Children, 19* (5), 187–198.

Epilogue: The Case Method Redux

Many persons have been curious about the case method. They have followed different paths in their attempts to learn about it. Those who have never experienced it have tried to learn about it by examining definitions, examples, practical guidelines, or philosophical principles.

Disappointed when they did not locate the information for which they were searching, some inquirers tried to gather information inductively. For example, they attempted to discern similarities between the case method and other types of instruction. They frequently compared it to the Socratic method.

Some persons tried to understand the case method by discerning the differences between it and other types of instruction. They frequently contrasted it with the didactic style of lecturing on which many professors have relied.

Persons who wanted to learn about the case method inevitably came across the approaches that professors of law and business developed. Although they discerned similarities in these approaches, they also discerned differences. In fact, the differences made some of them wonder whether the two groups actually were using the same instructional method (Barton, 2008).

LAWYERS USE THE CASE METHOD

When law professors implemented the case method, they used a distinctive approach. The primary materials that they gave their students were decisions that judges had written during legal proceedings. They did not append many contextual details to these decisions. They directed their students to read, recapitulate, analyze, and synthesize the decisions; they expected them to progress through these steps individually.

The law professors employed a distinctive type of pedagogy; they employed an equally distinctive type of assessment. Although they interacted with their students in class sessions and seminars, they gave them limited feedback about their progress in courses. They awarded grades exclusively on the basis of final exams. To ensure that they were being objective, the law professors read and evaluated the exams without knowing the identities of the students who had written them.

The professors of law used the case method to develop the academic and practical prowess of their students. They were confident that their idiosyncratic approach had helped their students acquire the skills that they would need in legal situations.

BUSINESSPERSONS USE THE CASE METHOD

When business professors implemented the case method, they used an approach that was highly distinctive. They gave their students narrative summaries of business incidents that they had written.

The business professors gave their students contextual information about the cases. This information included managerial reports, newspaper accounts, market analyses, personnel evaluations, accounting practices, legal documents, minutes from board meetings, stock prices, credit reports, and anecdotal reminiscences from characters in the cases.

The business professors directed their students to work in teams. In fact, they used the evaluations of team efforts when they were calculating individual grades. They also used comments that the students had made during class sessions to calculate their grades.

The business professors encouraged their students to place themselves in the positions of characters in the cases, appraise their situations, and then hypothesize about the courses of action that they would have taken. They encouraged the students to apply the insights that they had formed to current business problems.

The professors of business used the case method to develop the academic and practical prowess of their students. Although they relied on highly distinctive strategies, they were confident that they had helped their students acquire skills they would need in the business professions.

EDUCATORS USE THE CASE METHOD

When professors in multiple disciplines began to contemplate the case method, they examined the approach of the law professors and that of the business professors. Professors of education decided that they would replicate the approach that made the most sense in their discipline.

Recognizing that their students came from professions in which they collaborated with numerous constituencies, the education professors encouraged them to review and deliberate about cases cooperatively. They copied this strategy from the business professors.

The education professors were aware of the types of assessment that their students encountered in their jobs and decided that they would use comparable types of assessment. Therefore, they gave students continual feedback as they progressed through their classes. They copied this strategy from the business professors.

The education professors realized that educational students would focus their attention on the schools. However, they encouraged the students to look at the contextual information that influenced the schools. They copied this strategy from the business professors.

They borrowed another important strategy from the business professors. They encouraged their students to assume the roles of the characters in the cases, pose questions, extract information, and speculate about solutions. Then the education professors encouraged them to apply the insights that they had formed to current educational problems.

References

Allen, E. E. (1904). *Education of defectives*. Monographs on education in the United States, 15, 771–819.

American Association of University Women. (1992). *How schools shortchange girls: The AAUW Report—A study of major findings on girls and education*. New York: Marlowe.

Armstrong, O. K. (1940, September). Treason in the textbooks. *American Legion Magazine, 20* (3), 8–9, 51, 70–72.

Babcock, L., & Laschever, S. (2003). *Women don't ask: Negotiation and the gender divide*. Princeton, NJ: Princeton University Press.

Barker, D. C. (2002). *Rushed to judgment: Talk radio, persuasion, and American political behavior*. New York: Columbia University Press.

Barton, B. (2008). A tale of two case methods. *Tennessee Law Review, 75* (3). (Retrieved on 31 October 2008 from: http://ssrn.com/abstract=1021306.)

Belfiore, M. E., Defoe, T. A., Folinsbee, S., Hunter, J. M., & Jackson, N. S. (2004). *Reading work: Literacies in the new workplace*. Mahwah, NJ: Erlbaum.

Bencivenga, J. (1985, August 23). Students and teachers face more tests, but what do results mean? *Christian Science Monitor*, p. B3.

Berger, P. L., & Luckmann, T. (1967). *The social construction of reality: A treatise in the sociology of knowledge*. New York: Anchor.

Berry, C. (1923). The mentally retarded child in the public schools. *Mental Hygiene, 7*, 762–769.

Best, H. (1930). A comparison of the educational treatment of the deaf, the blind, and the feeble-minded. *American Journal of Sociology, 35*, 631–639.

Bloom, S. (2004). Neither liberty nor safety: The impact of fear on individuals, institutions, and societies. Part I. *Psychotherapy and Politics International, 2* (2), 78–98.

Bowers, C. A. (1964). The *Social Frontier* journal: A historical sketch. *History of Education Quarterly, 4*, 167–180.

Bowsher, J. E. (2001). *Fix schools first: Blueprint for achieving learning standards.* Gaithersburg, MD: Aspen.

Breitman, G. (Ed.). (1994). *Malcolm X speaks.* New York: Grove. (Original work published in 1965).

Brown v. Board of Education of Topeka. (1954). 347 U.S. 483.

Buckingham, D. (2007). *Beyond technology: Children's learning in the age of digital culture.* Cambridge, UK: Polity.

Burnham, S. (1920). *The making of our country: A history of the United States for schools.* Chicago: Winston.

Camhi, J. J. (1994). *Women against women: American anti-suffragism, 1880–1920.* New York: Carlson.

Cardozo, F. L. (1924). Test and measurements in public schools. *School and Society, 20,* 797–798.

Chancellor, W. E. (1913). The state publication question. *School Journal, 80,* 218–220.

Churchill, F. (1851). On the mental disorders of pregnancy and childbed. *American Journal of Insanity, 7,* 259–266.

Civil Rights: Brown v. the Board of Education. (Retrieved September 9, 2007, from: http://www.nationalcenter.org/brown.html.)

Claxton, P. P. (1919). Army psychologists for city public school work. *School and Society, 9,* 203–204.

Cockburn, A., & Haydn, T. (2003). *Recruiting and retaining teachers: Understanding why teachers teach.* London: Routledge.

Coleman, C. H., & Wesley, E. B. (1939). *America's road to now.* Boston, MA: Heath.

Coll, S. (2008). *The Bin Ladens: An Arabian family in the American century.* New York: Penguin.

Cornell, L. S. (1888). State uniformity of textbooks. *Addresses and Proceeding of the National Education Association, 28,* 225–233.

Cox, E. M. (1903). Free text-books. *Western Journal of Education, 8,* 88–98.

Creel, G. (1920). *How we advertised America.* New York: Harper.

Desolate valley. (1889, June 3). *New York Times.* (Retrieved on September 9, 2007, from: http://www.johnstownpa.com/History/hist30.html.)

Dewey, J. (1927). Introduction. In R. P. Barnes, *Militarizing our youth: The significance of the Reserve Officers' Training Corp in our schools and colleges.* (Pamphlet, pp. 3–4.) New York: Committee on Militarism in Education.

Dexter, E. G. (1904). *A history of education in the United States.* New York: Macmillan.

Dey, J. G., & Hill, C. (2007). *Behind the pay gap.* Washington, DC: American Association of University Women.

Diamond, J. (2005). *Collapse: How societies choose to fail or succeed.* New York: Viking.

Education for All Handicapped Children Act. Pub. L. No. 94-142. (1975). (Retrieved on 25 August 2007 from: http://thomas.loc.gov/bss.)

Fair Labor Standards Act of 1938 (FLSA, ch. 676, 52 Stat. 1060, June 25, 1938, 29 U.S.C. ch. 8). (Retrieved on 31 October 2008 from: http://www4.law.cornell.edu/uscode/html/uscode29/usc_sec_29_00000202----000-.html.)

Farrell, E. E. (1914). Introduction. In B. S. Morgan, *The backward child: A study of the psychology and treatment of backwardness* (pp. iii–vii). New York: Putnam's Sons.

Fishman, J., Deutsch, M., Kogan, L., North, R., & Whiteman, M. (1963). *Guidelines for testing minority group children.* Ann Arbor, MI: Society for the Psychological Study of Social Issues, American Psychological Association. (ERIC Document Reproduction Service No. ED001649.)

Fiske, E. B. (1988, April 10). America's test mania. *New York Times,* pp. EDUC 16– EDUC 20.

Freeland, G. E., Walker, E. E., & Williams, H. E. (1937). *America's building: The makers of our flag.* New York: Scribner.

Gardening: A patriotic duty. (1918). *Elementary School Journal, 18*, 643.

Gibson, C., & Jung, K. (2002). *Historical census statistics on population totals by race, 1790 to 1990, and by Hispanic origin, 1970 to 1990, for the United States, regions, divisions, and states.* Washington, DC: United States Census Bureau. (Retrieved August 7, 2007, from: http://www.census.gov/population/www/documentation/twps0056.html.)

Gilbert, G. M. (1951). Stereotype persistence and change among college students. *Journal of Abnormal and Social Psychology, 46*, 245–254.

Ginsburg, M. B., & Lindsay, B. (Eds.). (1995). *The political dimension in teacher education: Comparative perspectives on policy.* Philadelphia: Falmer.

Giordano, G. (1996). *Literacy programs for adults with developmental disabilities.* San Diego, CA: Singular.

Giordano, G. (2003). *Twentieth-century textbook wars: A history of advocacy and opposition.* New York: Peter Lang.

Giordano, G. (2004). *Wartime schools: How World War II changed American education.* New York: Peter Lang.

Goals 2000: Educate America Act. Pub. L. No. 103-227. (1994). (Retrieved on 14 October 2007 from: http://www.ed.gov/pubs/G2KReforming/index.html.)

Greene, J. P. (2006). *Education myths: What special interest groups want you to believe about our schools—and why it isn't so.* Lanham, MD: Rowman & Littlefield.

Heller, D. A. (2004). *Teachers wanted: Attracting and retaining good teachers.* Alexandria, VA: Association for Supervision and Curriculum Development.

Hildreth, G. H. (1933). *A bibliography of mental tests and rating scales.* New York: Psychological Corporation.

Hoff, D. J. (2002). A year later: Impact of 9/11 lingers. *Education Week, 22* (2), 1, 12–13.

Hood, W. R. (1922). *Some important school legislation, 1921 and 1922.* (U.S. Bureau of Education Bulletin, 1922, No. 43). Washington, DC: Government Printing Office.

Hutchby, I. (1996). *Confrontation talk: Arguments, asymmetries, and power on talk radio.* Mahwah, NJ: Erlbaum.

Integrating the texts. (1966, March 7). *Newsweek, 67*, 93–94.

Jessen, C. A. (1945). School-work programs for high-school youth. *Education for Victory, 3* (20), 5–12.

Katz, D., & Braly, K. W. (1933). Racial stereotypes of one hundred college students. *Journal of Abnormal and Social Psychology, 28*, 280–290.

Kuhn, I. C. (1952, April). Your child is their target. *American Legion Magazine, 44*, 18–19, 54–60.

Lerner, R., & Rothman, S. (1990, April). Newspeak, feminist-style. *Commentary, 89*, 54–56.

Lippmann, W. (1922). The abuse of the tests. *New Republic, 32*, 297–298.

Loretan, J. O. (1965). The decline and fall of group intelligence testing. *Teacher's College Record, 67*, 10–17.

Magee, E. S. (1944). Impact of the war on child labor. *Annals of the American Academy of Political and Social Science, 236*, 101–109.

McCluskey, N. P. (2007). *Feds in the classroom: How big government corrupts, cripples, and compromises American education.* Lanham, MD: Rowman & Littlefield.

McElroy, W. (2006). *The roots of individualist feminism in 19th-century America* (Parts 1 & 2). (Retrieved on 31 October 2008 from: http://www.ifeminists.net/e107_plugins/content/content.php?content.37.)

McGrath, E. J. (1958). Sputnik and American education. *Teachers College Record, 59*, 379–395.

Melendez, E. (Ed.). (2004). *Communities and workforce development.* Kalamazoo, MI: Upjohn Institute.

Muzzey, D. S. (1911). *An American history.* Boston, MA: Ginn.

National Association for the Advancement of Colored People. (1939). *Anti-Negro propaganda in school textbooks.* New York: Author.

National Commission on Excellence in Education. (1983). *A nation at risk: The imperative for educational reform.* Washington, DC: Author.

National School Boards Association. (1977). School board attitudes toward standardized testing. *NSBA Research Report, 1*, 25–29.

National Women's History Museum. (2007). *Cyber museum.* (Retrieved on 31 October 2008 from: http://www.nwhm.org/index.html.)

New York bill on history textbooks. (1923, March 31). *School and Society, 17*, p. 349.

No Child Left Behind Act of 2001. Pub. L. No. 107-110. (2002). (Retrieved on 14 October 2007 from: http://www.ed.gov/policy/elsec/leg/esea02/index.html.)

Nusser, J. (1996). Gender's contribution to the rise and fall of the Progressive Education Association, 1919–1955. (ERIC Document Reproduction Service No. ED399 340.) (Retrieved on 31 October 2008 from: http://www.eric.ed.gov/ERICWebPortal/custom/portlets/recordDetails/detailmini.jsp?_nfpb=true&_&ERICExtSearch_SearchValue_0=ED399340&ERICExtSearch_SearchType_0=eric_accno&accno=ED399340.)

O'Neill, M. (1988). Curricular reconstruction: Visions of the *Social Frontier. Educational Forum, 3*, 223–234.

Ogletree, C. J. (2004). *All deliberate speed: Reflections on the first half century of Brown v. Board of Education.* New York: Norton.

Paige, R. (2007). *The war against hope: How teachers' unions hurt children, hinder teachers, and endanger public education.* Nashville, TN: Nelson.

Parker, K. (2007, February 16). Yo, George, wassup? *Washington Post.* (Retrieved on 31 October 2008 from: http://www.townhall.com/columnists/column.aspx?UrlTitle=yo,_george,_wassup&ns=KathleenParker&dt=02/16/2007&page=full&comments=true.)

Patterson, J. T. (2001). *Brown v. Board of Education: A civil rights milestone and its troubled legacy.* New York: Oxford University Press.

Pew Research Center. (2007). *Muslim Americans: Middle class and mostly mainstream.* Washington, DC: Author. (Retrieved 18 June 2007 from: http://pewresearch.org/assets/pdf/muslim-americans.pdf.)

Plessy v. Ferguson. (1896). 163 U.S. 537.

Podsen, I. (2002). *Teacher retention: What is your weakest link?* Larchmont, NY: Eye on Education.

"Poll shows U.S. views on Muslim-Americans: Nearly half of those surveyed say some rights should be restricted." (2004). (Retrieved 18 June 2007 from: http://www.msnbc.msn.com/id/6729916.)

Reynolds, C., & Smith, S. (2002). Innocent lost: The impact of 9-11 on the development of children. *Annals of the American Psychotherapy Association, 5* (5), 12.

Rice, J. M. (1897a). The futility of the spelling grind. *Forum, 23,* 163–172.

Rice, J. M. (1897b). The futility of the spelling grind. II. *Forum, 23,* 409–419.

Rivers, L. W., Mitchell, H., & Williams, W. S. (1975). I.Q. labels and liability: Effects on the black child. *Journal of Afro-American Issues, 3* (1), 63–76.

Root, E. M. (1952, December). The propaganda program of our academic hucksters. *American Legion Magazine*, 18–19, 56–58.

Ruby, R. (May 30, 2007). A Six-Day War: Its aftermath in American public opinion. *Pew Forum on Religion & Public Life.* (Retrieved on 31 October 2008 from: http://pewforum.org/docs/?DocID=218.)

Russell, R. D. (1925). The use of educational and intelligence tests in the county schools of California. *American School Board Journal, 70* (6), 68.

Sacks, P. (1999). *Standardized minds: The high price of America's testing culture and what we can do to change it.* Cambridge, MA: Perseus.

Solmon, L. C., & Agam, K. F. (Ed.). (2007). *How stakeholders can support teacher quality.* Charlotte, NC: Information Age.

Solmon, L. C., & Schiff, M. W. (Eds.). (2004). *Talented teachers: The essential force for improving student achievement.* Charlotte, NC: Information Age.

Special report on book burning. (1953, June 29). *New Republic, 128,* 7–9.

Statistics Canada. (1994). *International adult survey.* Ottawa, Ontario: Author. (Retrieved on 31 October 2008 from: http://www.statcan.ca/english/Dli/Data/Ftp/ials/ials1994-96-98.htm.)

Statistics Canada. (1996). *International adult survey.* Ottawa, Ontario: Author. (Retrieved on 31 October 2008 from: http://www.statcan.ca/english/Dli/Data/Ftp/ials/ials1994-96-98.htm.)

Statistics Canada. (1998). *International adult survey*. Ottawa, Ontario: Author. (Retrieved on 31 October 2008 from: http://www.statcan.ca/english/Dli/Data/Ftp/ials/ials1994-96-98.htm.)

Tash, T. (1888). Free textbooks for free schools. *Addresses and Proceedings of the National Education Association, 28*, 220–225.

Taylor, J. S. (1912). Measurement of educational efficiency. *Educational Review, 44*, 348–367.

Tennessee Valley Authority Act. Pub. L. No. 73-17. (1933). Retrieved 25 September 2007 from: http://www.tva.gov/abouttva/pdf/TVA_Act.pdf)

United Nations Educational Scientific Cultural Organization (UNESCO). (2007). *Literacy*. (Retrieved 10 June 2007 from: http://portal.unesco.org/education/en/ev.php-URL_ID=40338&URL_DO=DO_TOPIC&URL_SECTION=201.html.)

United States Department of Education. (1993). *Adult literacy in America: A first look at the findings of the National Adult Literacy Survey*. Washington, DC: Author. (Retrieved 10 June 2007 from: http://nces.ed.gov/pubsearch/pubsinfo.asp?pubid=93275.)

United States Department of Education. (2007a). *Literacy behind bars: Results from the 2003 National Assessment of Adult Literacy Prison Survey*. Washington, DC: Author. (Retrieved 10 June 2007 from: http://nces.ed.gov/pubsearch/pubsinfo.asp?pubid=2007473.)

United States Department of Education. (2007b). *Literacy in everyday life: Results from the 2003 National Assessment of Adult Literacy*. Washington, DC: Author. (Retrieved 10 June 2007 from: http://nces.ed.gov/pubsearch/pubsinfo.asp?pubid=2007480.)

United States Department of Health, Education, and Welfare. (1956). *Education for national survival: A handbook on civil defense for schools*. Washington, DC: Author.

United States Department of State. (2005). *Report on global anti-Semitism: July 1, 2003–December 15, 2004*. (Retrieved on 31 October 2008 from: http://www.state.gov/g/drl/rls/40258.htm.)

United States Department of the Interior. (1946). *WRA: A story of human conservation*. Washington, DC: Author.

United States Office of Education. (1943). *Our armed forces: A source book on the Army and Navy for high school students*. Washington, DC: Author.

Updike, J. (1992). *Memoirs of the Ford administration: A novel*. New York: Knopf.

Valentine, T. W. (1857, August 26). *Letter to presidents of state teacher associations*. (Retrieved on 31 October 2008 from: http://www.nea.org/aboutnea/thecall.html.)

Victory Corps. (1942, November 9). *Life*, 53–54, 56.

War relocation centers: Education program for evacuees of Japanese ancestry. (1942, November 16). *Education for Victory, 1* (18), 7–9.

Weisberg, J. (2008). *The Bush tragedy*. New York: Random House.

Whitbeck, R. H. (1922). *High school geography*. New York: Macmillan.

Yerkes, R. M. (1923). Testing the human mind. *Atlantic Monthly, 131*, 358–370.

Author Index

Subject Index

About the Author

Gerard Giordano is a professor at the University of North Florida. He is the author of two tests, numerous book chapters, eight previous books, and nearly two hundred articles. He recently concluded a five-volume series of texts about the history of American education.